Ex Libris

Also by Susie Dent

Dent's Modern Tribes
Susie Dent's Weird Words
How to Talk Like a Local
What Made the Crocodile Cry?

WORD PERFECT

Etymological Entertainment for
Every Day of the Year

SUSIE DENT

JOHN MURRAY

First published in Great Britain in 2020 by John Murray (Publishers)
An Hachette UK company

6

Copyright © Susie Dent 2020

A CIP catalogue record for this title is available from the British Library

Hardback ISBN 978-1-529-31151-8
eBook ISBN 978-1-529-31150-1

Typeset in Bembo Std by
Palimpsest Book Production Ltd, Falkirk, Stirlingshire

Printed and bound in Great Britain by
Clays Ltd, Elcograf S.p.A.

John Murray policy is to use papers that are natural, renewable
and recyclable products and made from wood grown in sustainable
forests. The logging and manufacturing processes are expected to
conform to the environmental regulations of the country of origin.

John Murray (Publishers)
Carmelite House
50 Victoria Embankment
London EC4Y 0DZ

www.johnmurraypress.co.uk

For Thea and Lucy, my *raisons d'être*

CONTENTS

INTRODUCTION

'It is reasonable to have perfection in our eye that we may always advance toward it, though we know it can never be reached.' Samuel Johnson

Twenty-eight years ago I sat, rigid with fear, in Dictionary Corner for the first time, waiting for the cameras to turn to me. A newly fledged dictionary editor at Oxford University Press, I was a reluctant addition to the *Countdown* team, having resisted my boss's suggestion that I audition on at least three occasions. I am happiest when flying below the radar, and appearances on TV were clearly not on my wish list. But there I was, hiding behind Rula Lenska's glorious fox-red mane, trying desperately to look as though I knew what I was doing. I didn't, but somehow I got by that first afternoon, and that corner is now my second home. Most of all, the dictionary in front of me has become my greatest friend.

Perhaps it was always meant to be this way. I have been a linguistic magpie for as long as I can remember. These compelling birds, whose collective noun is the ominous 'tiding', have had a bad rap over the years. Whether lone harbingers of doom, or swooping thieves of chicks and jewellery, their dark reputation brings even the soberest amongst us to a shudder (or salute) in their presence. In the seventeenth century, 'magpie' was a metaphor for an idler or 'impertinent chatterer', and by the twentieth the epithet had attached itself to one who collects or hoards indiscriminately: as one dictionary put it, 'a petty pilferer'. That is surely an apt description of what I do, for I have collected odds and ends of language my whole life.

I was always the one who, during family dinnertime chats,

would be entirely lost in the ingredients on the back of a ketchup bottle. It was the same story for shampoo, on whose magical labels the swirling characters of French, Greek, Arabic and Cyrillic beckoned like the exotic jewels a magpie might smuggle away. No text was off limits – aeroplane safety instructions would be pored over, sometimes for an entire flight. It was there, squished between my parents, that I longed to know the difference between 'flammable' and 'inflammable', or to prove a possible link between 'monster' and 'demonstrate' (one of my many cul-de-sacs, as it happens, as there is no link, but even as I type this I am enjoying the fact that a cul-de-sac means 'bottom of the sack').

It was from earning pocket money posting pamphlets through letterboxes that I learned that the word 'pamphlet' was born not out of tedious bumf, but in a racy tale from the twelfth century, whose ardent hero was a relentless seducer named Pamphilus. His pursuits, devoured by the masses, were reprinted in little booklets or 'pamphilets', 'little Pamphiluses'. That bumf, by the way, before it became a byword for throwaway material, is short for the bumfodder that once wiped the bottoms of military personnel.

And so they went on, the petty pilferings from hundreds of mundane encounters that to me were anything but. I would file them away in my head – and eventually, in the only black book that interested me – marvelling in the simple shape of a word or musing over its origin. I would hoover up the new and unfamiliar, trying out a potential word from *Countdown*'s random letter selection and rejoicing when it was confirmed by the dictionary. These moments were the start of a linguistic adventure that has never come to an end.

Word Perfect might seem a strange choice of title. Like all lexicographers in the modern age, I sit very far from linguistic pedantry. I am, as John Humphrys once called me, one of those 'hippie chicks of English'. No modern dictionary-maker can afford to be prescriptive; rather we describe language as it is used, with its myriad meanings and contexts, and all its creases and crumples. A linguist's job is to map this evolving landscape, and to chart the journeys of words whose lifetimes will far exceed our own. We are, as Samuel Johnson beautifully described it, always 'chasing the sun'. For me, perfection is not a single moment in time when everything aligns and we are faultless, nor is it a finished state accomplished by rote. Instead I choose again Johnson's description – we keep it in our eye as we head towards it, knowing we will never quite catch up, but basking in that sun all the while.

I also like a definition from earlier times, when perfection conveyed maturity, ripeness, and full bloom. It is entirely fitting that the metaphors of trees and flowers have wrapped themselves around our language, from the 'anthology' – once a posy of flowers – to the 'book', which comes from the Old English for 'beech'. Not for nothing do lexicographers explore the 'roots' of the words they define. Johann Wolfgang von Goethe is said to have compared French to a country park, German to a dense forest, and English to a pretty garden. For all my love of German (and it's a deep love), English is so much more than that. If it is a garden, it is as full of thorns as roses, as gnarly as the bark of an old oak, and as mazy as a medieval labyrinth. It is also evergreen: locked away for weeks during the coronavirus, the dictionary was where I took my solace.

There was, for example, comfort in viewing our imposed quarantine through the filter of earlier times, when ships arriving in Venice at the peak of the Black Death were required to anchor for forty (*quaranta*) days of isolation. Ugsome lockdown days and nights were brightened by such rediscoveries as 'respair', an all-too-rare word for a recovery from despair, or the simple knowledge that 'chortle' was Lewis Carroll's blend of 'chuckle' and 'snort' (how we long to chortle again). Such were the things that sparkled in the darkness.

These were also the days when family sayings brought the warmth of home to those who were missing it so keenly. The pandemic bound us together with loved ones, either physically or Zoomed onto our screens, and threw us back upon the words of our childhood: verbal comforts that we pulled on like the cosiest of jumpers. They became the linguistic equivalent of 'huffle buffs', old Scots for the clothes in which we can breathe. *Word Perfect* includes many of the words and sayings that transport me straight home (a fit of sneezes, for example, will always be a 'snick-up').

In this book I have chosen a word for each day of the year. It is an anthology of words and phrases remembered through a moment in time. Some of these moments were decisive – the Battle of Copenhagen that had Nelson 'turn a blind eye'; the War of Independence that took the American language defiantly away from British English, thereby forever casting such authentically British words as 'fall' and 'sidewalk' into the list of Americanisms we love to hate. Other moments simply chimed with the time of year – the 'Yule-hole' at Christmas time, the 'crambazzlement' once the festivities are over, or the 'halcyon days' of summer heat.

Perhaps the greatest delight was choosing lost gems or obscurities from the corners of the dictionary. I made many fresh discoveries along the way. How could we ever have forgone the insults 'mumpsimus' and 'ultracrepidarian', when they so perfectly describe individuals that every one of us will recognise? And, to my greatest pleasure, I can confirm that we can all be 'gormful', 'gruntled', 'kempt', and 'couth' to our hearts' content. Now is surely the time to regain the lost positives of language.

Above all, the book has given me a chance to share the knowledge and love gained from a lifetime in the Corner, to prise open our language and revel in its secrets, surprises, surrealities, and occasional hiccups. Within its pages are 366 words and phrases that have made me smile, wonder, or simply 'suspire' (another word I'm determined to revive, meaning to 'breathe out with a sigh'). If *Word Perfect* gives you even a breath of the pleasure it has given me, this magpie's job will be done.

Susie Dent

JANUARY

CRAMBAZZLED

If there's one day of the year when much of the population will be feeling a little crapulous (a word defined in Samuel Johnson's great *Dictionary of the English Language* as 'sick with intemperance'), it's today. Though the English lexicon of drunkenness is vast, the term describing the aftermath is surprisingly patchy.

To be 'crambazzled', in old Yorkshire dialect, was to be prematurely aged through excess drinking. In other words, to achieve this status you will have partied hard for most of your life. The word has a deliciously decadent feel to it, conjuring images of being out for the count or looking entirely grisly and crumpled while you carry on your debauchery. You will also most likely be sporting a 'grogblossom': a nineteenth-century term for the telltale redness of face that results from too much booze.

If, on the other hand, you can see perfectly straight this morning and are devoid of what the Germans call a morning *Katzenjammer* (literally a 'cat's wailing' and a useful synonym for a severe hangover headache), literature will confirm that a tall, dark stranger arriving on your doorstep is a good thing. On the first day of the New Year, this is particularly so: dark-haired 'first-footers' have been prized above all others since Viking times.

In Scottish and northern English folklore, the first-footer is the person elected to cross the threshold of a house on New Year's Day morning. They are duly regarded as the bringer of fortune for the entire year. Technically anyone is eligible, though in Yorkshire traditionalists insist on male first-footers, while all candidates must have been absent from the house at the stroke of midnight.

First-footers are required to bear gifts, ranging from a

handful of coal to a pinch of salt and a dram of whisky, each symbolising a different piece of good fortune, whether it be financial luck or health and good cheer. Such gifts are known as 'handsels', from the Old English *handselen*, 'giving into a person's hand'. This word progressed to mean any good-luck charm or token, and by the eighteenth century traders were using 'handsel' for the first cash they earned in the morning – to them, an omen of good things to follow. Nowadays, it can also be used for the first use or experience of something that, if successful, will signal good days to come.

Unless that first experience is alcohol, in which case we are right back to crambazzlement.

---

2 January

JANUS WORDS

The month of January is named after the Roman deity Janus, god of beginnings, transitions, and doorways. He is traditionally depicted as having two faces, one that looks to the future, and one that looks back on the past. Janus was viewed as a protector of the state in times of war; the doors of his temple in the Roman forum, an enclosure with gates at each end, would be opened during times of battle, and closed in times of peace. He was also regarded as the door-keeper of all entrances, including the one to heaven; our modern word 'janitor' comes from the same Latin root.

The god's two faces inspired several terms in English. Janus cloth, for example, is a reversible material, while a Janus lock can be fitted to either a left- or right-opening door. But the most enduring legacy of the two-faced deity is the 'Janus word': a term that has two diametrically opposed meanings. The list in English includes:

- fast: firmly fixed; very quick.
- sanction: approval; (economic) disapproval.
- cleave: to split; to adhere firmly.
- clip: to attach something; to cut off.
- custom: usual; specially made.
- overlook: to look over something; to fail to see.
- dust: to make free of dust; to sprinkle with dust.
- screen: to hide from view; to show.
- left: went away from; remaining.

Janus words (also known as 'contronyms') are emerging all the time. Slang loves them – you only have to think of the reversed sense of 'wicked', 'sick', or 'bad' – and, of course, 'literally', which now has a very non-literal sense – to see how we love turning the traditional lexicon on its head. Even today, Janus is a working metaphor for looking both ways.

---

3 January

JOURNAL

This is the time of year when we begin to fill in the calendars we were gifted at Christmas. But how many of us still write a diary? The desire to record details of our lives is as old as handwriting itself. Early diaries were mostly kept as public records, before the medium embraced more private reflections on life. Today, we vlog and blog both the intimate and the prosaic details of our days, virtual footprints that can never (unfortunately on occasion) be erased.

Many of the earliest travel journals were written on the pilgrimages of Christians to the Holy Land. Some of the greatest explorers and early adventurers meticulously recorded their itineraries and discoveries in logbooks and diaries – they include Captain Cook, and naturalists like Charles Darwin.

Diary as autobiography began in the mid-seventeenth

century with Samuel Pepys, whose chronicles of London life include both dramatic scenes from history, such as the Great Fire of 1666, and more intimate scenes of drinking and entertainment with his friends (and of being caught short in the aftermath). Since then, the literary canon of journals has become immense. Tolstoy, Kafka, Virginia Woolf, and Sylvia Plath are among those most widely read, but there are thousands more, including surely the most famous diarist of all, Anne Frank.

The word 'journal' is from the French *journée*, 'day', a nod to the fact that the earliest examples were books containing the appointed time of daily prayers. The Romans similarly used *diurnus*, the ancestor of 'journal', both as an adjective meaning 'of the day', and as a noun meaning an account or daybook. 'Journal' is of course the parent of 'journalist', once specifically a writer for a daily newspaper, and is an unexpected sibling of 'journey', originally used for travels that lasted no more than a single day. Ultimately, all go back to an ancient root *dheu* meaning 'to shine', which lies at the heart of 'July', 'circadian', 'deity', and – appropriately – 'diary'.

---

4 January

HUMDUDGEON

It's about now that the incipient dread of returning to work begins to creep in. After the blissful timelessness of the Merryneum (see 28 December), and the blurry exuberance of New Year, the foreknowledge of picking up the same routine, not least in the darkness of January, delivers to most of us a distinct bout of 'ergophobia', the fear of work.

This is the time, then, when a bout of 'humdudgeon' might come in handy. First recorded in the bawdily brilliant collection that is Francis Grose's *A Classical Dictionary of the Vulgar Tongue* (1785), the word is comprised of *hum*, the first part of 'humbug', and *dudgeon*, a state of begrudging indignation that we know primarily in the phrase 'in high dudgeon'. In other words, a humdudgeon is an imaginary illness, particularly one brought about by an episode of low spirits.

Francis Grose was a retired army officer and contemporary of Samuel Johnson, as large in life as he was in girth. While Johnson looked to the greats of literature for his evidence of English, Grose gathered the evidence for his lexicon at night, visiting the taverns and brothels and prisons and byways of eighteenth-century London. This was the language of the common people, including those whose underground vocabularies had never been captured before – among them cutpurses, gangsters, and lowlifes. It's hardly surprising that the humdudgeon is first recorded in his vibrant and unsqueamish collection.

5 January

LICK INTO SHAPE

This is the point at which we really begin to put our resolutions to the test. Most New Year pledges are about self-improvement, whether you're a little too 'ventripotent' (a positive way in the 1600s of saying 'big-bellied'), or prone to 'quiddling' (attending to the trivial tasks in life as a way of avoiding the important ones). The majority of us, in other words, need to lick our lives into shape.

This expression, which sounds straightforwardly modern and suggestive of a military boot camp, hides within it an ancient belief that persisted beyond the Middle Ages. In the animal lore of the period, it was held that bear cubs were born as formless blobs, and needed to be energetically licked into bear shape by their mothers. In one of his later sermons, as Dean of St Paul's Cathedral, the poet John Donne states that 'Lyons are littered perfit, but Beare-whelpes lick'd unto their shape'.

All trace of inspiration for the expression was eventually lost, and the idiom took on various other verbs including 'knocked' and 'whipped' into shape. Nevertheless, the belief in this ultimate manifestation of maternal love persisted for centuries – in Shakespeare's *Henry VI, Part Three*, Gloucester compares his deformed body to 'an unlick'd bear-whelp, / That carries no impression like the dam [mother]'.

It is a beautiful image to keep us going when those tough resolutions come calling.

6 January

PANDICULATE

Dark mornings are, for most of us, the only catalyst we need for a good stretch and yawn, a combination that is technically known as 'pandiculating'.

The specialist terms for bodily functions are typically pretty dull. They tend to be borrowed from Latin and Greek, and remain within the confines of medical or anatomical diction- aries for good reason. The act of sneezing, for example, is more properly known as 'sternutation', while kissing is 'oscu- lation'. The latter is alternatively, and slightly chillingly, defined in the *Oxford English Dictionary* as 'the mutual contact of blood vessels'; in the dictionary it sits close to 'oscitation', the medical term for yawning (from the Latin *os*, mouth).

None of these quiver with colour. Pandiculating, while still having a medical ring to it, is nonetheless a pithy description for something many of us do every day on waking: issue a large yawn while stretching our sleepy limbs. It too comes from Latin, this time from *pandere*, to stretch, which is also at the heart of 'expand'. It is recorded in a seventeenth-century dictionary with the definition 'a stretching in th' approach of an Ague' (a cold or fever). Most of us don't need that excuse. Incidentally, if you find yourself pandiculating after seeing someone else do the same thing, the contagion of bodily actions is known as 'echopraxis'.

Finally, in Joseph Wright's glorious nineteenth-century collection of dialect, we also find the word 'yawmagorp'. Wright defines it as either a yawn itself, or an affectionately mocking term from Yorkshire, Lancashire, and Leicestershire for a yawning, stretching person – in other words, a lounger. 'Yawm', from the same counties, means 'to move about awkwardly or slowly; to stand gaping or idling', while 'gorp' is a riff on the idea of gawping in a vacant, day-dreamy kind of way.

7 January

GYM

Gyms are never fuller than in January, when resolve remains firm and the Yule-hole (see 27 December) is a reminder of a blowout Christmas past. Gym is of course short for 'gymnasium', a highly important building in ancient Greece. There it was considered an essential community space, not only as a training arena for athletic games, but also as a place for socialising and engaging the mind.

The three great public gymnasia in Athens were each asso-ciated with a celebrated school of philosophy. Antisthenes founded a school at Cynosarges (meaning 'White Dog'), from which the word 'cynic' derives; Plato, whose name lies behind the principles of platonic love, founded a school that gathered at the Academy, and Aristotle founded the Peripatetic school at the Lyceum (the fact that he liked to walk around a lot while teaching gave us the modern meaning of 'peripatetic': 'moving from place to place').

It seems a stretch to get from these famously intellectual institutions to the modern gym, where sweaty 'curlbros' gather. And yet in ancient Athens the body beautiful was equally important. Gymnastics was an integral part of education; contests would be held in honour of the gods, while the training of athletes was a matter of public pride and status. Physical prowess was the greatest indicator of good preparation, and bodies would be oiled to best exhibit the contours of a muscly physique. One consequence of such concentration on the aesthetic was that exercise was undertaken naked. Which is how the word 'gymnasium' began – in the Greek *gymnazein*, meaning literally 'to train naked'.

Incidentally, not all thoughts in these ancient gymnasia were quite so lofty. 'Muscle' is a shortening of the Latin *musculus*, 'little mouse' – so-called because the shape and movement of the biceps, when flexed, were thought to resemble tiny rodents scuttling beneath the skin.

8 January

DYSANIA

When the alarm goes off on a cold January morning, there is little incentive to throw off the duvet and embrace the day. 'Alarm', from the Italian *Alla arme!*, 'To arms!', began as a military call to soldiers to prepare for imminent attack – which is fairly representative of the body's reaction to the insistent buzzing from the bedside table.

The medical term 'dysania' may feel particularly relevant at this time of year. Dysania is a condition characterised by the physical impossibility of getting out of bed. While it may be a symptom of a serious disease, the term has been hauled into mainstream vernacular because it so clearly supplies a need.

Dysania is often paired with 'clinomania', an equally useful term for the near-irresistible desire to lie down.

9 January

DONG-DING

On this day in 2007, the Apple Inc. CEO and co-founder Steve Jobs announced the iPhone, fulfilling for many his own words from twenty years earlier: 'I want to put a ding in the universe.'

'Ding', imitating a ringing sound, has been around for some five hundred years. But its first appearances were far more violent – in the fourteenth century, it meant to deal heavy blows, or crush. To 'huff and ding' was, as the *Oxford English Dictionary* puts it, 'to throw oneself violently about; to bounce and swagger'. The ding that is the sound of a bell seems to have been a riff on 'ding-dong', which made one of its earliest appearances in an Italian–English dictionary as a definition of the verb *tintillare*: 'to jangle, to gingle, to ding-dong, or ring shrill and sharp, as some bells do'.

Today we might use ding-dong for a bell, an argument, a riotous party, or an exclamation of sexual frisson. It would of course never be dong-ding, just as we can never dally-dilly or shally-shilly on our way to a song-sing while wearing flop-flips. Nor walk in a zag-zig to a saw-see, have a chat-chit while eating a Kat-Kit, or (sadly) play a game of pong-ping. All of these follow an ancient protocol that we follow entirely unconsciously, and that goes by the technical name of 'ablaut reduplication'. Essentially it dictates that, in any duplicating word combination, we always put the *i* sound (as in 'pit'), or the *e* (as in 'see'), first, before an *a* or *o*. Even with three elements, the 'rule' stands: the order must be *i* (or *e*)/*a*/*o* – never bash-bosh-bish, or eeny-miney-meeny-moe.

The same 'law' is found in many languages. The Japanese have the beautiful *kasa koso* (the rustling sound of dry leaves), while the Germans might speak of *Quitschquatsch* ('fiddlesticks'), a *Wirrwarr* (muddle), or of *Krimskrams* (their version of the French *bric-à-brac* – which is another).

We've all been doing this for centuries, yet the reason ablaut reduplication exists has never been fully nailed down. Sound is unquestionably key – when we produce an *i* or *e*, we position our tongue higher in our mouth, whereas the *a* or *o* pushes it lower. This high vowel/low vowel sequence produces a pleasing rhythm, even if it's one we reserve mostly for these playful combinations. Such unconscious knowledge of what to put where is just one example of native speaker's luck.

Another rule we don't know we know governs English adjectives, and would remain unknown to most of us had the writer Mark Forsyth not pointed out a hidden (and apparently arbitrary) blueprint when it comes to ordering our descriptions. The rule is 'opinion-size-age-shape-colour-origin-material-purpose'. Thus you will never have a green great dragon, or a young small girl admiring her red shiny new shoes in the marble long old mirror. Exceptions to this order are rare, though among them is the 'big bad wolf', which happens to observe . . . the rule of ablaut reduplication.

10 January

CROSSING THE RUBICON

The crossing of a small stream in northern Italy, on this day in 49 BC, became one of the most pivotal events in ancient history, and the inspiration for a phrase that has come to signal the point of no return.

The significance of the Rubicon River (just north of modern-day Ravenna) lay not in its size, but in its location, marking the official boundary between Italy proper (directly controlled by Rome) and Cisalpine Gaul, a region on the southern side of the Alps governed by Julius Caesar. Such was

Caesar's popularity with the people that he was seen as a threat to the power of the Roman Senate; the antipathy towards him from its senators meant that his days were effectively numbered. Caesar was ordered to disband his army, and his nemesis Pompey the Great, a tenacious military commander, was entrusted with enforcing the edict.

Caesar knew full well that crossing the Rubicon would have dramatic consequences. According to the law of the Roman Republic, a general was forbidden to lead an army out of the province to which he was assigned. There was no coming back – the journey would be forever viewed as an act of war.

Writing around a century and a half later, the historian Suetonius reconstructed the moment that ensured Caesar's heroic status in the Roman imagination. As the governor of Gaul deliberated his next move, Suetonius imagines that a divine messenger of extraordinary height and beauty appeared, snatching a trumpet and rushing to the river to sound the note of war. Caesar is said to have cried out *Alea iacta est* – 'The die is cast.'

Caesar threw the die, and took the irrevocable step of crossing the river, thereby sealing not only his own future but also that of the Roman Empire. 'Crossing the Rubicon' was first recorded as a military aphorism in a chronicle of 1624 – fittingly, the idiom has itself never looked back.

---

11 January

LOTTERY

The first recorded lottery in England was drawn on this day in 1569, at the western gate of the old St Paul's Cathedral. The concept of the lottery had already been in existence for centuries: it is believed that the building of the Great Wall of China was partially funded by public money and the drawing of lots, and the sale of tickets to win various items was used in ancient Rome to fund repairs to the city or give aid to the people. Prizes varied widely – it is said that those offered by the hard-partying Emperor Elagabalus ranged from the 'gift' of six slaves to a cheap and cheerful vase.

For Queen Elizabeth I, on that day in 1569, the matter in hand was the Spanish presence in the Netherlands and its potential threat to her Protestant rule. The pressure was on to shore up her navy and coastal defences, and in 1566 she granted a royal charter to raise money for the reparation of the 'havens and strength of the realm, and towards further public works'. Lottery tickets were issued, 400,000 of them, with a possible jackpot of £5,000. Smaller prizes included silver-plated items, and tapestries from the queen's own collection.

At ten shillings a ticket, the cost of entering such lotteries was well beyond the reach of most ordinary citizens. Syndicates were formed and money pooled to buy a single ticket. The attraction was more than the cash alone – the Crown also promised all ticket-buyers an amnesty of any crimes committed in their past, with the exception of murder and treason. For Elizabeth, such promises were worth it: with its boosted resources, her navy went on to defeat the Spanish Armada.

The word 'lottery' is based on a Germanic word for an object used in a chance selection. 'Lot' appears in a number of enduring expressions, such as to 'throw in one's lot', while reference to a 'lot' draws on the idea of a great number or multitude of things. Meanwhile, the method used for these early lotteries, whereby pairs of slips were drawn from two separate pots – one containing participants' names and the other with either prizes or nothing written upon them – led to the idiom 'drawing a blank'.

12 January

FEEFLE

The debate over the number of Inuit words for snow has been flurrying, if not raging, for decades, held up as proof that not only does our culture determine language, but that our language in turn shapes our view of the world. In the 1960s the anthropologist Frank Boas gently raised the possibility that the structure of languages such as Inuit allows for more variety in its way of describing things. Yet objections to his perceived headline accumulated, and what became known as 'The Great Eskimo Vocabulary Hoax' became a fixture in linguistic textbooks. Even so, to this day most people will tell you that the Inuit have hundreds of words for the white stuff.

In fact, Inuit and other language groups are able to add suffixes to almost any word, thereby creating many more words – this goes for any category, including snow. Consequently there is indeed a large vocabulary for snow, but the argument largely comes down to what you consider to be a 'word'. If all that wasn't enough, in 2015 a new contender in the snow stakes arrived. According to the first historical thesaurus of Scots, that language has over four hundred words for snow, with more being discovered all the time.

The historical Scottish word-hoard includes the wonderful 'feefle', meaning to 'swirl'; 'smirr', a smattering of snow; 'unbrak', the very beginning of a thaw; 'flindrikin', a slight snow shower; and 'flother' and 'figgerin', both a single flake of snow that might be a harbinger of more.

13 January

GRAMMAR

During the Middle Ages, superstition and rationality competed for supremacy in many areas of learning. The study of magic, and the belief in alchemy – the transmutation of metals into gold in the search for the panacea or 'universal remedy' – became the chief objectives of early chemistry. A translation of Bartholomew de Glanville's influential *De Proprietatibus Rerum* ('On the Properties of Things') of 1398 states boldly that 'the asshes of a cokatrice [a serpent, identified with the basilisk, fabulously said to kill with a glance] be acountyd good and proffytable in werkyng of Alkamye: and namely in tornynge and chaungynge of metalle'.

On 13 January 1404, the English Parliament passed the Act of Multipliers, forbidding alchemists to engage in the creation of precious metals: 'that none from henceforth should use to multiply gold or silver, or use the craft of multiplication; and if any the same do, they incur the pain of felony'. Behind the prohibition was the fear of economic anarchy: that the alchemists would create such wealth as would easily surpass the royal coffers.

Nonetheless, education was popularly supposed to include the essential magic arts. These were folded into the notion of 'grammar', a synonym for learning in general. In fact 'grammar' remained attached to this melting pot of language, literature, and occult sciences for 350 years, until the aspects of magical beauty and allure split off to become, in Scots, and largely thanks to the writings of Sir Walter Scott, 'glamour'. 'Grammar', meanwhile, narrowed to embrace the purely linguistic portion of the academic discipline, where it remains to this day.

For lexicographers, it is a strange but reassuring thought that grammar and glamour were once the closest of siblings.

14 January

COLOR

On this day in 1784, the United States was ratified as an independent and sovereign nation. The conclusion of the American War of Independence meant far more than the autonomy of government in the new United States of America – it also decided a battle for linguistic independence, in which rejecting the King's English was tantamount to rejecting the king.

Noah Webster was at the forefront of the movement to separate American English from its British counterpart. No longer would the United States look to the British for guidance on how to speak and write – instead, Webster argued, it must look to itself.

Webster wrote prolifically on the need for a new, independent language, one that replaced arcane and complicated rules with new, simplified, and vigorously American ones. This was linguistic patriotism to rival anything seen on British shores. It enshrined such spellings as 'color', 'honor', and 'rumor' in the American lexicon.

Not that these were new ideas – spelling, at the time the *Mayflower* set sail, was in a state of flux, if not chaos. This was a time when Shakespeare spelled his name differently, twice in his own will, and when the Bard himself (or his compositors at least) heartily embraced spellings that we now consider to be wholly 'American'. In the First Folio of Shakespeare's plays, 'honor' is found almost 500 times – 100 times more than 'honour'. In the same works, 'humor' outscores 'humour', and 'center' pips 'centre' with ease.

Webster embraced such spellings because they were easier, more phonetically correct. And it's hard to argue with him. For anyone tripping up over 'aluminum', 'sidewalk', or even the ubiquitous 'Wow!', it pays to remember that the British used every single one of them before they crossed the Atlantic.

15 January

HIBERNACLE

If you're looking to escape to a winter retreat, 'hibernacle' is for you. The word is the equivalent of the 'hibernaculum', the place a hibernating animal passes the winter months and a term that has been variously used in relation to a hedgehog's sanctuary, a greenhouse, a frog's muddy hideaway, and a caterpillar's cocoon clinging to a snowy twig. 'Hibernacle', 'hibernaculum', and 'hibernate' are all the offspring of a Latin verb, *hibernare*, to pass the winter.

What we choose to do in our hibernacle is of course entirely up to us. If we are 'dormitive' (inclined to sleep throughout the winter), the answer is obvious. Most of us, however, will probably opt for 'snudging', another perfect word for dark January days, this time from the seventeenth century, for the act of 'remaining snug and quiet'. In fact historical and dialect dictionaries hold a cosy lexicon of words for snuggling – including 'croozling', 'snerdling', 'snoodling', 'snuzzling', and 'neezling'.

16 January

SCREAMER

On this day in 1939, the *Superman* comic strip made its debut. At its height, it was syndicated in over three hundred publications, reaching an audience of around twenty million.

In the unlikely event that a superhero was ever asked for their favourite point of punctuation, the answer would surely be the '!'. From Captain Marvel's 'Shazam!' to Robin's 'Holy . . . Batman!' and Superman's own 'Up, up, and away!', the exclamation mark is as necessary to their stories as the hero's evil nemesis who threatens to destroy the world. The lead writer of *Superman* comics for many years explained that reproduction of comics on pulp paper was such a messy job that he began to use exclamation marks rather than full stops at the end of sentences, because they were clearer in print. His own name was duly changed to Elliot S! Maggin.

This is a punctuation mark with a fittingly lively history. The most plausible of the many theories attached to its origin is that it descends from the Latin word *io* ('joy') – represented by a capital 'I' over a lowercase 'o'. Since its early introduction in the sixteenth century, it has inspired a host of nicknames. In 1551, John Hart, making a list of the major English punctuation marks, included one that he called the 'wonderer'. Ben Jonson, arguably England's greatest punctuator (who even inserted a colon, or what he called a 'double prick', between his first and last name), called it the admiration mark; others of his time knew it as the 'shriek' and the 'screamer'. Since then, it has been variously called a 'boing', 'pling', 'bang', 'gasper', 'slammer', and 'Christer'.

Whatever you choose to call it, a pile-on of them is generally seen as a linguistic no-no. As the writer Terry Pratchett put it: 'All those exclamation marks. Five? A sure sign of someone who wears his underpants on his head.'

---

17 January

BAFFLING

On this day in 1773, Captain James Cook commanded the first expedition to the Antarctic Circle, with the aim of ending the ancient debate over the existence of *Terra Australis*. This 'South Land' had been postulated as early as the fifth century, and was regularly charted on maps even though no proof of it existed. Its presence was assumed because it seemed unthinkable that the land in the northern hemisphere was not balanced by a similar mass in the southern hemisphere. On 17 January, *Resolution* became the first ship to venture south of the Antarctic Circle. Cook's sweeps across the Pacific finally proved that there was no *Terra Australis* further south of Australia itself, which was eventually to take the name of the mythical continent.

Cook's contribution to modern geography is undisputed, but his presence in the dictionary is less keenly felt. Nonetheless, his meticulous journals and accounts of his voyages have provided early evidence for a host of words, especially ones originating in languages indigenous to the lands he explored. The *Oxford English Dictionary* records his name alongside quotations for 'taboo', 'tattoo', 'albatross', 'cannibalise', 'chocolate', 'gum', 'mangrove', 'mocking bird', and 'kangaroo'.

An extract from Cook's writings also gives us the word 'coconut', written at the time as 'cocoanut'. Cook may well have known the word's eerie history: that *coco*, in Portuguese, described a terrifying mask used to frighten children into obedience. Look at any coconut and you'll see three holes at its base, reminiscent of a horrible grin.

Such exoticisms are unsurprising legacies from an adventurer like Cook. But he also recorded some home-grown expressions, among them the adjective 'baffling', which he used of winds that blew about and made straight sailing nigh impossible. Even by that time, the word 'baffle' had coursed a strange and fittingly unpredictable path. A Scottish word from the sixteenth century, to baffle was originally to expose someone, and in particular a perjured knight, to public ridicule. One of the (literally) baffling rituals included making an image of the said offender hanging from his heels, and subjecting it to shouting and the fierce blowing of horns. Later on, 'baffle' came to mean to hoodwink or gull, setting the path for the bewilderment and confusion now attached to it. The metaphor of billowing sails, buffeted this way and that aboard a ship such as *Resolution*, is still a vivid one today.

> **18 January**

BERSERK

One of the first polar bears to be exhibited in the United States became part of an early menagerie in Boston on this day in 1773; the nine-month-old cub had been captured in Greenland. Forty years earlier, a Captain Atkins had successfully caught a 'Large White Greenland bear' during a whaling voyage. The poor creature, described as 'white as Snow tho somewhat sullied by the Dirt of the Cage', was brought back to the US, where it lived amidst the bustle of the Boston wharves.

Bears have long held particular sway over our emotions, a fact reflected by their presence in our language (*see* 'lick into shape', 5 January). The animal, regarded with a mixture of fear and amusement and the subject of the cruellest medieval entertainment, crouches behind much in our language. The Welsh for bear, *arth* or *arthen*, inspired the Gaelic names Art and Arthur; Ben is one of several Germanic names containing the root *bera*, bear, while Orson is a name inherited from the Normans with its roots in the French *ours*, bear.

The bear-goddess Artio was venerated at what is now Berne ('bear city') in Switzerland, while the Arctic and the Antarctic were inspired by two constellations in the northern hemisphere, the Great Bear (*Ursa Major*), also known as the Plough, or the Big Dipper in the United States, and the Lesser Bear (*Ursa Minor*).

The Vikings were in particular awe of the creature, again attested by personal names such as Björn. Norse mythology tells of ancient warriors who fought with wild or uncontrolled ferocity, and who prepared themselves for battle in a terrifying war dance known as 'berserker rage'. *Berserkr* translates as 'bear-coat', and looks to the bear-skin coats worn by the warriors into battle, believed to convey superhuman strength. Going berserk these days has some hairy history behind it.

19 January

COMPUTER

In his fiery satire *A Tale of a Tub* (1704), Jonathan Swift wrote of 'A very skilful Computer, who hath given a full Demonstration of it from Rules of Arithmetick'. The computer in question was some three centuries ahead of machines like the Apple Lisa, the first personal computer to use a graphical user interface, launched on this day in 1983.

These first computers were officers and accountants who made computations and calculations, also known as 'calculators'. The word, recorded as early as 1613, kept this sense of human agency until the mid-twentieth century, when the first programmable electronic digital computers began to emerge.

Of course, devices that facilitate counting and computation have existed for centuries. One of the earliest was the tally-stick, long pieces of bone or wood onto which tally marks would be 'scored' as a means of keeping count. The abacus – originally a board strewn with sand, whose name comes from the Hebrew for 'dust' – is said to have been used in Babylonia from as early as 2400 BC, while the idea of 'calculating' itself comes from the Latin *calculus*, a pebble, reflecting the ancient use of stones for counting.

In the Middle Ages, the monarch's accountants would use a chequered cloth as the basis for their computing of royal revenues, moving counters from square to square. This process gave us the name of the office of the 'Exchequer', as well as the idea of 'checking' for accuracy. Ultimately, both 'chequered' and 'check' originated in the name of the game of 'chess'. Which brings us right back to computers – the modern kind – against whom human chess masters have traded blows for decades.

---

20 January

LALOCHEZIA

If winter days make you feel unusually 'forswunk', a term from the thirteenth century meaning exhausted from a sense of drudgery, then 'lalochezia' might be for you. This Greek word, which combines *lalos*, speech, and *chezo*, to relieve oneself, is defined as the use of foul language in order to alleviate stress, unhappiness, pain, or frustration.

Most of us will recognise the instinct to exclaim or mouth obscenities when things go awry, whether it's the stubbing of a toe, a spot of car rage, or a general sense of resentful ennui. We may not be proud of it, but now we at least have the evidence of science to back us up. Swearing has become the popular subject of linguistic and medical research in recent years, and much has focused on its value in psychological and physiological terms. Experiments have shown, for example, that a person is able to immerse their hand in icy water for 120 per cent longer if they are shouting 'Bollocks!' (or similar) while doing so, as opposed to exclaiming something neutral but far less cathartic.

Swearing, clearly, can be good for the health, though if you're foreswunk as well as forswunk (tired before you even begin), it might take a lot of mouthing off to see you through. (*See* 'fuck', 27 May; 'the dog's bollocks', 14 August.)

---

21 January

DAPHNE

While in winter our gardens lie mostly dormant and quiet, they are lit by a few plants that begin to spring to life at the start of the year. One of the most beautiful of these is surely the daphne, a plant yielding lustrous clusters of flowers that fill the air with scent.

The name 'daphne' comes from the Greek for 'laurel' or 'bay'. In ancient mythology, Daphne was a nymph who became the unwilling object of obsession for Apollo, who persisted in hunting her down. In desperation, Daphne pleaded with her father – in most sources the river god Peneus – to help her; he did so by transforming her into a laurel tree (*see* 25 July).

Before her metamorphosis, Daphne was a naiad, a female spirit or nymph who in myth presided over fountains, wells, and other sources of fresh water. Those associated with rivers were known as the Potamides, believed to inspire those who drank from their waters. Among them was Lethe, the Greek spirit of forgetfulness and oblivion who inhabited the waters of the River Lethe in the Greek underworld. Those who drank from it forgot all memories of their earthly life. It is to the name of this river in Hades that we owe the word 'lethargic' today.

22 January

ARSLE

We all have days where progress seems impossible, and we are left with the distinct impression of going backwards. One word for this is 'arsleing'.

'Arsle' is a dialect word, found in Cumbria, Yorkshire, and Lancashire and documented from at least the 1800s. Its origin may lie in the Dutch *aarzelen*, which in turn comes from *aars*, 'backside'. Rather than simply arsing or 'futzing' about, however, it carries the definite sense of retreating – the English equivalent of the French *reculer* (which similarly has *cul*, arse, at its heart). For a while, 'arsleing' carried the various meanings of sitting restlessly, wandering aimlessly, and moving backwards. It is at its most useful in describing the latter – a single, pithy verb for conveying the fact that you are going nowhere, slowly.

23 January

JINGOISTIC

On this day in 1878, Disraeli ordered the British fleet into the Dardanelles to resist Russia – a move celebrated by a music-hall song that went on to become wildly popular. Its chorus included the two words 'by jingo', thus shunting the term 'jingoism' from its relatively unremarkable existence into the mainstream.

Jingoism is defined as extreme patriotism, especially in the form of an aggressive or bellicose foreign policy or a chauvinistic dismissal of foreigners. Its beginnings, unlikely as it seems, lie in a conjuror's patter.

'Jingo' is first recorded in the forms 'hey jingo!' or 'high jingo!' in the late seventeenth century. It was the classic refrain used by conjurors when an item was revealed as though by magic – an alternative to 'abracadabra'. In the same period, 'by jingo!', one of many euphemisms for 'by God' or 'by Jesus', became a general exclamation of surprise or exaggeration. It was in this form that we find it in the music-hall song of the 1870s, written by George Hunt for the actor and singer Gilbert Hastings 'The Great' Macdermott, a regular performer at the London Pavilion. Its refrain consisted of these lines, which were quickly picked up as a mantra in support of Disraeli's actions:

> We don't want to fight but, by Jingo!, if we do,
> We've got the ships, we've got the men, we've got
> the money too.

On 11 March 1878, the *Daily News* was one of the first to call London's outspoken protestors 'jingoes' – 'the new type of music-hall patriots who sing the Jingo song'.

> ## 24 January

THE ACID TEST

On 24 January 1848, James Wilson Marshall, a foreman working for the pioneer John Sutter, was overseeing the construction of a water-powered sawmill in Coloma, on the American River, when he noticed a shiny metal gleaming on the bed of a channel below the mill. The discovery of what turned out to be nuggets of gold sparked one of the biggest migrations in US history. Despite Marshall's efforts to keep the discovery a secret, the news soon leaked and hopeful prospectors began to flock to Coloma; the Gold Rush had truly begun. It's said that by mid-June, three-quarters of the male population of San Francisco had departed for the newly discovered mines.

English owes several words and expressions to this frenzied time. Settlements were dug into the earth surrounding the mines to house the fast-increasing population and to provide saloons, shops, and brothels – these were the first 'diggings', a word later abbreviated to the 'digs' of modern slang.

One of those to arrive in California was the Bavarian immigrant Levi Strauss, who had the idea of making durable trousers for the miners from a heavy canvas that had previously been used for making tents. Those trousers were to become known as Levi's, one of the most popular brands of jeans in the world.

Using simple pans in which to rinse the gravel, those who isolated nuggets of the precious metal found that everything, quite literally, 'panned out'. In their bid to distinguish gold from base metal, gold prospectors performed a test that relied on the ability of nitric acid to dissolve other metals more readily than gold. This was the very first 'acid test', a metaphor today for any definitive evaluation, and the curious precursor of San Francisco's very different acid test parties of the 1960s, whose attendees were given drinks of Kool-Aid spiked with lysergic acid diethylamide, or LSD.

---

25 January

WHISKY

This is Burns Night, celebrating the life and work of one of Scotland's best-loved poets, and cherished author of 'Auld Lang Syne', Robert Burns. A Burns supper heralds an evening of food, singing, poetry, and copious amounts of whisky.

The production of Scotch whisky is recorded in documents as early as the fifteenth century, when King James IV commissioned Friar John Cor at Lindores Abbey, Fife, to turn eight barrels of malt into *aqua vitae*. As a distinct term, 'whisky' is first recorded in 1715, in an ominous sentence from the poet and antiquary James Maidment: 'Whiskie shall put our brains in rage.' If an issue of the *Gentleman's Magazine* from 1753 is anything to go by, anxiety over the effects of the liquor had spread as far as Ireland: 'In one dram shop only in this town [i.e. Dublin], there are 120 gallons of that accursed spirit, whiskey, sold.'

But rather than following the trajectory of gin, which was to become the number one public vice of eighteenth-century London, whisky steadily moved to become one of Scotland's most revered legacies. It is seen, indeed, as the 'water of life', the meaning not only of *aqua vitae* but also of the word 'whisky' itself, from the Gaelic *usquebaugh*.

One surprising hand-me-down from Scottish whisky is the expression 'the real McCoy', a mark of authenticity that has been variously attributed to the American boxer Kid McCoy, a famous cattle baron, and a Prohibition era rum-dealer. The earliest example we have, however, refers not to a McCoy but a Mackay, specifically Messrs G. Mackay and Co. of Edinburgh, who were popular whisky distillers. 'A drappie o' the real MacKay' was a popular slogan advertising the strong stuff in the late 1800s.

26 January

HOOCH

On this day in 1838, Tennessee passed the first Prohibition law in the history of the United States, rendering it illegal to be caught selling, manufacturing, or transporting alcohol. This led, inevitably, to a highly profitable black market, and the popularisation of a shady practice known as 'bootlegging'.

Bootlegging today is a fairly blanket term for the sale of any illegally made product, or for unlicensed recording of a performance, but the name has an entirely literal beginning. During the early periods of Prohibition, black-market traders would hide their ill-gotten bottles of alcohol down their boots. These dealers might have referred to the smuggled booze as 'moonshine', liquor that was both distilled and transported under cover of darkness, or by the light of the moon. 'Hooch' was another name from the period for alcohol acquired illegally.

'Hooch' is a shortening of Hoochinoo, itself a corruption of Hutsnuwu, the name of an Alaskan indigenous people that is said to translate as 'Grizzly Bear Fort'. In his study of the region, the Presbyterian missionary Sheldon Jackson wrote about 'reaching Angoon, the chief town of the hootznahoos – but we did not remain long as the whole town was drunk'. The behaviour he found there, he noted, was not unusual, thanks to the strong liquor that the people drank in abundance. The process of manufacturing hooch was described by another visitor as 'weirdly horrible' – no explanation was offered, but ingredients were said to consist largely of yeast, molasses, berries, sugar and graham flour (quite an innocuous mix compared with some concoctions of the day, such as 'balderdash', a dubious mixture of beer and milk, with the occasional addition of pigeon dung and quicklime). Whatever its taste, the sheer strength of hooch and its effects made the term a byword for any strong liquor – especially the bootlegged kind.

27 January

CHAFF

This was a day in 1841 when Charles Dickens, having completed *The Pickwick Papers*, *Oliver Twist*, *Nicholas Nickleby*, and *The Old Curiosity Shop*, declared himself to be once again 'very busy'. His mission was to complete the novel that had the longest and most troubled gestation of all his works, *Barnaby Rudge* – a story that he believed would seal his fame, but that he also felt hung over him 'like a hideous nightmare'.

While it may not be the writer's most famous work, it did introduce one word that might appease all those whose toes curl at the sound of 'bants' or 'bantz' – those of us who also object to any hint of 'chillaxing' and other words that are self-consciously designed to be cool but fail miserably. 'Chaff', for Dickens and his circle, meant good-humoured banter – light and kind-hearted and designed to lift the mood of the other person. It may be a riff on the literal chaff of wheat – husks separated by threshing and winnowing and of little importance in the end.

Should you fancy a little more bantz for your buck, you can always opt for 'badinage' – a French-born fancy for humorous, witty, or frivolous conversation, at home in the salons of seventeenth-century Paris and London (and so about as far away from chillaxing with your homies as you can get).

28 January

SERENDIPITY

The wonderfully onomatopoeic 'serendipity', which is often chosen as English-speakers' favourite word alongside 'nincompoop', discombobulate', and 'mellifluous', means the making of happy and unexpected discoveries by chance. It was explained on this day in 1754 by its creator, the writer and politician Horace Walpole, in a letter to the diplomat Horace Mann. Walpole tells how he based the word on the title of a fairy tale, *The Three Princes of Serendip*, the heroes of which 'were always making discoveries, by accidents and sagacity, of things they were not in quest of'.

The story tells of three princes who, in the course of their journeys and philosophical discussions, follow the tracks of a camel. Through a combination of luck and deduction, following such clues as the patches of grass where the camel had grazed, and the imprints it had left in the ground, they conclude the animal is lame, blind in one eye, missing a tooth, bearing a pregnant woman, and carrying honey on one side and butter on the other. When they later encounter the merchant who has lost the camel, they report their observations to him, whereupon he inevitably suspects them of stealing it and denounces them to the king. When they are sentenced to death, their only chance of survival is for the camel to be found, which it duly is, thanks to their own detective work. The princes go on to have many more adventures, punctuated by happy coincidence and the fortunate alignment of circumstances, hence 'serendipity'.

As for Serendip, this was an Old Persian name for Ceylon (and in more recent times Sri Lanka). It is said to come from the Sanskrit *Siṃhaladvīpa*, 'Dwelling-Place-of-Lions Island'.

---

29 January

SNOTTINGER

The word 'hankie' is, of course, short for handkerchief. The first element, 'hand', is clear enough, but 'kerchief' has a more complicated history. It comes from the anglicisation of a French word, *couvrechef*, 'cover-head', which originally referred to a woman's headdress. Over time, the word extended to mean a piece of cloth with which one could mop one's brow as well as nose. The French term was mangled to 'kercher', and then 'kerchief', with 'hand' tacked on for transparency. Eventually, both gave way to the diminutive 'hankie'.

Very pleasingly, the Victorians liked to call a hankie a 'snottinger', a word that echoes older nicknames such as the 'muckender' or 'muckinger'. 'Snottinger' can be found in a slang dictionary of 1865, sitting alongside the 'snotter' and the 'snot-hauler', both defined as 'a pickpocket who commits great depredations upon gentlemen's pocket-handkerchiefs'.

Other Victorian slang terms are just as delightful. Sausages, for example, were dubbed 'bags o' mystery', because you never knew what was in them. Not dissimilarly, 'trousers' was a word never to be uttered in polite company, since these clearly housed the unthinkable. Instead, the Victorians developed a whole lexicon of euphemisms for the garment, including 'round-me-houses', 'sit-upons', 'unmentionables', and 'inexpressibles'. If the trousers' contents needed to be aired (linguistically at least), then 'periwinkles', 'jelly-bags', and 'apples' were whispered slang for testicles, while the penis went by such magisterial names as the 'holy poker', 'Adam's needle', and 'staff of life' (far coarser terms existed, of course, but they were tucked firmly beneath the doilied table).

On the street, an 'arfarfan'arf' was a drunkard (who had had more than a couple of halfs); your 'daddles' were your hands; and a semi-polite form of swearing was to exclaim 'Damfino!' ('Damned if I know').

30 January

MAVERICK

This was the day, in 1965, when Britain came to a standstill to mark the death of a man seen by many as the greatest leader the nation has ever had, and by others as a political maverick with an undeniable gift for eloquence but unforgivably racist beliefs. Whatever your viewpoint, few would deny he was a man who got the job done, a patriot from whom leaders still take lessons today – including Boris Johnson, his biographer, who is said to see in himself many parallels. The man was of course Winston Churchill, whose body was carried, on a cold, clear January day, to St Martin's Church in Bladon, near Woodstock, Oxfordshire. The procession, watched on the BBC by millions around the world, was declared by his wife Lady Clementine Churchill to be not 'a funeral, but a triumph'.

The word 'maverick' is freely used today of anyone who ploughs their own furrow, and refuses to bend to social norms or, as was said of Churchill, to the will of the establishment. The inspiration for the word was a land baron and legislator of the nineteenth century, who, depending upon which account you believe, was obnoxious, lazy, or extremely fairminded. No matter which of these was true, he was certainly unconventional.

Maverick was a busy man – he managed not just thousands of acres in Bexar County, Texas, but was also a practising lawyer and a member of the Texas Congress. It is perhaps for this reason that many of his cattle were left unbranded, a fact frowned upon by Maverick's closest neighbours, who saw the animals roam freely and mix with their own. Maverick himself is said to have claimed that this was in the interests of his animals, but many were less generous in their attribution of his reasoning. It's said that whenever they spotted an unbranded animal they would tut-tuttingly observe, 'There goes another maverick.'

From an unbranded calf, the term was later transferred to any independent, free-roaming individual with a rebellious turn of mind.

31 January

CAKEISM

There is no foreign equivalent of the strangely illogical English expression 'have one's cake and eat it'. The proverb puzzles because it is in fact the wrong way round: all becomes clearer with the original incarnation of the proverb: 'you can't eat your cake and have it', recorded from the middle of the sixteenth century in northern English and Scottish dialect. In other words, you cannot simultaneously eat your cake and retain it – the two states are incompossible (i.e. mutually incompatible).

The proverb received an unexpected breath of life during the arduous Brexit process, when Boris Johnson characterised his policy on both cake and leaving the EU as 'pro having it and pro eating it too'. In October 2016, the European Council president Donald Tusk called upon proponents of the 'cake philosophy' to carry out a scientific experiment: 'Buy a cake, eat it, and see if it is still there on the plate.' Clearly some members of the Conservative Party were none too keen on the idea. In November 2016, a page of notes scribbled by one

MP's aide was caught on camera, revealing the phrase: 'What's the model? Have your cake and eat it.'

The embarrassment of the leak swiftly led to a formal denial that having one's cake and eating it was official government policy. Nonetheless, a new phrase entered the Brexicon with matching speed: 'cakeism': the belief that you can have all the benefits of something, with none of the disadvantages.

FEBRUARY

MUD-MONTH

February only became the name of the second month of the year in the Julian calendar in the thirteenth century. It is a borrowing from the Latin *Februa*, the eventual name of a Roman festival of purification and fertility that was held on the 15th of this month, during which people were ritually washed. The festival involved a particular celebration known as the *Lupercalia*, a reference to the Lupercal cave in the ancient city of Rome where Romulus and Remus were said to have been suckled by a she-wolf. The festival entailed the sacrifice of animals whose hides were then made into thongs and worn by young men of patrician families known as the *Luperci* ('brothers of the wolf'), who would ritually run naked around the city.

Before its Roman past was reignited, February went by some unexpected names. In Old English, the month was known as 'Solmonað', 'Mud-month'. A less common but equally earthy moniker was 'Kale-month'. Clearly this time of the year was associated with labours of the land. Perhaps the Anglo-Saxons eventually felt the need to inject a little more romance (or nudity) into proceedings.

AMETHYST

The majestic violet amethyst is the birthday gemstone for February. Its powers were once believed to extend far beyond its beauty. Roman women, for example, are said to have treasured the stone in the belief it would keep their husbands faithful, while early Christians associated the gem's reddish hues with the suffering of Christ. But its popularity was greatest among drinkers, for whom the amethyst held a very specific attraction. It was traditionally believed that putting an amethyst in alcohol prevented intoxication, so that drinkers could carouse to their hearts' content without feeling the effects.

This reputation is largely down to a myth, attributed to classical times but in fact created by the French poet Rémy Belleau during the Renaissance. Its protagonist is Bacchus, the god of wine, who turns his wrath upon the goddess Diana as punishment for refusing his advances. In revenge, he pledges to unleash his tigers on any person who dares to come his way – that person happens to be Amethyst, who calls on Diana for help and is swiftly turned into a statue of perfect crystal, stained with the colour of wine. From that moment on, any drinking vessel or wine pendant fashioned from the purple quartz was said to bestow magical powers of sobriety. The legend survives in the name of the stone, which comes from the Greek *amethustos*, 'not drunken'.

┌─────────────────────┐
│   **3 February**   │
└─────────────────────┘

TAWDRY

This day marks the feast day of Blaise, a fourth-century physician and the patron saint both of wool-combers (he was martyred after being attacked with sharp, iron-toothed combs) and all those afflicted with complaints of the throat. One traditional blessing is administered to sufferers through the touch of two candles held in a crossed position against the neck.

Afflictions of the throat inform the story of another saint, who gave us an altogether unexpected English word. Etheldreda was the daughter of King Anna of East Anglia, who fled an unhappy marriage to found an abbey in Ely, now the site of the city's cathedral. Her death in 679, according to the Venerable Bede, came from a tumour of the throat, which Etheldreda herself accepted as divine retribution for the vanity of wearing necklaces in her youth.

Centuries later, Etheldreda became the patron saint of Ely under the popular name of St Audrey. The city held an annual fair in commemoration of her religious devotion, at which stalls would sell 'St Audrey Lace' – neck-bands of fine lace and ribbons. The name was eventually corrupted to 'tawdry lace', and, as the quality of the fair's finery diminished, 'tawdry' came to describe anything cheap and shoddy. It is an ill-fitting testimony to a woman who devoted herself to what she considered the highest of principles.

---

4 February

DISMAL

While the British love the word 'discombobulated', the Scots, it seems, will always opt for 'dreich'. This is the adjective that regularly tops the polls when it comes to the nation's most expressive word.

'Dreich' is multi-purpose, a term that pithily conveys a sense of something long-drawn-out, of lingering gloom, tediousness, and heaviness. Today it is used largely to describe a dreary, bleak, dismal day with heavy clouds and little light.

That word 'dismal' has its own story to tell. Since ancient times, the belief has persisted that certain days of the year are unlucky. Medieval calendars would mark these days – twenty-four in total – with the letter *D*, short for *dies Aegyptiaci*, 'Egyptian days', for the reason that these had been precisely identified by Egyptian astrologers. No event of any importance would be scheduled on these days of malevolence, of which 4 February was one. In particular, no doctor or barber would ever consider letting blood, and any significant journeys were postponed. One twelfth-century manuscript includes a verse above the calendar page for September, warning that the third day from the beginning of the month, and the tenth from the end, are notably unpropitious days: *Tertia septembris et denus fert mala membris* ('The 3rd and 21st of September are unlucky for the limbs'). Quite what consequences were foretold is left to the imagination.

Another term for these inauspicious times of year was even stronger: *dies mali*, 'evil days'. The Latin phrase became, in English, 'dismal', and the reference to those specific days of astrological malevolence was retained at first. Over time, the term moved to variously describe the Devil; a calamitous event; a bout of the blues; and as a local name for dreary, swampy ground in North Carolina. The adjective followed a parallel route – by the seventeenth century, it had landed on its modern definition: inspiring gloom and depression. In other words, very dreich.

---

5 February

STEALING SOMEONE'S THUNDER

If anyone has ever stolen your thunder, you might be consoled by the story behind the idiom, which is gratifyingly literal.

It is rare for etymologists to pinpoint the very first use of a word or phrase. In this case, however, several contemporary sources recount the events that gave rise to the very idea of stealing someone's thunder, i.e. winning praise for oneself by pre-empting someone else's attempt to impress (and we've all been there).

The story involves an eighteenth-century dramatist and critic named John Dennis. On 5 February 1709, a production of Dennis's play *Appius and Virginia* opened at London's Drury Lane Theatre. The venue was badly in need of successes following the loss of six weeks of performances to royal mourning the previous autumn, when Queen Anne's husband, Prince George of Denmark, had died. Unfortunately, Dennis's play was not to be one of them. It was judged to be ponderously classical and downright boring, and survived only four nights before it was unceremoniously closed.

Even the inclusion of a theatrical first failed to save the play. Dennis had improved on a traditional device to produce the sound of thunder by inventing a contraption that mimicked it more closely – no records exist of how it worked, but some believe he used a sheet of tin, while others suggest it involved rolling a drum over wooden troughs. Whatever it entailed, it was clearly successful enough to be pinched by the company who succeeded Dennis's ill-fated play, and who were staging a production of *Macbeth*.

Perhaps out of solidarity, Dennis himself went along to the opening night, only to be outraged by an all too familiar sound booming from the stage. First-hand accounts suggest he stood up in fierce indignation and shouted, 'Damn them! . . . they will not let my play run, but they steal my thunder.'

If only Dennis knew that one of his inventions – an unwitting linguistic one – was to prove as enduring as the words of any of his rivals, including one William Shakespeare.

---

6 February

BUMBERSHOOT

Umbrellas have inspired plenty of nicknames. In Britain, 'brolly' is the most popular: a term first used at Oxford and Cambridge universities in the 1800s. 'Bumbershoot' is a predominantly American nickname, a word of whimsy recorded since the late 1890s. In America it has come to be seen as quintessentially British. So much so that when Dick Van Dyke sang about his bumbershoot in the film of *Chitty Chitty Bang Bang* (1968) it was intended to emphasise his

Englishness (viewers on this side of the Atlantic were politely baffled). Its origins are elusive, but 'bumber' is very likely to be a riff on the *umbr* of 'umbrella', while the 'shoot' is an alteration of the *chute* of a 'parachute' (since an open parachute looks a little like an umbrella).

As for umbrellas themselves, they were once all about shade – the first examples were used as protection from the sun. The heart of the word lies in the Latin *umbra*, shade – hence 'penumbra' ('almost shadow') – and 'umbrage': the shadow of suspicion. 'Taking umbrage' was thus the predecessor to today's unspeakable act of 'throwing shade'.

---

7 February

COCK AND BULL STORY

History offers various synonyms for a liar, from the fourteenth-century 'leasing-monger' to the Victorian 'pseudologist', with nods to the 'falsificator', 'gabber', and 'wrinkler' along the way.

All of them might be appropriate for this day, which saw the premiere, in 1840, of *Pinocchio* in New York City. The story is based on a tale by Carlo Collodi, in which the eponymous puppet is created by the woodcarver Geppetto in a Tuscan village. The name Pinocchio may come from the Tuscan dialect for 'pine nut', or the standard Italian *pino*, pine tree. As with Disney's creation, Pinocchio's nose grows longer with every fib he tells.

The word 'fib' is short for 'fible-fable', a sixteenth-century byword for nonsense in which 'fible' offers a rhyming duplication. In blunter terms, Pinocchio's schnozzle was particularly sensitive to 'cock and bull', an expression to which two inns in Stony Stratford jealously lay claim. Popular legend maintains that these two inns, in a village near Milton Keynes, were once stopping posts for rival stagecoach companies, where passengers could be refreshed and horses changed. The Cock and The Bull are said to have run a competition to see which of them could produce the most outlandish story and convince travellers of its veracity so that they would swiftly deliver the gossip to London.

For all its colour, the story is appropriately enough a load of old cobblers ('cobblers' awls' = balls, in which an 'awl' is a shoemaker's tool). The true source of 'cock and bull' has been lost, but it was almost certainly a riff on a French expression from the 1600s – a *coq-à-l'âne* ('cock to the donkey') story was an incoherent, rambling one, with a fair bit of pseudologising thrown in.

---

8 February

RAGAMUFFIN

A day of mystery and menace, 8 February lingers in the mythology of Devon, thanks to the discovery, in 1855, of thousands of cloven hoofmarks along a snowy stretch beside the Exe estuary in South Devon.

The footprints appeared to inexplicably travel across the river, through haystacks, over walls and roofs, and up drainpipes. They came right up to cottage doors before tracking back upon themselves. No single theory as to their origin made sense, apart, it seemed, for one – that this was Satan's stalking ground. While several theories have been put forward to explain the phenomenon dubbed 'Devil's Footprints', none of them nail it to complete satisfaction, and the mystery remains unsolved.

English abounds with names for the Prince of Darkness: Mephistopheles, Old Nick, Beelzebub (from the Hebrew for another nickname, 'Lord of the Flies') – all have inspired fear for centuries. Other words hide their satanic past with ease – such as 'the blues', a shortening of the 'blue devils' that were said to bring depression and melancholy.

'Ragamuffins' are equally clandestine companions to Lucifer. 'Ragged', 'ragman', and 'ragamuffin' all appeared in the early Middle Ages as bywords for the Devil himself. The allusion in each seems to be either to the Devil's shabby appearance, or to his incarnation as a cloven-hoofed animal with tatty, matted fur. As for 'muffin', it probably serves here simply as a fanciful suffix. What intrigues more is that the first evidence of the word appears in a surname: an 'Isabella Ragamuffyn' was alive and well (and presumably unpopular) in Oxford in 1344.

Whatever the origin, by the sixteenth century 'ragamuffin' had shifted from a hellish demon to someone of ragged and dirty appearance, with morals and behaviour to match.

9 February

TOADY

These are the weeks in which frogs and toads spawn in ponds across Britain before hatching into tadpoles. 'Tadpole' is a curious word that translates literally as 'toad-head' – perhaps because, in its early stages, a tadpole seems to consist of nothing but a tail and a large head. The 'pole' here, incidentally, is a sibling of the voting poll, originally a head count.

Frogs held unusual importance in medieval and Renaissance medicine. It was believed, for example, that holding a live frog in a child's mouth would cure the patient of a throat infection. Conversely, many frogs and toads were considered to be poisonous, and it was this belief that inspired one of the shadiest tricks in the repertoire of seventeenth-century quacks and charlatans.

Quack is short for 'quacksalver' – a Dutch term that translates as 'ointment-rubber'. It was a popular epithet for the bogus doctors who stunned crowds at markets and fairs across sixteenth-century Britain in their efforts to sell their medicinal wares. One of their most notorious stunts involved the quack 'allowing' his assistant to swallow a supposedly poisonous toad. The master would then promptly 'save' the assistant by administering a miracle potion, one that he would then sell to the captivated crowd as a universal cure-all.

Thanks to such quackery, the charlatan's assistant became known as a 'toad-eater', a word that soon took on the figurative meaning of an obsequious parasite whose sole aim was to please his master at any price. By the nineteenth century, 'toad-eater' had been shortened to 'toady': the diminutive -y suffix adding emphasis to the contemptible nature of a sycophant.

---

10 February

TOFF

During the Middle Ages, students admitted to universities would often hold minor clerical status, and donned garb similar to that worn by the clergy. These vestments evolved into the academic long black gown, together with a hood and cap. The latter, when worn by titled undergraduates and the sons of peers in the House of Lords, were often ornately decorated with gold tassels or 'tufts'. It is these embellishments, the symbols of extreme privilege, that gave us the modern English word 'toff'.

The word 'snob' may also have its birthplace in these privileged institutions. Originally a dialect term for a cobbler, it became attached to Cambridge townsfolk, considered outsiders by members of the university. From there it was only a short step to its use for a 'lower-class' person and, eventually, to social climbers who sought to imitate those of greater wealth and status, as well as those who looked down on the wannabes who did exactly that.

From such social divisions the term 'town and gown'

emerged. Enmity between the two populations has a long and occasionally bloody history, none more so than in the city of Oxford, when one particularly deadly encounter on the feast day of St Scholastica, 10 February 1355, led to the death of sixty-three students and thirty townspeople.

The seed of the riot was a dispute in the Swindlestock Tavern between two Oxford students – Walter Spryngeheuse and Roger de Chesterfield – and the taverner, John Croidon. The students are said to have complained churlishly about the quality of their drink, leading to an altercation in which they threw their drinks in the taverner's face and assaulted him. Some two hundred students entered the fray, attacking the mayor and other local councillors. As the situation escalated, locals from the surrounding countryside arrived, armed with bows, axes, and the battle cry, 'Havoc! Havoc! Smyt fast, give gode knocks!' They broke into the academic halls and slaughtered any students they could vanquish, many losing their own lives in the process.

For nearly five hundred years thereafter, on 10 February, the mayor and bailiffs of Oxford, together with sixty-three townspeople representing the number of scholars slain, marched to the University Church of St Mary the Virgin, where the vice chancellor of the university awaited them. The bailiffs would hand over 63 pence, usually in small silver coins.

Although the ceremony was stopped in the nineteenth century, some would say that the relationship between town and gown remains fragile – and that 'toffs' and 'snobs' remain firmly on the linguistic landscape, despite strong efforts to move them on.

GERRYMANDERING

Gerrymandering, or what is otherwise known as 'redistricting', is generally viewed as one of the great curses of modern politics. The term arose from one particular episode in American political history, involving a bill signed on 11 February 1812 by Elbridge Gerry, then Governor of Massachusetts. The bill effectively redistributed the State Senate election districts so as to favour his Democratic-Republican party over the rival Federalists. This wasn't the first time that political machinations had redefined district boundaries, but it is surely the most notorious.

Gerry was considered to be one of the Founding Fathers. A signatory to the Declaration of Independence and a trusted friend of the second US President John Adams, he was as well known as he was eccentric. A picture of him in Washington's Smithsonian Institution shows a shock of white hair and a startlingly direct gaze. His newly drawn senatorial districts were freakish in shape, denounced by his opponents as mere 'carvings and manglings'.

It's said that the word 'gerrymander' was created at a dinner party attended by Federalists, intended as a mockery of the hated bill. A drawing of a salamander-like creature, with a long neck and snake-like head, appeared in the *Boston Gazette*, where it was nicknamed the Gerry-Mander. In a separate account, by the Republican senator and historian Henry Cabot Lodge, the word arose from a different incident, when the editor of the *Centinel* newspaper hung a map of the new voting boundaries in his office: 'Stuart, the painter, observing it, added a head, wings and claws, and exclaimed, "That will do for a salamander!" "Gerrymander!" said Russell, and the word became a proverb.'

However it came about, the portmanteau has since become a byword for any manipulation of electoral boundaries in the interests of political expediency.

12 February

TREADMILL

We may feel as if we're walking an endless treadmill during these days of winter – we may even be electing to exercise on real ones if our resolutions still hold – but we are at least afforded the occasional break. This was patently not the case for those on an original treadmill: a machine with a disturbing and unforgiving past.

The origins of the treadmill can be traced back as far as ancient Rome, when treadwheel cranes were used to carry heavy stones and masonry. Their use in construction and agriculture – particularly in the milling industry – continued. But it was the grinding of air rather than corn that took over in the nineteenth century, when an English engineer named Sir William Cubitt identified what he saw as a just and fitting antidote to the idleness of prisoners at a gaol in Bury St Edmunds. Cubitt believed that a new version of the traditional treadmill, powered by humans, might 'reform offenders by teaching them the habits of industry'.

Cubitt's punitive treadmills rotated around a horizontal axis that required the user to step upwards continually, so that they were effectively, like an Escher painting, walking up an endless staircase.

Many models were wide enough for several prisoners to walk side by side for six or more hours a day, climbing up to four kilometres in the process. The exercise was, in most cases, entirely pointless – achieving nothing but the Victorian ideal of atonement. In some prisons, mills were installed so that the punishment at least had some purpose. Brixton Prison was one of these, enforcing hard labour through the relentless grinding of corn. The back-breaking, demoralising work caused many an early death and starvation – no amount of prison rations could replace the calories the prisoners would expend day in, day out.

For all their popularity at banishing perceived idleness and complacency, penal treadmills were eventually abolished. As for the treadmills we pound in the gym, their forerunners were designed to diagnose heart and lung disease, and were invented at the University of Washington in 1952. The fact that they were given the name of those torturous machines of old may feel appropriate after a sweaty hour on the eternal conveyor belt.

---

13 February

TARTLE

English is full of linguistic gaps. What do we call the email you leave until later because you need to give it a considered response, and then forget about all together? What about the compulsion to stare at the person you're overtaking in your car? What do you call the sudden grip of fear that the person trending on Twitter has died?

Happily, some of the apparent holes in today's language can in fact be filled by a good riffle through a dictionary from the past. The seventeenth-century Scots word 'tartle' is one of those. It is defined in the *Dictionary of the Scots Language* as 'to hesitate, to be uncertain as in recognizing a person or object'. In other words, tartling involves the embarrassed and extended pause you make when forced to introduce to a friend someone whose name you have completely forgotten. The flow of ums, erms, and ahs that duly follow are also known as tartles.

If you're looking for something more expressive, you

might look to Australian slang, where the term for someone who is very familiar but whose name escapes you is apparently known as a 'shaggledick'. History hasn't yet recorded why.

---

14 February

FIRKYTOODLING

There is, famously, no synonym for love, no single word that captures its spectrum of emotions and possibilities. Love is as unique in language as it is in life.

The vocabulary surrounding love is a different matter – whether it's a fancy term for the hots ('concupiscence' if you need it this Valentine's Day), or a byword for being excessively fond of your wife ('uxorious'), English will always oblige.

According to the lexicon of TV shows like *Love Island*, sex is otherwise known as 'dusting' or 'cracking on'. This is as nothing compared to those terms offered by a historical thesaurus, which might suggest 'hot cockles' (1500s), doing the 'service of Venus' (1600s), and enjoying some 'fandango de pokum' (1800s). Energetic flirting ('sticking it on someone', in blunt twenty-first-century slang) was gloriously known to the Victorians as 'firkytoodling'.

Firkytoodling is defined as 'indulging in physically intimate endearments', or 'preliminary caresses' – in other words, having a bit of foreplay. Its origin is unknown, though there may be a sinister connection with the verb to 'firk', meaning to 'beat'. (That may sound far-fetched, but the verb to 'fuck' is probably from the Latin *pugnare*, which also meant to 'hit'; *see* 27 May.)

Any good love-lexicon will give you other useful phrases too: a 'belgard' is a longing, infatuated gaze, as from eyes that glimmer with 'lovelight' – a radiance that only deep affection and attraction can give. Not that this is always successful –

'sphallolalia' is flirtation that, for all its intensity, leads absolutely nowhere (*see* 25 November).

The thesaurus entry for love may be a little light, but firkytoodling is surely worth a second glance.

15 February

HUFFLE-BUFFS

The *Dictionary of the Scots Language* defines 'huffle-buffs' simply as 'old clothes'. For those that love them, however, they are so much more than that.

The clue lies in the word's sounds – shuffling, fluffy, soft, and possibly a little on the baggy side. For huffle-buffs are the old, shabby, but wonderfully homely clothes we tend to put on at the end of a very long week and – with luck – not take off again until Monday morning. They are, in other words, the ultimate in comfort wear. It seems that even in the eighteenth century, when the word is first recorded, people had a need for clothes in which they could lounge, mooch, and expand as much as they pleased.

16 February

SNICK-UP

It's said that on this day in the seventh century, during a deadly epidemic of bubonic plague, Pope Gregory the Great decreed that 'God bless you' was the proper protective response to a sneeze. His formula was apparently intended to protect both the sneezer and sneezee from disease, or alternatively to commend a doomed soul to God. Other cultures clearly agreed: the Spanish, Germans and Russians are among many that wish each other 'health' (*Salud, Gesundheit,* and *Búdte zdoróvy* respectively).

The practice of blessing someone after a sneeze goes back earlier still. Tiberius Caesar allegedly made a point of saluting anyone sneezing even from his chariot. Superstition commonly held that a sneeze was the body's way of ridding any evil spirits possessing it; the act was also thought to cause a temporary cessation of the heart.

The medical term for sneezing is 'sternutation'. 'Sneeze' itself began as the onomatopoeic 'fnese', in which the hard 'f' conveys the sound both of a blocked nose and a puff and a snort. When the Germanic combination of 'fn' became wholly unfamiliar, the 'f' was misread as an 's'.

If you happen to suffer from a 'snick-up' – a seventeenth-century byword for a fit of fneses – there is a verbal etiquette for that too. Two sneezes in Spanish will earn you a *dinero* (money), while three will allow you *amor*, love. In the Netherlands, if you manage three sneezes you may hear the response *morgen mooi weer*, 'good weather tomorrow'. If hayfever strikes, and your snick-up starts to stack up beyond three, then – linguistically speaking – you're on your own.

---

17 February

FROBLY-MOBLY

Dark murky mornings can have you yearning for a duvet day. While claims of a humdudgeon (*see* 4 January) might land nicely with your boss, you are perfectly entitled to feel 'frobly-mobly' (or, if you prefer, the slightly flabbier 'flobly-mobly').

Put simply, frobly-mobly is the eighteenth-century equivalent of 'meh'. It was described in one glossary of local and provincial words as meaning 'indifferently well' – in other words, neither one thing nor the other.

---

18 February

GIGGLEMUG

There is something intensely irritating about someone who is permanently jolly, especially first thing in the morning and before coffee. Happily there is, at least, a label you can throw at them. In nineteenth-century slang they would be known as a 'gigglemug' – someone who is perpetually and annoyingly cheery, and the beaming successor of the sixteenth-century 'grinagog'.

Gigglemugs become especially hard to face if you yourself are a 'humgruffin', a word defined in the *Oxford English Dictionary* as a 'terrible or repulsive person' or, less strongly, someone whose natural demeanour is grumpy, cantankerous, and prone to sullen brooding.

---

19 February

PERENDINATE

Most of us are all too familiar with the word 'procrastinate', which is made up of the Latin *pro*, 'forward', and *cras*, 'tomorrow'. In its literal sense, to procrastinate is to put something off until the next day (also known, in various regional dialects, as 'spuddling', 'niffle-naffling', or 'futzing about').

Should you need a little more time, Latin can offer you an extra day in the form of 'perendinate', a verb meaning 'putting something off until the day *after* tomorrow'. The *dies perendinus* was the fuller term for what we once, beautifully, called in English the 'overmorrow' (very similar to the standard German term for the day after tomorrow, *übermorgen*). In fact English is full of the most beautiful markers of time that have inexplicably faded from view. A 'sennight', for example, was the Anglo-Saxon 'week' – it is a contraction of 'seven nights', just as 'fortnight' is a shortening of 'fourteen nights'. 'Yestreen' was last or 'yesterday' night – how much clunkier are our modern alternatives.

If of course you want to remain as vague as possible when it comes to deadlines, you can always rely on the Spanish *mañana*, or borrow the Devonian 'dreckly', a version of 'directly' that actually means anything but – if you promise to do something dreckly, you'll get to it some day.

20 February

FREAK

On this day in 1932, Tod Browning's horror film *Freaks* was screened, starring real sideshow characters. It was highly controversial in its day, resulting in a ban on any UK screening for over thirty years.

The word 'freak' had an unlikely beginning. Its ultimate ancestor is an Old English verb 'frician', meaning to dance, and in its first incarnation in English in the mid-sixteenth century it meant 'a sudden causeless change of mind, a capricious humour or notion'. Authors of the time drew on the idea of sudden whimsy to describe 'fickle freakes of fortune', and those so taken by a flight of fancy that they make the most impulsive of decisions. When nature behaves unpredictably, it may run off course, and any human being considered of abnormal character or appearance was therefore equally the sign of a freakish universe. The progression to our modern definition was already underway.

By the nineteenth century, the 'freak show' reached its heyday. Human displays of people we now know to be afflicted by distinct medical conditions regularly attracted gawping crowds across most towns in Britain. Alongside the bearded ladies and those of unusual height or shortness, P. T. Barnum's shows included such 'attractions' as 'The Human Skeleton', 'The Living Torso', and 'The Girl with Four Legs'.

The trajectory of 'freak' changed once more when the hairy peaceniks of the 1960s emerged on the streets of San Francisco. The term was now intrinsic to the counterculture lexicon, in which a 'freak flag' was long hair, and the unfortunate freak who experienced a bad trip from a hallucinogen was described as 'freaking out' when he or she lost control.

The suitably strange journey of the freak is matched by a similar term, 'geek', a version of the dialect 'geck', 'fool', and first applied to freaks who would entertain the crowds by biting the heads off live chickens or snakes. The idea of an extreme obsessive, who would do anything for their cause, lingered for decades, before shifting to encompass the far cooler enthusiasm we hail today. Freaks, on the other hand, have never quite managed to escape the cold.

---

21 February

SNACCIDENT

Among the most useful portmanteaux in recent times (*see* 2 August) is the word 'snaccident' – a very recent mash-up of 'snack' and 'accident', which denotes the inadvertent eating of a whole packet of biscuits or other delicious treat when you meant to have just the one. Fortunately for any snaccident sufferers, Alka-Seltzer was introduced on this day in 1931.

22 February

DISASTER

On this day in 1797, the last enemy invasion of Britain took place, when a rather ragtag collection of French warships arrived at the Pembrokeshire coast in preparation for what became known as the Battle of Fishguard. After brief skirmishes with the local population (including the plucky 'Jemima the Great' who, pitchfork in hand, rounded up twelve Frenchmen and locked them in the local church), and retaliation by hastily assembled British forces, the invaders from Revolutionary France were forced into unconditional surrender. It was, for both French pride and prowess, a disaster.

For centuries, superstition held that the stars influenced both human nature and fate. Shakespeare was only too aware of the steadfast belief in astrological power. Romeo and Juliet are the 'star-crossed lovers', while in *King Lear*, Gloucester's bastard son Edmund mocks a blind subservience to influences beyond our control: 'we make guilty of our disasters the sun, the moon, and the stars: as if we were villains by necessity; fools by heavenly compulsion . . .'

Shakespeare chose the word 'disaster' in full knowledge of its linguistic origins. The term came into English via the Old Italian adjective *disastro*, 'ill-starred', with the strong implication that all misery and misfortune are the result of the inauspicious position of the stars.

Stars are hidden in many more English words: they lie at the heart of 'asterisk', for example, by way of the Latin *aster*, 'little star'. 'Phosphorus', from the Greek for 'light-bringing', was the name given to the morning star Venus as it appeared in the sky before sunrise; the chemical element was so-named because it burns very brightly. Lucifer, an old name for a match, was the Latin equivalent, while Satan, who went by the same name, was thought to be a rebel angel, a 'fallen star'. And both 'consider', which originally described the act of observing the stars, and 'desire' (to wish upon a star) are rooted in another Latin term for 'star', *sidus*.

---

23 February

MINGING

S lang, as the linguist Carl Sandburg famously said, is a language that 'rolls up its sleeves, spits on its hands, and goes to work'. Arguably the greatest example of sleeves rolled up – for all sorts of reasons – was published on this day in 1996: Irvine Welsh's novel *Trainspotting* offers the darkest of journeys into the bowels of Edinburgh and the lives of its doper antiheroes and, with it, the gnarly depths of Scottish slang.

Beyond Welsh's phonetic transcriptions (*heid* for 'head', or *isnae* for 'is not', among others), and his straight Scottishisms (*blooter*, to strike hard; *cludgie*, a toilet; *minging*, the multi-purpose insult), one of his writing's most striking features is its use of local rhyming slang. Here, an 'Ian McLagan', the keyboard player from the English rock band Small Faces, is code for sex ('shagging'), 'mantovani' is the collective term for women ('fanny'), and the 'Hampden roar' is the sound of the football ground ('score'). You have to work a bit harder to get to the murky bottom of 'Danny McGrain', a former Scottish footballer whose name is a byword for a vein, and a 'Christopher Reeve', meaning a 'drink', aka a 'peeve', itself probably from the Scottish *piver*, to urinate.

Once those have been deconstructed, the reader is faced with what the slang master Jonathon Green counts as 1,300 unique slang terms, all implanted thickly but effortlessly into *Trainspotting*'s prose. Welsh offers a unique glossary of a counter-language that consummately suits his junkie rebels.

24 February

SHORT SHRIFT

The 'shrove' of Shrove Tuesday, celebrated in this month of February, is a form of the verb 'shrive', which in its Anglo-Saxon form meant the taking of confession by a priest, and the absolution of the penitent's sins.

Shrift is an offspring of the same verb. A condemned criminal would only have a short time to be given 'shrift' – and thereby absolved of their sins – by a priest or prison chaplain before their execution. Shakespeare used it in this original sense in *Richard III*: 'Make a short shrift, he longs to see your head.' It is this dark past that lies behind our modern meaning of giving someone short shrift, which is to treat them in a cursory and dismissive way.

Shrove Tuesday, preceding Ash Wednesday, was thus named for its religious significance. Today it is marked by feasting and celebration before the beginning of Lent and abstinence. On this day, believers and non-believers alike eat copious amounts of pancakes, hence the secular name of Pancake Day. In other countries it is known as Mardi Gras, French for 'fat Tuesday': the last day of feasting before fasting begins and the setting for the famous carnival, itself a word formed from the Latin *carnelevare*, 'Shrovetide', but which translates literally as 'the putting away of meat'.

25 February

BUNKUM

A riffle through the *Oxford English Dictionary* delivers a
feast when it comes to political epithets – mostly one
that would give any politician severe indigestion. Morality,
integrity, corruptibility – all are called into question in its
pages.

Whatever a politician's level of probity, talking – a lot –
remains a key job requirement. And, for all that we rely on
the voices of our representatives to echo our own, English-
speakers have long framed such talk as nonsense. The first
record of the term 'flapdoodler', a deliverer of 'humbug',
comes from a glossary of nineteenth-century slang which
defines the typical culprit as a 'charlatan, namby-pamby political speaker'.

There are many other names for these apparent deliverers
of 'pish' and 'twaddle', as well as for the 'flimflam' itself. A
word that has travelled far beyond the world of politics is
'bunkum'. This we owe to a rambling and inconsequential
speech delivered on this day in 1820 by a congressman representing Buncombe County, North Carolina. So long-winded
did it become that other members apparently gathered around
the perpetrator, begging him to finally sit down – but still he
soldiered on, declaring earnestly that he was doing all this 'for
Buncombe'. Buncombe became 'bunkum', and a byword for
political flummery that has endured ever since.

26 February

POUND

As early as 1895, it was mooted that 'the English pound sign . . . is believed to be the oldest monetary abbreviation now in use'.

The first one-pound note was issued on this day in 1797 by the Bank of England, although the curious-looking £ symbol had already been around for some time to designate a pound sterling. The Bank of England museum holds a cheque dated 7 January 1661, in which the sign is clearly visible.

The symbol is a representation of the letter L, with one or two crossbars added to indicate an abbreviation. The L itself stood for the Latin word *libra*, meaning 'scales' or 'balance' – hence the traditional icon of the star sign Libra, and a Roman unit of weight. It was generally written as *libra pondo* – in which *pondo*, the ancestor of the English 'pound', meant 'by weight'. *Libra* also gave us the abbreviation 'lb', for a pound in weight. A pound sterling originally had the value of a pound weight of sterling silver – 'sterling' having got its name from early Norman coins that were adorned with little stars.

The pound note was withdrawn from circulation in England in 1988, and replaced by a coin that bore around its patterned, grooved edge the inscription *decus et tutamen*, taken from Virgil's *Aeneid*, meaning 'adornment and protection'. The phrase was originally inscribed on a shield presented to a victorious warrior; it was chosen as an inscription by the Bank of England because the motto was both an embellishment and a safeguard – in the days when coins were made of precious metal, coin-clipping, whereby coins were filed down, was a serious threat. Today's twelve-sided design is intended to be even harder to counterfeit.

In Scotland, the pound coin bore the Latin phrase *nemo*

me impune lacessit, 'no one attacks me with impunity' – a motto of the Order of the Thistle and the Scottish kings. The Welsh coin was decorated with an evocative line from the Welsh national anthem, *pleidiol wyf I'm gwlad*, 'I am loyal to my country'.

27 February

BUGBEAR

On 27 February 1939, Borley Rectory, renowned as the most haunted building in Britain, burned down in suspicious circumstances. It had been the home to many grim imaginings thanks to various apparent spirit sightings by the psychic researcher Harry Price. His findings were reported daily in London newspapers; years later, they were all largely discredited.

Tales of ghosts, goblins, and monsters of all sorts have been used to thrill and instil fear for millennia. The first 'bugbears' were recorded in the middle of the sixteenth century. They appear in a spine-tingling description in a play of the time, which lists such terrors as 'Hob Goblin, Rawhead, & bloudibone, the ouglie hagges Bugbeares, & helhoundes . . .' At this point, a bugbear was an imaginary evil creature that was said to devour naughty children – a terrorising image used by exasperated parents to coerce their children into good behaviour. The 'bug' is probably a variation of 'bugy' (a word of uncertain origin) while the 'bear' added the spectre of bloody destruction. Nightmares – in which a 'mare' was a spirit believed to produce a feeling of suffocation in a sleeping person or animal – would duly follow.

It didn't take long before bugbear became a byword for a source of (usually needless) fear or dread. In a letter of 1783, the great dictionary-maker Samuel Johnson mused that 'hystericks are the bug bears of disease, of great terror but little danger'. Today's bugbears, usually focused on language and usage, are more pet hates than terrorising beasts, but the idea of annoyance or abhorrence remains the same. The French equivalent, which also slipped into English, is bête noire, 'black beast'.

28 February

DORD

'Ignorance, Madam, pure ignorance' – thus the reply from Samuel Johnson to the observation that his definition of the word 'pastern' contained a significant mistake. Johnson had defined a 'pastern' as 'the knee of a horse' – it is, in fact, part of a horse's foot. Such straight-up matter-of-factness was characteristic of Johnson's approach. The verb to 'worm' he defined as 'To deprive a dog of something, nobody knows what, under his tongue, which is said to prevent him, nobody knows why, from going mad'. Elsewhere, his etymologies were also a little suspect: 'May not the word "spider"', he mooted, 'be "spy dor"', the insect that watches the dor?'

Happily – though not all will agree – English has no government. The absence of a single authority leads most of us to look to dictionaries to provide the ultimate say on whether a word exists and is therefore 'allowed'. These days, the presence of any errors may not be taken so lightly. Among dictionary compilers, a particularly notable mistake was spotted on this day in 1939. It concerned 'dord', one of the most notorious 'ghost' words in modern lexicography.

Dord was an accidental creation by the editors of the *New International Dictionary*, Second Edition, published in 1934: 'dord (dôrd), *n. Physics & Chem.* Density.' The word was therefore 'officially' presented as a synonym for 'density' – the only snag being that there is no such word.

The story of 'dord' began innocently enough. The dictionary's chemistry editor used the once-traditional method of compiling dictionaries, in which each entry would be presented on a separate slip of paper. In this case, the slip read '*D* or *d*, cont./density.' In other words, 'D', or 'd', is the abbreviation for the word 'density'. The entry was somehow misinterpreted as presenting a single word, one that was duly assigned a part of speech (noun), as well as a pronunciation.

The mistake stood for over five years, until an editor noticed that 'dord' lacked an etymology and uncovered the error. 'Dord' was duly excised from the English language, but its reputation lives on. As lexicographical spectres go, it's really rather sweet.

---

29 February

BACHELOR

Today is Leap Day, or, in Ireland, Bachelor's Day. A leap year offsets the difference between the length of the solar year (365.2422 days) and the calendar year of 365 days. For some it also offsets any gender stereotyping by encouraging women to initiate a marriage proposal.

The swapping of the traditional roles is said to have originated in a deal struck between St Brigid of Kildare, an early Christian nun, and St Patrick, whereby one day in the year would be set aside for women to 'win' their beloved. Other suggestions are available, and historians have yet to find the definitive reason for women pushing on this specific day to 'join giblets' with another (*see* 9 March). Perhaps the intention was simply to upend the traditional order, in the same way that 29 February trips up the usual order of the calendar. Whatever the reason, tradition once dictated that any man who dared *refuse* a proposal must subsequently buy the rejected woman a silk gown or a new pair of gloves.

The word 'bachelor' entered English in the late 1200s, when it designated a young knight who was not yet of age and who therefore followed the banner of another. A century later, Geoffrey Chaucer described such a man as 'yong, fressh, strong, and in Armes desirous'.

The implication of youth and inexperience was extended to any novice, including junior members of a City guild, and students who were taking the first degree at a university and who were not yet a master of the Arts. The sense of an unmarried man quickly followed – again it's Chaucer who gives us one of the earliest records of this sense, but this time in a far more pessimistic vein: 'Bachelers have often peyne and woe'.

Such a gloomy outlook didn't, of course, last long. The stereotypical view of a bachelor's life became one of glamour, glitz, and girls. Meanwhile, in the glossary that is unique to the media, 'confirmed bachelor' was throughout much of the twentieth century code for 'gay'.

On the whole, bachelors have fared a lot better than their spinster counterparts, whose name reflects the fact that many unmarried women, for lack of a husband, were forced to spin for a living. By the eighteenth century, the term had all the pejorative associations of 'old maid'. Whoever heard of an eligible spinster?

MARCH

WELSH RAREBIT

Welsh is descended from a Brittonic language of Roman Britain – its closest relatives are Cornish and Breton. It is surely one of the world's most beautiful languages, yet neither Welsh nor its speakers have had an easy ride. Their name was bestowed by the wary Anglo-Saxons, for whom *Wealh* simply meant 'foreigner' – the term had been liberally applied to Celtic peoples collectively who, for the speakers of the Germanic-based Old English, seemed to speak in a strange, unintelligible tongue. This makes Welsh the curious etymological sibling of the 'walnut', the name of which means 'foreign nut', in contrast to the native hazelnut, while the county Cornwall also shares its history with Wales – its name means 'headland of the Celts', thanks to the settlement of Celtic tribes in Britain's south west. Indeed, Cornwall was referred to by the Anglo-Saxons for a time as 'West Wales'.

The first day of March is the day of St David, the patron saint of Wales. It sees celebrations throughout the country, while Welsh expatriates don leeks and/or daffodils (the national vegetable and flower). Samuel Pepys, writing in the seventeenth century, noted how Welsh celebrations in London for St David's Day would spark wider counter-celebrations among their English neighbours, where life-sized effigies of Welshmen were symbolically lynched, and bakers would make 'taffies' – gingerbread figures baked in the shape of a Welshman riding a goat.

Within the historical dictionary's pages are multiple expressions coined by the English to express disdain or ridicule towards their neighbours. Welsh itself was used by Shakespeare as a byword for gibberish – 'it's Welsh to me' sat alongside 'it's all Greek to me' for centuries. For lawyers, a 'Welsh brief' was one that was unduly long or unintelligible, while to renege on a deal was to 'welsh' on it. To use a 'Welsh comb' was to cursorily put your fingers through your hair.

As for the rightly famous Welsh rarebit – the 'rabbit' alternative came first rather than after. The dish was dubbed Welsh rabbit to snidely imply that the impoverished Welsh couldn't afford any meat, and were thus forced to resort to cheese on toast. Only later was 'rarebit' substituted because, ironically, it sounded more 'posh'.

---

2 March

APRICITY

When Florence Nightingale was inspecting hospitals in the Crimea in the 1850s, she observed something that significantly affected her patients' recovery: the positions of the wounded soldiers. She noticed that, just as a plant leans towards the sun, the patients lay facing the window, even if that made their bodily positions more painful. 'It is not only light, but direct sunlight they want', she wrote, observing the tangible effects of the sun on physical health.

The sensations induced by the warmth of the sun on our skin are as hard to articulate as they are exquisite. We bask in its rays unthinkingly, yet science continues to back this basic desire. Sunlight is proven to strengthen the immune system and to increase our levels of serotonin, which in turn impact upon our mental health – yet it is in increasingly short supply. Thanks to artificial light and our addiction to screens, modern living means that our days are too dark, and our night-times too bright. In her book *Chasing the Sun*, Linda Geddes explores how one Norwegian town has installed giant rotating mirrors high on a nearby mountainside in order to reflect sunlight down into the town square for two hours a day in winter. The aim is to alleviate what Icelanders call *skammdegist-hunglyndi*, the heavy mood of the short days.

Even on our own short days, we are occasionally offered the beauty of 'apricity'. This is a word that means, quite simply, the warmth of the sun on a chilly day. Its root is the Latin *apricari*, to 'bask in the sun'. The *Oxford English Dictionary* has only one record of it, from 1623. Surely this is one word that deserves a rescue from obsolescence.

---

3 March

ROBIN

One of the most significant linguistic consequences of the Norman Conquest was the virtual eradication of native Old English personal names. In late Anglo-Saxon England, those such as the male Godwine and Wulfsige, and the female Godgifu and Cwēnhild, were steadily replaced by continental ones introduced by the new Norman rulers. Even those from the Viking strongholds in eastern and northern England, such as Gunnhildr, were eventually abandoned. Beyond the middle of the thirteenth century, only such heavily traditional names as Ēadweard, Ēadmund, Cūðbeorh, and Ēadgýð resisted substitution, becoming during the Middle English period Edward, Edmund, Cuthbert, and Edith. Otherwise, the stock of names given to us by the conquerors were largely continental German names with a French pronunciation, among them what were to become William, John, Alice, Maud, Richard, and Robert.

In late medieval England, pet forms of first names really came to the fore, perhaps because of the need to distinguish individuals within small, close-knit communities. Marion, Janet, Dick, Hick, Dob, Hob, Nob, Dodge, Hodge, and Nodge were all riffs on popular first names such as Richard, Robert, and Roger, while Ned and Ted took over from Edward or Edmund, and Bib, Lib, Nib, and Tib became affectionate nicknames for Isabel. Jack, the most common pet form of John in medieval

England, was a French borrowing of a Flemish shortening of Jankin.

The forename Robin was another of these, a direct result of the Norman influx. A pet form of Robert, it can be found in English records from the early 1200s, but it was in evidence much earlier in France. The beautiful garden songbird that also bears the name, and which usually begins to breed during the month of March, was originally known as the 'redbreast', but acquired a pet name in much the same way as the magpie, originally the *pica*, took on a version of the name Margaret (*see* 'pi', 14 March).

4 March

SWANSONG

This day in 1877 saw the premiere of *Swan Lake*, at the Bolshoi Theatre in Moscow, with the first major ballet score to be composed by Pyotr Il'yich Tchaikovsky. The critics hated it, lamenting the convoluted music, the choreography, even the orchestra. One hundred and fifty years later *Swan Lake* is the most commonly staged ballet in the world. Despite the clamour of the critics, it isn't the inauspicious beginning of *Swan Lake* that has lingered in the imagination – rather it's the mystique of the Swan Queen, and the undulating arms of the attendant swans that we remember. Such has been the story's impact that it would be natural to assume a linguistic legacy in the form of 'swansong' – the final, glorious performance of one's career. In fact, while the ballet no doubt popularised the idea, the expression itself stems from a belief dating as far back as the third century BC.

Swans, the ancients maintained, are born mute, and remain so all their lives until the moment of their death, when they burst into exquisitely plaintive song. The Roman poet Ovid, in his *Metamorphoses*, relates how the nymph Canens 'with tears, in weak, faint tones, poured out her mournful words of grief; just as, in dying, the swan sings once, a funeral song'.

In reality swans have a wide range of vocal sounds, but the legend persisted until at least Shakespeare's time. In *Othello*, the dying Emilia proclaims that she 'will play the swan / And die in music'.

---

5 March

FRIDGE

In the first week of March 1930, the very first range of frozen food went on sale in eighteen stores in Springfield, Massachusetts. A year earlier, Goldman Sachs had bought the General Seafoods Company for $22 million from Clarence Birdseye, a New Yorker who had learned the process of freezing food while working as a fur trader in Labrador, Canada. It was here that the indigenous Inuit showed him the method of preserving fish under thick layers of ice. When thawed, they tasted as fresh as the day they were caught. Birdseye recognised the opportunities such techniques might bring, and on returning home he borrowed space in a New Jersey icehouse, spent a handful of dollars on an electric fan, some ice and brine, and began experimenting. By January the next year, ads were promising American housewives that they could buy 'June peas as gloriously fresh as any you will eat next summer'.

Some two decades before, the first electric fridge had been invented, known as the *Domelre*, or DOMestic ELectric REfrigerator. The first self-contained refrigerator began to be mass-produced by the company Frigidaire a few years later. Refrigerator itself, from the Latin *frigidus* – 'cold' – was shortened to the simpler 'fridge' in the 1920s when Frigidaires were all the rage. It is probably thanks to the popularity of that brand that English acquired the mysterious 'd' in fridge (though, to be fair, 'frig' would never have cut it).

6 March

WEARING THE WILLOW

The first tabloids hit the press in the late nineteenth century. They were small, round and white, and had nothing to do with scurrilous headlines. Rather these were pills that compressed medicines such as quinine and morphine – the literal meaning of 'tabloid' is 'little tablet'.

By the early twentieth century, many pharmaceutical remedies were sold in this form – including aspirin, the abbreviated term for acetylated spiraeic acid (today's acetylsalicyclic acid) that was trademarked by Bayer on this day in 1899. Its natural source is the *Spiraea*, a family of shrubs that includes jasmine, clover, and, notably, the willow tree, which is rich in the compound.

Medicines derived from willow date back to ancient times. In the fifth century BC, the Greek physician Hippocrates recommended chewing on willow bark to relieve pain or fever, while tea made from the tree was said to relieve labour pains during childbirth.

And yet for all its restorative and healing properties, willow has long been synonymous with sadness and grief. The weeping willow, its back apparently bent over in dejection, is an ancient metaphor for sorrow, and to 'wear the willow', either metaphorically or literally, was to mourn the loss of a loved one. In *The Merchant of Venice*, reference is made to Dido, Queen of Carthage, and her despair at being deserted by the Trojan hero Aeneas:

> In such a night
> Stood Dido with a willow in her hand
> Upon the wild sea banks and waft her love
> To come again to Carthage.

Similarly, Ophelia, in the account given by Gertrude in *Hamlet*, dies by climbing into a willow tree and falling into the river below. It's a curious trail that links the willow tree to both the relief of pain, and its direct cause.

As for those tabloids, when newspapers began to appear in a condensed form, they happily took on a word that looked right back to the original meaning of 'tablet', a sheet for writing upon.

---

7 March

BIRDIE

The first rules of golf were published on this day in Edinburgh in 1744, 287 years after the earliest mention of the game. That first record is in an Act of Parliament passed by James II, in which he attempted to ban the sport in favour of archery. This was no whimsical decision – the constant threat of invasion meant that military skills needed to be kept sharp, and both football and golf were clearly proving too much of a temptation for those who should be flexing their bows. Such was the pull of other leisure pursuits that golf needed two further bans enforced by Parliament, in 1471 and in 1491.

The game, however, eventually won, and even endeared itself to another royal, Mary, Queen of Scots, who is said to have had a team of 'cadets' (the forerunners of the modern 'caddie') lift up her long skirts whenever she prepared to tee off. She herself allegedly ran into a spot of bother when her political enemies considered her playing a game of golf just hours after the demise of her second husband, Lord Darnley, as clear evidence that she was behind his murder.

The origins of the word 'golf' are ancient: they are likely to be part of the Viking legacy and their Old Norse *kólfr*, a 'stick' or 'club'. This fact has never quite put paid to the belief that the term is an acronym for 'Gentlemen Only, Ladies

Forbidden'. While being patently wrong on the etymological level, the stubborn belief in the myth is understandable. Mary Stuart may have managed it, but most women have been fighting for a level playing green for centuries.

As for its terminology, the golfing lexicon is as rich and confusing to outsiders as that of cricket. It famously delights in avian metaphors such as 'birdies', 'eagles', and 'albatrosses'. Reputedly, 'birdie' first came to golf in 1899 during a game between Ab Smith, his brother William, and George Crump, which took place at the Country Club in Atlantic City. The story goes that, on the par-4 second hole, Ab hit his second shot to within inches of the hole and excitedly announced he had hit 'a bird of a shot', 'bird' being contemporary American slang for something outstanding. He duly holed his putt and, it is said, from that moment on such a shot was named a birdie.

---

8 March

AMAZON

The Amazon warriors were a legendary race of women, renowned for their fighting skills and immortalised in modern popular culture thanks to the fictional superhero *Wonder Woman*, the Amazon warrior and the daughter of Hippolyte, Queen of Paradise Island. Her story begins when her mother reluctantly sends her to the United States to aid the fight against hate and oppression: 'In America', she says, 'you'll indeed be a *Wonder Woman*. Let yourself be known as Diana, after your godmother, the goddess of the moon.' Diana Prince was introduced to the world on this day in 1941, in *All Star Comics*, amid the bleak landscape of the Second World War.

The Amazons were believed at first to be characters of Greek mythology, as fictional as Diana Prince herself. But recent archaeological research has unearthed evidence of women at least fitting the description of the Amazons living as far back as the ninth century BC. They belonged to a nomadic Eurasian race known as the Scythians, renowned for their horsemanship and their skills with the bow and arrow. The women fought on horseback alongside the men, and have been found buried alongside their weapons bearing injuries consistent with battle wounds.

The etymology of 'Amazon' seems to derive from an apocryphal belief that the women cut off one of their own breasts in order to improve their bow(wo)manship – 'Amazon' may thus come from the Greek for 'lacking' and 'breast'. This, however, is not backed up by any physical evidence, and most linguists today see the word as having alternative, ancient origins, such as the Iranian *ha-maz-an*, meaning 'one-fighting-together'.

Those ancient Scythian horsewomen have inspired more than archetypal embodiments of female physicality and strength of will. The Amazon River is believed to have been named by the Spanish conquistador Francisco de Orellana, who likened the ferocious local Tapuya tribeswomen to the legendary warriors of Greek mythology. This river in turn gave us the name of one of the world's most powerful companies, when in 1994 Jeff Bezos renamed Cadabra (a company whose title apparently sounded a little too close to 'cadaver') and heralded Amazon as the world's largest bookstore.

Not bad for a group of nomadic tribeswomen.

---

9 March

JOINING GIBLETS

On 9 March 1796, Napoleon Bonaparte married Josephine de Beauharnais, whom he was to call his eternal *dolce amor*.

To 'wed', originally, was to wager something precious – such as one's money, life, head, or occasionally horse. The idea was of a pledge, although cynics might infer that its later development into matrimony was more about a gamble on happiness.

The act of marriage has enjoyed several names over time, including, in the seventeenth century, 'joining giblets', a curious turn of phrase given that 'giblets' are generally applied to any unessential appendages of the human or animal body. The earliest records we have of the expression suggest a degree of mirth or mockery, 'If your ladyship's not engaged, what's the reason but we may join giblets without any pribble-prabble?'

The knot that we tie when getting wed is said to originate in the ancient custom of 'handfasting', in which the hands of the betrothed were ceremonially tied together with ribbon. Centuries later, knots of coloured silk were traditionally tied to a bride's dress and kept by guests after the ceremony as lucky charms. The actual expression 'tying the knot' is first recorded in a glossary of Yorkshire dialect from 1828, where you'll find a typically blunt definition of the marriage cere-mony: 'to tie a knot wi the tongue, at yan cannot louze wi yan's teeth'.

This idea of being 'fastened' to someone is there in other terms for getting married, from 'buckling' and 'yoking' to 'getting hitched' and 'holy wedlock' (or 'deadlock', depending on your point of view). In fact, the potential for cynicism is everywhere: it even flows through the word 'honeymoon', the period immediately following a marriage and characterised by love, happiness, and expensive holidays. It sounds poetic enough, but the original allusion was to love that wanes as steadily and predictably as the moon.

The duties of today's best man may be as nothing compared with those in Anglo-Saxon England. It is said that standing to the left of the groom in those days was crucial – if anyone tried to stop the marriage, the best man could dexterously draw his sword with his right hand and fight off the oppos-ition. That opposition might well have included the bride's parents, always a challenge – in fact any best man looking for justification of a mother-in-law joke might enjoy the fact that the root of 'matrimony' is the Latin word *mater*, 'mother'.

On a happier note, the word 'bridal' began with the 'bride-ale', a wedding feast of merry-making and copious amounts of beer that ran as freely through the guests as blood flows through the *vena amoris*, the 'vein of love' once thought to run directly from the wedding finger to the heart.

---

10 March

IPSEDIXITISM

If you're looking for a word to describe dogmatic assertion without proof, 'ipsedixitism' is an excellent choice.

Coined in 1885, it originated in the writings of Roman orator Cicero in his theological treatise *De Natura Deorum* (*On the Nature of the Gods*); he translated it from the Greek motto of followers of Pythagoras – *ipse dixit*, 'he said it himself'. In other words, these disciples thought, if Pythagoras said it, it must be true. A few centuries later, it was extended to uphold the teachings of another ancient Greek philosopher, Aristotle.

In modern terms, *ipse dixit* is restricted largely to legal use, where it is used to criticise or refute arguments based solely on the word of one individual or administration. As for 'ipse-dixitism', this can be freely used for any pontifical statement based on the assumption that if someone, somewhere, said it, then it must be true, i.e. without any allowance for proof or doubt whatsoever – the kind very possibly made by a mumpsimus (*see* 20 April).

---
11 March

COCKTHROPPLED

It might seem unlikely that a national day would be set aside to celebrate a wanderer who travelled barefoot across the American frontier with a cooking pot on his head and apple seeds in his hand. And yet on this day each year, the American folk hero Johnny Appleseed is celebrated – largely with an overindulgence of apples. Thanks to the fruitful exploits of this nomad, it's said that orchards sprang up across the land, bringing blossomed prosperity to the nation. His story had a real-life namesake – a nurseryman named John Chapman, a charitable and dedicated maverick who introduced apples to large parts of the United States.

For all their constancy in our lives, apples feature in relatively few expressions in English. We might speak disparagingly of someone who is a 'rotten apple', exhort our children to eat an apple a day to keep the doctor away, or comment on someone's prominent Adam's apple. This last term, originally applied to an ancient hybrid of the citron, pomelo, and lemon, came to describe the protuberance in the front of the neck, the implication being that it is a relic of the apple of sin that became stuck in our ur-progenitor's throat. In English dialect, you might alternatively hear someone described as 'cockthroppled': implying they have either a neck like a rooster, or an extremely large Adam's apple.

Perhaps the most puzzling of all modern fruity expressions, though, is the apple of one's eye, an evocative phrase that turns up in the King James Bible – 'He kept him as the apple of his eye' (Deuteronomy) – and in Shakespeare's *A Midsummer Night's Dream*: 'Flower of this purple dye, / Hit with Cupid's archery, / Sink in apple of his eye.' The expression is one of the oldest in English, being first recorded in a work by King Alfred in the ninth century. In those times, the pupil of the eye was regarded as a solid, spherical object, and was commonly known as the apple. Because sight is such a precious gift, the 'apple of my eye' was transferred metaphorically to an object of love and affection.

As for 'pupil', this comes from the Latin *pupilla*, 'little doll', and rests on the beautiful image that when we look into the eyes of another we see a tiny, doll-like reflection of ourselves.

---

12 March

AVOCADO

Today, at sunrise, the Aztec New Year begins. The language most commonly used in the Aztec empire, Nahuatl, is now the most widely spoken indigenous language in Mexico. It has given us a valuable handful of English words, passed on by the Spanish conquistadors. They include, possibly, the word 'Mexican' itself, inspired by *Mexitl*, the Aztec god of war. But, alongside 'cocoa' (from the Nahuatl *cacahuatl*), 'chilli', and 'tomato' (from *tomatl*, 'love-apple', because it was regarded as a potent aphrodisiac), by far the most frequently used word from Aztec is the name of the fruit that has taken over twenty-first-century menus and palates like no other – the avocado.

The name of this new superfood began with the Aztec *āhuacatl*. Both the fruit and its name were eagerly adopted by the Spanish conquerors of Central America though, understandably, their tongues struggled with this exotically strange word. In their mouths it quickly became *aguacate*, followed by the far more familiar-sounding *avocado* (no matter that it was already the Spanish word for an 'advocate' or 'lawyer'). The name moved into English in the late 1600s as the 'avigato pear', when it was quickly mangled into 'alligator pear' (a nickname still used in parts of California), before settling on today's avocado. These alterations unwittingly added a figleaf to the original Aztec name, for in Nahuatl *āhuacatl* means 'testicle', on account of the shape of the fruit.

Such is the ascendancy of the avo that, in 2016, Australian millennials were warned that their likelihood of being able to afford their own homes would rise significantly if they curbed their enthusiasm for the fruit. More recently, Virgin Trains jokingly offered customers a third off the cost of a rail ticket if they presented an avocado at the time of purchase. From ancient beginnings, the testicular delicacy is gaining currency every which way.

13 March

OFF ONE'S TROLLEY

In 1888, the second day of one of the worst winter storms in American history brought a renewed pummelling of the Atlantic coast. The Great Blizzard, as it became known, claimed over four hundred lives and paralysed infrastructure. The East River froze over, and high winds, together with more than a metre of snow, demolished power and telegraph lines, leaving thousands stranded in Manhattan alone, among them Mark Twain. Those stuck in Madison Square Garden found themselves being entertained by P. T. Barnum and his team of performers. It was a bleak and surreal time, the impact of which was felt for decades. The storm was the catalyst for the moving of power lines and transport underground, resulting ultimately in the New York City subway.

One expression to emerge from the aftermath of the Great Blizzard was 'off one's trolley', used today as metaphor for wild and erratic behaviour. Emerging just a few years later, the trolley in question was a trolley car, an electric-powered coach that ran along metal tracks set into the roadway. After the havoc of the storm, the use of overhead cables for Manhattan's trolleys was abandoned; they picked up their supply instead from an electrified third rail. If the car became derailed, its power was lost. The analogy in 'off one's trolley' is therefore between a vehicle that has literally come off the rails, and a person who is no longer acting sanely.

14 March

PI

Known in America as Pi Day, and officially ratified as such by the House of Representatives in 2009, the date of 14 March – or 3/14 – represents the first three digits of the famous mathematical constant. As any attentive school pupil will be able to tell you, this is the ratio of a circle's circumference to its diameter, and can be used in a number of different formulae. Archimedes is often credited with the first calculation of pi, although its existence was understood as far back as the Babylonian era.

The word 'pi' was first used in Latin in the mid-eighteenth century by Swiss mathematician Leonhard Euler, as an abbreviation of Greek *periphereia*, 'periphery'. The pi symbol is similarly π, the Greek letter with which the word begins. There have been poems, short stories, haikus (or pikus), and even a book written in what is known as Pilish, a language in which the letter counts of sequential words follow the digits of pi. Michael Keith's 10,000-word composition *Not A Wake*, for example, begins 'Now I fall, a tired suburbian in liquid under the trees', reflecting the first letters of pi – 3.1415926535.

Today is of course entirely distinct from National Pie Day, although enthusiasts of Pi Day apparently bake a good few pies in celebration of their favourite irrational number. The edible homophone has far earthier, if unexpected beginnings, owing its origin to the medieval Latin *pica*, 'magpie', reflecting the idea that the assorted ingredients of a pie are rather like the miscellaneous items collected by the much-maligned bird.

---

15 March

IDES OF MARCH

Today marks the date of the assassination of Julius Caesar, dictator of Rome, an act that was famously dramatised by William Shakespeare. The Roman calendar, whose year began in March, was based upon phases of the moon. Months were divided into three periods: the *Kalends* or *Calends*, marking the new moon; the *Nones*, the first quarter moon; and the *Ides*, the full moon. The first day of each month was the *calends*, when payments fell due and were noted in the book of accounts, or *calendaria*. These were the forerunners of the modern 'calendars', which count the number of days from the first of each month.

The Ides of March, 44 BC, is notorious as the date in history which saw Caesar's downfall, but 15 March was also the annual date of a new year festival dedicated to Anna Perenna, Roman goddess of renewal, life, and the returning year (her name is thus a sibling of 'pcrennial'). This festival is said to have involved the sacrificial expulsion of an old man or criminal in a ritual designed to purify or cleanse society; its origins lay in the ancient Greek ceremony of atonement known as *pharmakos*, in which the pharmakos itself was the scapegoat. The name is of course at the heart of 'pharmacy' and 'pharmaceutical', as the sacrifice was said to represent a remedy for the ills of society.

16 March

FANATIC

On 16 March 1872, the first FA Cup Final was played at the Kennington Oval in London. The match, between the Wanderers and the Royal Engineers, kicked off what is now the oldest football competition in the world.

This was not, however, the start of football, a sport that has been played in some incarnation since the third and second centuries BC. It was particularly popular in the Middle Ages, when Henry VIII enjoyed a kickabout, wearing boots made especially for him by the royal cobbler at the cost of four shillings.

The type of game enjoyed by Henry was not for the faint-hearted. It was sniffily described by a contemporary, Sir Thomas Elyot, as full of 'beastly fury and extreme violence'. Such was the frantic behaviour exhibited by players and spectators, apparently whipped into a diabolical frenzy, that Henry later tried to outlaw the game among his commoners. That frenzy will surprise no one sitting in today's terraces.

Football and obsession have never been far apart. 'I'm off to the temple' was the early twentieth-century fan's way of saying they were going to watch the match at their team's home ground. The phrase holds an unexpected link between the modern fan and an obsessive of Roman times, for *fanaticus* was the Latin for 'belonging to the temple' and, by extension, 'inspired by a god'. The term soon encompassed the frantic and manic behaviour of someone possessed by a spirit or demon – and, centuries later, any fervent pursuit.

For today's fans, the god of football inspires every emotion imaginable and, like those fanatics of the temple, usually to the extreme. If a Roman were to witness a modern supporter's screaming, stripping, and swearing, he might well put it down to a demon. ('Profanity', incidentally, is linked to a different kind of worship – *pro fanum* is Latin for 'outside the temple', hence unsacred.)

For most, football occupies a plane higher even than Cloud Nine, the one regularly referred to after a home win. The playwright J. B. Priestley recognised this early on, observing: 'To say that these men paid their shillings to watch twenty-two hirelings kick a ball is merely to say that a violin is wood and catgut, that *Hamlet* is so much paper and ink. For a shilling, Bruddersford United AFC offered you Conflict and Art.'

17 March

ACUSHLA

On St Patrick's Day, it's worth remembering that the English language owes a number of essential words to Gaelic. They include 'slogan', 'brogue', 'banshee', 'craic', 'galore' (from the Irish *go leor*, 'till plenty'), 'trousers', and 'smithereens', thought to come to us from the word *smidiríní*, 'little bits'.

'Hooligan' is another import from Ireland, a version of an ancient Irish surname that became a staple of music-hall comedy and a series of newspaper cartoons. In the closing decade of the nineteenth century, it was picked up by criminal gangs around London, when the 'Hooligan Boys' received several mentions at court hearings and in news bulletins expressing outrage at increased violence in the city. The hot summer of 1898 saw a marked increase in burglaries and other criminal activities, prompting headlines such as 'Savages in South London: Uncaged Yahoos'. The Hooligan Boys were a particular threat, and the press leapt on the word 'hooligan' as a catch-all term for any disruptive or rowdy individual.

But while there can occasionally be a few hooligans at St Patrick's Day celebrations across the world on this day, with its parades, green shamrocks, and copious amounts of Guinness, the word that sums up the sentimental spirit of the festival, particularly for Irish exiles, is at the opposite end of the spectrum of Irish borrowings – namely the evocative word *acushla*, a term of affection thought to be derived from the Irish *a chuisle mo chroí* – 'pulse of my heart'.

---

18 March

HECKLING

The early years of the nineteenth century brought the formation of the first labour organisations uniting workers. By the time trade unions were legalised in 1824, growing numbers were joining to consolidate the fight for better pay and working conditions. The concept of worker solidarity gained an enormous popular boost on this day in 1834, when six labourers from Tolpuddle, Dorset, were sentenced to transportation to Australia as punishment for setting up a union to tackle poor pay. The bloody French Revolution remained fresh in British minds, and both government and landowners were loath to tolerate any form of organised protest. The outcry at the workers' sentence provoked a mass demonstration through the streets of London, and the submission of an 800,000-signature petition to Parliament. The labourers would thereafter be known as the Tolpuddle Martyrs.

An unlikely by-product of trade unionism is the taunting we know today as 'heckling', a word whose origins are said to come from a particularly belligerent union in Scotland.

A hackle, or heckle, is a steel comb used in the textile industry for removing knots and dirt from flax or hemp fibres. Before the process became mechanised, heckling was no easy task, requiring great concentration and hard work. No. 10 Glasgow Vennel, in the Scottish town of Dundee, was home to a notorious heckling shop, said to be stiflingly ill ventilated and highly unsuited to such back-breaking work.

The poet Robert Burns was among those who carried out hour upon hour of monotonous heckling in the establishment, which was divided into a 'but-an-ben': the 'ben' end being where the flax was dressed before it was stored at the 'but' end. By 1880, the shop's workers had established a union to fight for better conditions, using their strength in numbers and, it's said, a fair amount of shouting. The heckling shop quickly gained a reputation for activism and general haranguing, which led to one theory as to how the 'heckling' of an audience got its name.

A simpler explanation of the term compares the thorough combing, splitting, and straightening of a knotty expanse of flax, with the thorough and persistent questioning of a politician or performer. As for Robert Burns, he wisely abandoned the arduous occupation, for – as his brother Gilbert put it – it agreed 'neither with his health nor inclination'.

---

19 March

EYESERVANT

In a sermon delivered in 1555, a congregation heard the damning verdict that 'the most part of servants are but eye-servants'. A few decades later, the general warning to householders seemed to be 'Keepe not an eye-servant within thy doore'.

The label is a description of a servant or employee who is industrious and obedient only when their master is looking. They pay, in other words, both lip- and eye-service – any service, in fact, as one nineteenth-century writer put it, 'but service of the heart'.

20 March

BOOK

March is the month of both World Book Day and International Happiness Day, and it's hard to imagine anything that has brought more happiness over the centuries, barring love, than books.

The history of the book is inextricably intertwined with trees, in ways that extend far beyond the production of paper. The original word, in Old English, was spelt *boc*, 'beech', for it was on the bark on that tree, or upon beechwood itself, that runes were cast and inscriptions engraved; to this day the German for a letter of the alphabet is *Buchstabe*, 'beechstaff'. 'Folio', which today refers to a book of a very large size, is from the Latin for 'leaf' (itself a term for a book's pages), while 'volume' takes its name from *volumen*, 'roll', referring to the roll of papyrus manuscript that was wrapped around a spindle.

The very first albums, meanwhile, were less to do with music and everything to do with reading. In ancient Rome, *albus*, meaning both 'white' and 'blank', was used for a tablet on which public notices were displayed. (Britain was called Albion in allusion to the white cliffs of Dover.)

It seems entirely appropriate that the tree – whose name shares an ancient root with 'true', because truth is loyalty, steadfastness, and solidity – was the birthplace for books. Not for nothing do lexicographers talk about the 'roots' of the words they define.

21 March

VERNALAGNIA

The beginning of spring is always a cause for celebration. It is a time when buds are erumpent and burst through the soil with vigour.

But it's not just plants that emerge from wintry torpor – humans, of course, tend to be filled with burgeoning joy and renewed energy. They may even experience distinct 'vernalagnia', a recently invented word that combines the Latin *vernalis*, 'relating to spring', and *lagnia*, 'lust'. Quite simply, vernalagnia describes romantic feelings brought on by the advent of spring.

22 March

SYMPOSIUM

If you occasionally need an excuse for knocking off work early and migrating to the pub, 'I'm just off to a symposium' might do the trick. Etymologically speaking, it's fairly accurate, for a symposium was essentially an ancient Greek drinking party.

Symposia were traditionally held in private homes and involved drinking, eating, and a lot of energetic debate on philosophical, political, poetical, and topical matters. They were all-male affairs whose participants were from the highest echelons of Greek society, known as the *aristoi*. The only women permitted were the *hetairai*: high-class prostitutes who were well trained in music and dance – and who probably knew a thing or two about the topics of discourse too.

For the most part, symposia were occasions of entertainment, which for the Greeks most definitely included philosophical debate alongside the plentiful libations; the word 'school', after all, comes from the Greek for 'leisure'. Plato's philosophical text *Symposium*, written around 385–370 BC, depicts a friendly contest of extemporaneous speeches given at a convivial gathering of a group of notable men, including Socrates and Aristophanes. Their frank orations, dedicated to Eros, god of love and desire, amply fulfil the axiom *in vino veritas*. There is beauty too: Aristophanes tells a fantastical story of human evolution, of how humans were at one time two people conjoined, until Zeus cut everyone in half. Love, then, according to Aristophanes, is the pursuit of the other half of ourselves, whom we need to become whole.

To the background of the impromptu musical and poetry recitals, a shared cup, or *kylix*, was passed around throughout the evening. The long-stemmed vessel was an ideal receptacle for those reclining on a couch and 'humicubating' (eating and drinking while lying down). At the end of the speeches, the revellers might take to the streets in noisy and tipsy abandon.

Today's business or academic conferences seem decidedly lukewarm by comparison.

---

23 March

HURRICANE

Today is World Meteorological Day. The language of weather has changed significantly in recent years. In the race to be both informative and exciting, TV, radio, and online weather segments love nothing more than a scattering of hyperbole as well as showers, prefaced with fanfares such as 'we're in for a lot of weather today'. Storms have started to 'take aim' before they 'pack a punch', while in recent years we have been introduced to the phenomena of 'thundersnow', 'frostquakes', and 'firenados'. Happily, some discerning forecasters are also espousing descriptions such as the scent of 'petrichor' (*see* 31 July), or the joy of 'apricity' (*see* 2 March).

The traditional lexicon of weather, particularly the dramatic kind, is still well worth exploring. The story of the word 'hurricane', for example, which conjures evocative images of chaos and destruction, begins with an ancient, one-legged deity. Hurakán was one of the more powerful gods in the diverse Mayan pantheon, playing a large part in the creation of man. His name, generally understood to come from a native word for 'one leg', suggests a connection with another Mayan deity known as god K, who is also depicted as a monoped, as well as a serpent representing a lightning bolt. Hurakán is most commonly associated with the wind, storms, and fire, and it is no coincidence that the Taino natives of South America, as well as the Caribs and Arawak natives of the Caribbean, believed the weather to be controlled by a deity of the same name.

When Christopher Columbus arrived in the Caribbean in 1492, he encountered the Arawak and their word for a powerful wind. Although tragically these peaceful people did not long survive the coming of the Spanish, one part of their culture lives on in the term, which eventually found its way into English, and which originally applied specifically to a tropical cyclone in the Caribbean before being picked up in wider meteorology. In both mythology and reality, hurricanes have inspired awe and terror for some four thousand years.

24 March

WUTHERING

The film *Wuthering Heights*, released this day in 1939, combined the searing talents of Merle Oberon and Laurence Olivier. The poster issued on release carried the tagline 'I am torn with Desire . . . tortured by hate!' The word 'wuthering' had been a good choice by the story's author, Emily Brontë, for through it flows an equally distinct sense of drama.

'Wuthering', also spelled as 'whithering', is defined in the *Oxford English Dictionary* as a regional word for a 'rushing, whizzing, or blustering'. To 'wuther' or 'whither' is to rage like the wind. Such words were well known to Brontë and her fellow inhabitants of Yorkshire. She described the suitability of 'wuthering' to the house belonging to her tempestuous hero Heathcliff, being 'descriptive of the atmospheric tumult to which its station is exposed, in stormy weather'.

But there may be an added layer to the story. According to Emily's biographer Winifred Gérin, the author based the name of Heathcliff's dwelling on a local Elizabethan farm-house named 'Top Withins', situated on stark moorland just west of Haworth, in the heart of Brontë country. In the local rural lexicon, 'withins' are willow trees, based on an ancient word for 'withies', flexible branches of willow used for binding into halters or leashes. If this is true, then Emily Brontë might well have been thinking of her own stormy wind in the willows when creating the place name and title of her story.

---

25 March

LADY

Today is Lady Day, one of the four quarter-days of the year. 'Lady' here is a reference to Our Lady, the Virgin Mary; 25 March marks the Feast of the Annunciation, commemorating the announcement of the Incarnation by the angel Gabriel.

The earliest meaning of lady was 'kneader of bread'. It comes from the Old English *hlafdige*, combining an early form of 'loaf' and a word meaning 'knead', from which 'dough' also derives. In the same way, 'lord' comes from the Old English *hlafweard*, 'keeper of bread'. It was ever thus, you might think, and yet in spite of the implications of humility and subservience, a lady in Anglo-Saxon times was a powerful woman who ruled over the household, and who was responsible for making its staple food.

It's remarkable that the associations of bread with subsistence and status remain to this day. 'Dough' is still a slang byword for money – the wherewithal for living – while today's 'bread-winners', for all their change in roles, are still kissing-cousins with the lords and ladies from ten centuries ago.

The metaphor of food extends beyond position in society to embrace friendship and enmity too. A 'parasite', for example, was someone who sat next (*para*) to you and took food (*sitos*) from your table. Even the word 'mate' is a riff on 'meat', which for the Anglo-Saxons designated all food, whether plant- or animal-based, as opposed to 'drink' – we preserve this more general sense in proverbs such as 'one man's meat is another man's poison'. Over the centuries that followed, as the variety of foods available increased, some kind of differentiation was needed, so 'green meat' came to denote vegetables, and 'sweet meat' began to be used for any item of confectionery. And, once again, friendship was defined in terms of someone who sat with you at your table: your 'mate' was someone with whom you shared your 'meat'.

As for the kneaders of the dough, the first 'companions' were people with (*com*) whom you might share your bread (*panis*). The Anglo-Saxon ladies would have approved.

26 March

BLOWING HOT AND COLD

In the spring of 1484, at England's first ever press in the almonry of Westminster Abbey, William Caxton printed the first translation of Aesop's *Fables*. It was some eight years before the 'discovery' of America.

The identity of the Greek fabulist Aesop remains unclear. There is no extant evidence of his writing, and yet, century after century, fables were collected and credited to him. His stories bear the characteristic hallmark of animal behaviour that throws light upon the moral behaviour of men and women. For linguists, his legacy goes even further, for Aesop's canon has given us enduring expressions like 'sour grapes', 'pride comes before a fall', 'quality not quantity', the 'lion's share', and 'look before you leap'.

To 'blow hot and cold' by continually changing one's mind is another coinage attributed to the storyteller, born in the fable of the man and the satyr. In the story, a traveller who becomes hopelessly lost in a forest encounters a satyr – the mythic, goatish wood-dweller – who offers him both lodging for the night and a passage to safety out of the woods in the morning. On the way to the satyr's home, the man blows on his hands. The satyr asks why he does this, to which the man replies, 'My breath warms my cold hands.' On arrival at their destination, the two sit down to some steaming hot porridge. The man blows on his first spoonful and again the satyr asks him why. 'The porridge is too hot to eat and my breath will cool it,' he answers. At this the satyr orders him to leave, crying 'I can have nothing to do with a man who can blow hot and cold with the same breath.'

27 March

DEODAND

This day in 1848 marks a day in history few will remember: the final abolition of the 'deodand'. This word, from the Latin *deo dandum*, 'given to God', would have been all too familiar to those in the eleventh century, when any item of property or 'chattel', deemed to have caused the death of an unsuspecting human being could be seized upon as penance.

96

The law was often invoked following a death caused by horses or other livestock, carts, or machinery – anything, in fact, considered to be under the ownership of another. Thenceforth it became a deodand, under a law of forfeit that continued intermittently until the mid-nineteenth century. Any sum of money demanded in addition to a deodand was known as *wergild*, also known as 'man price'. This term for blood money includes the Anglo-Saxon name for a man, a *wer* (as opposed to a woman who was known as a *wyf*). *Wer* survives today only in the word 'werewolf'.

Those objects thought to be the cause of death were also known as 'banes', from the Old English *bana*, first recorded in one of the foremost texts on English history from around 800 AD. Its meaning in the text is equivalent to 'agent of death', therefore to describe something or someone as 'the bane of my life' was tantamount to calling them a murderous arch-enemy, a fact reflected in the name of Batman's nemesis and fictional supervillain Bane, and in that of a poisonous plant of the buttercup family, wolfsbane, which superstition believed to be a 'slayer of wolves'.

28 March

SCUTTLEBUTT

For all their destruction, wars have proved consistently productive when it comes to new vocabulary. Many of the terms are sober descriptions of battle, while others give a nod to life in between the fighting. One of these is 'scuttlebutt'.

Scuttlebutt is an eighteenth-century term for a water butt on board a ship: one that had been scuttled by making a hole in it, so that water could be withdrawn. It was traditionally the place where sailors would gather to have a drink of fresh water and a chat – the precursor to today's watercooler.

In Australia, it is the 'furphy' you need to watch out for.

Now a term for any urban myth or erroneous story that is widely believed until eventually discounted, the word is thought to have derived from water carts made by J. Furphy & Sons of Shepparton, Victoria, many of which were used to transport water to troops during the First World War. The carts, carrying the firm's logo, became a focal point for soldiers gathering to exchange gossip and the occasional tall tale. (Others, it must be said, believe the furphy originated in the use of the word for a fart: in other words, a load of hot air.)

29 March

FORSLOTH

For anyone who has squandered a morning, afternoon, or entire day by futzing about and achieving very little, it may be some solace to know that such loafing is nothing new. In the thirteenth century, they knew all about it too. It was then that the word 'forslothing' was born: the perfect, pithy description of wasting time through idleness. To forsloth the day away is to forfeit it for no other reason than being a supreme sluggard.

In fact, a glance through a historical thesaurus will provide you with a whole lexicon of lounging, including 'tiffling', 'piddling', and 'picking a salad' from the fifteenth century, the wonderfully ornate 'fanfreluching' in the seventeenth, and 'moodling', 'fannying', and 'fart-arsing' from the last hundred years.

30 March

ETHER

Among the deepest mysteries of the cosmos, few have inspired such ferocious debate as the existence of 'ether', or 'æther'.

The word for the rarefied substance once believed to permeate all space is a nod to the Greek sky god Aether, the son of Nyx, primordial goddess of the night. Aether gave his name to the material believed by the ancient Greeks to have filled the spaces between the earth, moon, and stars; it was the pure upper air that provided breath to the gods.

Later on, ether was held to be the mysterious substance that light necessarily travelled through: a kind of fifth element that permeated the universe. For years, scientists attempted to prove, or disprove, its existence, until Einstein put paid to the debate with his twin theories of relativity in the early part of the twentieth century. Some scientists, however, maintain that what his experiments show was not the lack of ether's existence, but that ether wasn't essential to the results.

Today, the term carries a different meaning, as the collective name for a class of alcohol-like chemical compounds used as an early form of anaesthetic. It was on this day in 1842 that Dr Crawford Young used ether as an anaesthetic for the first time, successfully removing a tumour from the neck of a patient who would otherwise have died.

But the original mythology lives on in the word 'ethereal', once a poetic designator of things celestial and godly that occupy the upper regions of space beyond the sky, and used today of something otherworldly, with a lightness and delicacy that is beyond the reach of mere mortals.

---

31 March

CATCHFART

A French dictionary of 1688 lists the following entry:

> A Catch-fart, '*un Attrape-pet, Surnom burlesque que l'on donne aux Pages qui portent la Queue de leurs Dames* ['a burlesque surname given to pages who hold on to the tail of their mistresses'].

Clearly the British thought they had priority over the term, for it became a firm slang expression for a footman or lackey who followed their master so closely they were in the firing line for more than instructions. Today, it is a suitable epithet for anyone who follows the political wind – the seventeenth-century equivalent of a windsock.

APRIL

1 April

GOBEMOUCHE

Today will no doubt offer a few hours of more fake news than usual, a spot of children's mischief, and a fair amount of pinching and punching. Those who are on the receiving end are of course April fools or, as they are still known in some parts of northern Britain, 'gowks', an Old English term for cuckoos.

Birds crop up in more than one guise when it comes to deception. To 'grope a gull', in the street slang of Shakespeare's day, was to thoroughly swindle or hoodwink an unsuspecting victim. Those 'gullible' enough to be groped have gone by many more names throughout the years, including 'easy weener' (1600s), 'camel-swallower' (1800s), and 'stiffy' (1900s). Perhaps the idea of swallowing a camel seemed a little far-fetched to some, and in the course of the nineteenth century the swallowee became an insect. A *gobemouche*, in the fashionable French of the time, is one whose mouth opens so wide in credulity that they offer free entry to any passing fly (*mouche*). The French *gober*, 'to eat', also gave us the English 'gob'.

It may be old, but 'gobemouche' is surely a word to keep in the dictionary, where it is defined as someone who believes anything and everything they are told.

2 April

TURN A BLIND EYE

This expression for wilfully overlooking something you know is wrong is thought to have been inspired by one of the most significant events in British naval history.

The Battle of Copenhagen, which began on the morning of 2 April 1801 at the height of the French Revolutionary Wars, pitched the British against the Danish. The latter were acting as part of a coalition of countries, including Russia, who were intent upon ensuring free trade with France in defiance of Britain's position. The British government assembled a fleet off Great Yarmouth with the intention of breaking up the league. The fleet was under the charge of Admiral Sir Hyde Parker, with Horatio Nelson his second-in-command.

Nelson was a formidable enemy, despite having lost his sight in one eye from a cannon shot some seven years earlier. By 1 p.m. the battle was in full swing, and heavy gun smoke prevented Parker from having a full view of the British line. He decided nevertheless that he could see enough signals of distress from his ships to conclude that Nelson might also be stricken and be awaiting orders to retreat. These he gave and, via a series of flags, Parker ordered Nelson to disengage.

On spotting the flags, Nelson's signal officer queried whether the command should be repeated to the other ships. Nelson's response, reported in *Life of Nelson*, a biography published just eight years later, was apparently: 'You know, Foley, I have only one eye. I have a right to be blind sometimes.' Nelson then raised his telescope to his blind eye and said, 'I really do not see the signal.'

Nelson's words coincided with a strong swing to the British, as their superior weaponry took hold. By 2 p.m., the Danish fleet had fallen silent, and victory belonged to him. His success led directly to his being given command of the Channel Fleet, which was to take him to the Battle of Trafalgar.

The idea of 'turning a blind eye' had been in existence for over a century by the time Nelson took on the Danes. But there can be little doubt that his decision to 'miss' a direct order lodged the expression firmly in the fervent nineteenth-century imagination.

3 April

WOLF'S HEAD

On this day in 1882, one of the most notorious outlaws in US history was killed in Missouri. Jesse James, through his daring, violent robberies, and leadership of the most wanted gang in America, was betrayed by fellow bandits Charley and Robert Ford, who shot him in the back following secret negotiations with the state's governor. James remains a legendary figure of the Wild West, seen by some as America's Robin Hood, and by others as a terrorist and master of his own myth.

Centuries earlier, James would have amply earned the epithet of 'friendless man', a synonym in Old English for a hunted outlaw. He might also have heard a cry, enshrined in Anglo-Saxon law, of 'Wolf's head!', a clarion call to the public to hunt down a bandit like a wild animal. Such an exclamation rings odd to modern ears, but there are plenty of similar examples from history: on the streets of nineteenth-century London, an equally urgent cry was 'Hot beef!', rhyming slang for 'Stop thief!'

For anyone daring to capture this particular wolf's head, a reward of $5,000 awaited. Those reading the WANTED poster for James and his band, which brandished the caption 'These men are desperate', were urged to contact Pinkerton's Detective Agency, hired to track outlaws such as Butch Cassidy and the Sundance Kid. The agency's logo of an unblinking, ever-watching eye, with the promise 'We never sleep', has since become synonymous with the expression 'private eye', originally a riff on the initials of 'private investigator'.

4 April

MAGNOLIA

We wouldn't be painting our walls a certain warm off-white shade had it not been for explorers in the seventeenth century, who set off for the Americas with the aim of finding rich sources of bark from a Peruvian plant that, thanks to its high quinine content, was hailed as a cure for malaria. The plant was later to be named 'cinchona' after the Countess of Chinchón, wife of the Peruvian viceroy, who herself was said to have been cured by its bark.

Charles Plumier, the official Royal Botanist to Louis XIV of France, was tasked with documenting the miraculous plant, and catalogued many other specimens from his travels. In 1703 he wrote about a flowering tree that he had found on the island of Martinique, known locally as the 'talauma', to which he gave the genus name *Magnolia* in honour of his compatriot, Pierre Magnol.

Magnol was born in Montpellier into a family of physicians and chemists, at a time when both professions involved the study of plants. In 1676 he published the *Botanicum Monspeliense*, documenting the flora of his home environs, and describing over thirteen hundred species noted by the author himself.

Today there are over two hundred species in the family that bears his name. According to fossil records, the ancestors of the *Magnoliaceae* genus were in existence over 95 million years ago. Today, magnolia flowers are associated with dignity and purity, and their delicate hues, exquisite blossoms, and intoxicating scent have made them a favourite choice in spring wedding bouquets. The plant has found its way into Chinese medicine, popular culture, and even into the kitchen, where magnolia petals can be pickled. It is the state flower of both Mississippi and Louisiana, and is the subject of a number of popular songs and films, including that of *Steel Magnolias* – an expression describing women who combine both femininity and fortitude.

5 April

TITCH

'Titch' and 'titchy', used of someone or something diminutive, have long been staples of the children's lexicon. Yet their story involves one of the most scandalous court cases of the nineteenth century.

In the late 1860s and early 1870s, a widely publicised series of court cases revolved around the claim of a butcher from Wagga Wagga, Australia, that he was the long-lost heir to the Tichbourne baronetcy, held by a noble Catholic family who were holders of England's ninth largest fortune. Roger Tichbourne, the eldest son and heir, was said to have perished aboard a ship bound for South America, but his mother refused to believe her son had died, sending agents far and wide until she heard the news she was longing for: that her son had 'turned up'.

The butcher, known locally as Thomas Castro, duly travelled to England to meet the family he claimed as his. Tichbourne's desperate mother claimed that he shared the same 'malformation of the genitals' as her missing child, and welcomed him as her long-lost son. This was in spite of the fact that Castro was plump and fair, while her son had been slim and dark, and that he had no memory of his childhood. Castro duly petitioned to have the current tenant of the estate ejected. The subsequent court case lasted 102 days and was among the most closely followed and sensational of its day.

Castro was discovered to be in fact Arthur Orton, the youngest son of a butcher from Wapping, and his case collapsed. He was found guilty of perjury, raised large sums from the general public for an appeal, but lost again. When he was released from prison in 1884, he lived off his reputation and even became a folk hero thanks to his defiance of the establishment. He embarked on a nationwide tour of music halls and circuses, he went to the United States, came back penniless, and eventually died in 1898 in poverty and relative obscurity.

The relationship between the Tichbourne claimant and the word 'titch' is not entirely straightforward. Far from being a small man, Orton was extremely overweight. But such was his notoriety that his pictures appeared for months in every newspaper, and enterprising music-hall stars found they could profitably trade on a passing similarity. One such 'Young Tichborne' is mentioned in the *Era* (a newspaper largely devoted to theatrical notices) in 1874, the year that the claimant was sentenced to two sequential seven-year terms in prison. Another who went by the name was a child performer with the real name of Harry Relph, who in 1884 changed his stage name to 'Little Tich' to ride the wave of fame that Orton had inspired. A double jointed acrobat who could tiptoe on shoes that were 28 inches long, and who stood at just 4 feet 6 inches, Relph was as famous for his small stature as for his colourful character roles. In the end, it was his smallness, not his alliance with the name of the Tichbourne claimant, that went on to shape the meaning of the word 'titch'.

6 April

ROBOT

In 1941 Isaac Asimov coined the first written use of the word 'robotics' in his short story 'Liar', which appeared in an issue of the US magazine *Astounding Science Fiction*. The prolific Russian author, who died on this day in 1992, described the study and manufacture of autonomous humanoid machines as 'robotics', and its proponents as 'roboticists'. In a story written in the same year called 'The Runaround', Asimov lists his three laws of robotics:

1. A robot may not injure a human being or, through inaction, allow a human being to come to harm.
2. A robot must obey the orders given to it by human beings, except where such orders would conflict with the First Law.
3. A robot must protect its own existence as long as such protection does not conflict with the First or Second Law.

The laws are quoted as being from the 'Handbook of Robotics, 56th Edition, 2058 AD'.

Despite the entrenchment of the laws in subsequent science fiction, Asimov did not actually invent the word 'robot'. The first use of the term in a modern sense had been some twenty years earlier, in a play by Karel Čapek from the 1920s entitled *Rossum's Universal Robots*. The word *robota* in the Czech language means 'forced labour' and was given to the android-like automatons in the play who embodied the concept.

As for Asimov, when asked about the extended application of his three laws to humans, he replied: 'Yes, the Three Laws are the only way in which rational human beings can deal with robots – or with anything else. But when I say that, I always remember (sadly) that human beings are not always rational.'

---

7 April

HAIR OF THE DOG

While it would be another eight months before Prohibition was officially over, Franklin D. Roosevelt's signature, on 23 March 1933, repealed an Act that had enshrined the belief that alcohol was both unchristian and dangerous. Arguably no other subject had so divided the nation since the Civil War. The many loud voices opposing the Act, including those resorting to speakeasies and bootlegging joints, declared that the legalisation of beer would both boost the flailing economy and put a million people back in work. It would also have the side effect of freeing the nation's jails: at the time of the president's signature, it's estimated that in Illinois alone over three thousand Prohibition offenders were behind bars.

Fifteen days after Roosevelt's momentous decision, beer of a strength of 3.2 per cent began to flow freely in states that turned from dry to wet overnight. Today, 7 April is celebrated as National Beer Day (and the night before, of course, as New Beer's Eve).

If the results of overindulgence leave us feeling 'wamble-cropped', many of us reach for a 'hair of the dog'. This idiom, a shortened version of 'a hair of the dog that bit you', is about as literal as you're likely to find. It is rooted in a medieval remedy that instructed anyone bitten by a stray dog to find the offending animal and pluck out one of its hairs. A poultice containing the hair was believed to cure the wound. Later, the idea of quaffing a small tot of alcohol to mitigate a hangover was thought (conveniently perhaps) to follow a similar model.

Tearing through the streets for a hair is as bizarre a remedy as many others proposed over the centuries, albeit for the bite of alcohol rather than that of a rabid dog. Romans are purported to have sworn by raw owls' eggs mixed with sheep's lungs; bull's penis soup is the national cure of Bolivia, while a seventeenth-century physician named Jonathan Goddard produced a tincture for various ills known as 'Goddard's Drops', said to consist of dried viper and powdered human skull — specifically, however, the skull of someone who had recently been hanged.

More recently, the writer Kingsley Amis recommended a more metaphysical approach. The best cure, he mooted in *On Drink*, was to address head-on the melancholy felt the morning after. In other words, we should confront 'the ineffable compound of depression, sadness, anxiety, self-hatred, sense of failure, and fear for the future' by having a good old-fashioned cry.

8 April

APHRODISIAC

This day marks the discovery, in 1820, of a mutilated masterpiece. A farmer on the Greek island of Melos (Milos in modern Greek) was digging in his field when his spade hit something unusual. He pulled a piece of marble from the ground and, to an audience of French naval officers, proceeded to uncover what was to become known as the *Venus de Milo*.

To this day, the true form and likeness of the sculptured beauty remains an enigma. For some she is Aphrodite, Greek goddess of love, while others consider her to be the sea goddess Amphitrite, who was faithfully worshipped on the island. Over two thousand years old, she remains arrested in time, and worshipped by thousands of visitors to the Louvre where she is now housed.

Likenesses of ancient gods are preserved in language as much as art. From Aphrodite, the English gained the word 'aphrodisiac', an inspirer of passion, while from her Roman equivalent, Venus, we took the word 'venereal', as well as the French *vendredi*, 'Friday', day of Venus (it was Freyja, traditionally seen as her Norse equivalent, who gave us the English 'Friday').

The *Venus de Milo* is surely one of the most gorgeous works of ancient Greek sculpture. She is tantalisingly incomplete: we know for example that the goddess originally wore metal jewellery, where now only its fixing holes remain. Had it survived intact, that word 'gorgeous' would have been even more fitting – derived from the old French word *gorge*, 'throat', the adjective referred originally to bedazzling jewellery worn around the neck.

9 April

QUISLING

This was the day, in 1940, when a man once known as a quiet, intelligent dreamer changed the course of the Second World War and simultaneously left his mark on the English language.

The twelve years that Norwegian Vidkun Quisling had spent in the Soviet Union destroyed his allegiance to Communism, and inspired instead a desire to set up a right-wing political party in his own country. In 1939, Quisling held secret talks with Adolf Hitler, asking the Germans to support a *coup d'état* and help his National Union party assume power. Hitler refused, but when later the Führer's own army took occupation of Norway after a brutal military campaign, he instated Quisling as a puppet leader, thereby ensuring the Norwegian's vilification as a traitor to his homeland.

To the end, Quisling proclaimed his innocence, but his accusers remained deaf to his pleas, remembering perhaps Quisling's own lack of mercy towards anti Nazi protestors. He was executed by firing squad at the end of the war in 1945. Today, 'quisling' retains the very specific definition of someone who betrays their own country by collaborating with an enemy occupier.

10 April

COMET

To see it is a once-in-a-lifetime event. It inspired Giotto's Star of Bethlehem in his *Adoration of the Magi*, and is represented by a flash of light streaking across the sky of the Bayeux

Tapestry. Halley's Comet, named after the seventeenth-century scientist who both identified it and correctly predicted its return, is the only short-period comet that is visible to the naked eye; it passes Earth only every seventy-five to seventy-six years. On this day in 837, the marvel of the skies made its closest approach to Earth, an event recorded by Chinese astronomers. It has struck awe in stargazers ever since.

The word 'comet' comes from the Greek *komētēs* 'long-haired star', alluding to the appearance of a head of streaming hair. These fast-moving balls of gas and ice were historically said to be harbingers of doom, unwelcome prophetic occurrences that would inspire fear among the masses. Those who witnessed one fully expected a year of pestilence, or political upheaval. Its appearance in 1066 was taken as an omen of certain death for King Harold.

Such fear persisted throughout the centuries, so that even as late as 1852, a Victorian periodical noted that:

> Their sudden appearance in the heavens, and the imposing and astonishing aspect which they present, have, even in recent times, inspired alarm and terror.

The magazine notes a recent exception, however:

> The splendid comet of 1811 escaped somewhat of the general odium; for as it was supposed to be an agent concerned in the remarkably beautiful autumn of that year, and was also associated with the abundant and superior yield of the continental vineyards, the wine of that season was called the comet wine.

Greek has given us much of our celestial vocabulary. The word 'meteor' comes from the Greek *meteōros*, meaning 'lofty', which perhaps explains why we speak of a 'meteoric rise' when meteors actually plummet. We take the word 'asteroid' from the Greek *asteroeidēs* 'star-like', and can see its derivatives in the words 'astronomy', 'asterisk' (little star), and the beautiful image behind the 'astronaut', who is a 'star sailor'.

Finally, the word 'galaxy' has even more in common with our own spiral-formed Milky Way than you might think. From *galaktos* comes the word for milk, and the Greeks referred to the collection of stars in the night sky as *galaxias kyklos*, or 'milky circle'. It ties into the creation story that the galaxy was created from milk spilled from the teat of Hera, queen of the gods.

Halley's Comet will next appear in the night sky in 2062. Whether it will be viewed as a predictor of disaster, or as the impetus for some heavenly wine, will be up to the historians of the future.

11 April

ANTHOLOGY

An anthology is literally a collection of flowers. At the root of the Greek word *anthologia* are *anthos*, 'flower', and *logia*, 'collection'. In English, 'anthology' was applied metaphorically to a collection of the 'flowers' of verse, poems by various authors that had been chosen for being especially fine. The same metaphor operates in reverse in the word 'posy', a shortening of 'poesy', or poetry. A posy of April's flowers would be particularly beautiful.

The daisy, for example, is a sure sign that spring has arrived. The story of its name is as entrancing as it is simple – it is a shortening of 'day's eye', because the flower opens its petals at dawn, revealing its sunny yellow disc, and closes them again at dusk.

Other flowers that bloom in this month are shot with golden threads from Greek mythology. The iris, for example, is a nod to the messenger of the gods, personified by a rainbow. The name of the sweet-smelling hyacinth, also drawn from these ancient narratives, harbours a darkly beautiful tale.

Hyacinth was a handsome Spartan prince, and lover of the god Apollo, son of Zeus. His unsuccessful suitors included Boreas, god of the south wind, and Zephyrus, god of the west wind, but his star-crossed relationship (*see* 22 February) with Apollo was to have a tragic end. During a game one day, Apollo threw a discus high into the clouds, and Hyacinth ran after it, hoping to impress the Olympian. In the Ovidian version of events, the spurned Zephyrus blows the discus off course; in others, it is an unfortunate ricochet; but in both accounts the discus inexorably kills the young Spartan, leaving behind a grief-stricken Apollo. From Hyacinth's blood he created the flower whose name we still know today, and inscribed upon its petals the lamentation '*Ai Ai*', 'alas'.

As it happens, the Greeks associated this myth not with the flower we call a hyacinth, of the family *Liliaceae*, but a gladiolus, larkspur, or iris, which each carry distinctive markings. Perhaps the tragic story of a fallen hero was too good for botanists to resist, especially as the original name for hyacinth was the far more prosaic 'crowtoe' – it would be difficult to make a poetic anthology with that.

---

12 April

DEADLINE

Douglas Adams famously mused, 'I love deadlines. I like the whooshing sound they make as they fly by.' A sentiment most of us might share, but, only 150 years ago, that 'whoosh' may have been the literal one of a bullet.

The sense of the term that we know today, of a time or date by which something must be done, didn't emerge in English until the beginning of the twentieth century. At the height of the American Civil War, it denoted a physical rather than a metaphorical boundary, specifically one around military prisons. If any inmate stepped beyond it, they were liable to be shot. Records show that several crossings of the 'dead line' around Andersonville, a Confederate prison for Union soldiers, had fatal consequences. Accounts from captive soldiers make frequent reference to the terrorising power of the dead line, while Union officers wrote of their prisoners: 'They are fast losing hope and becoming utterly reckless of life. Numbers, crazed by their sufferings, wander about in a state of idiocy. Others deliberately cross the "Dead Line" and are remorselessly shot down.'

This wasn't the only use of the word 'deadline', though it was certainly the most extreme. In printing, it was a standard term for a guideline marked on a press that prevented type slipping outside it and subsequently off the page. Today, it is the pressing time limit that looms largest in the mind, with all sense of bloody history forgotten.

13 April

COCKTAIL

Today, in 1953, saw the publication of Ian Fleming's first James Bond novel, *Casino Royale*. A riffle through the pages of the *Oxford English Dictionary* reveals a strong presence for Fleming and his vocabulary. He provides the first records, for example, of 'ninja', as well as 'SMERSH', the former Soviet security service (a Russian abbreviation of *smert shpionam*, literally 'death to spies'). Among his most memorable catch-phrases, of course, is his very particular request for a certain cocktail – a vodka Martini, shaken not stirred.

Many a Martini connoisseur has pointed out that this instruction is the reverse of the usual state of affairs. For a perfect mix, ingredients should certainly not be shaken, lest the melting of the ice and the dilution of the Martini spoil the taste. Bond aficionados might counter that this was a deliberate choice by a spy who wished to surreptitiously lower the potency of his drink. We may never know the answer, but, for a linguist, by far the greater mystery is the etymology of the word 'cocktail'.

The most commonly told theory for the origin of this curious-looking word is that it stems from the French *coquetier*, 'egg cup'. It is said that the cocktail was an eighteenth-century invention by Antoine Amédée Peychaud, an apothecary and mixologist from Santo Domingo in the Caribbean. At get-togethers with fellow freemasons, Peychaud would offer brandy toddies, flavoured with his own make of bitters, which would be duly served up in egg cups. The drink is said to have gradually taken on the name of the cup, which was mangled to 'cocktay' and eventually to 'cocktail'. Compelling as this account is, there is little evidence as yet to support it. It is however a lot more appetising than another suggested inspiration, the 'cock-ale', a dubious drink from the seventeenth century in which a cask of ale was 'flavoured' with the addition of an old rooster, together with raisins, mace, and cloves.

Perhaps, in the end, the best explanation is the most prosaic one – that 'cocktail' comes from the practice of decorating a drink with rooster feathers, much like we do today with paper umbrellas.

---

14 April

YOUR NAME IS MUD

President Abraham Lincoln was assassinated on this day in 1865. In June of the same year, Dr Samuel Mudd was found guilty of conspiracy to his murder. Even now, the extent of his true involvement in the crime is argued over by historians.

Much of the evidence against Mudd focused on the fact that he was seen in the company of John Wilkes Booth: both were Confederate sympathisers with a fierce opposition to the abolition of slavery. It was Booth who shot Lincoln in the president's box at Ford's Theatre in Washington, during a performance of the play *Our American Cousin*. As an acclaimed actor himself, Booth had full access to the theatre; after pulling the trigger, he is said to have sprung onto the stage and to have broken a leg in the process (although Mudd was later to say Booth's injury came from a high-spirited getaway horse). He made his way to Maryland, where Mudd attended to him.

Booth was later killed by Union soldiers and Mudd was convicted as a conspirator. National feeling ran high, with one author later describing the mourning of the president's death as 'the mightiest outpouring of grief the world had yet seen'. Mudd was eventually pardoned by President Andrew Johnson and released from prison, but his name has never been fully cleared. That fact, some maintain, is the origin of the expression 'your name is mud'.

It's a riveting story, but etymologists have cleared Mudd, if not of his crime, then with any eponymous association in language. The *Oxford English Dictionary* states that the use of 'mud' to mean the lowest or worst part of something is over five centuries old. Furthermore, the expression 'his name is mud' is chronicled in a sporting slang glossary of 1823, some forty years before Lincoln's assassination. The relevant entry reads:

Mud, a stupid twaddling fellow. 'And his name is mud!' ejaculated upon the conclusion of a silly oration.

In this, at least, Dr Mudd is innocent. But his insistence that slavery was divinely ordained might suggest that linguistic retribution is better than none.

15 April

CONTRAFIBULARITY

There are few more important anniversaries in the history of English lexicography than the publication of Samuel Johnson's *A Dictionary of the English Language*. For all its magnificence, its quirks and eccentricities, it also represents an admission that English can never be pickled and preserved, and that change is both inevitable and necessary.

Johnson set out to create a portrait of English that was fit for kings, drawing his evidence from the literary greats. And yet, in the time between starting and completing his work, he also recognised a crucial truth. Having wanted to clean up a language threatened by decay, to freeze it in as pure a state as he could muster, he realised that English must rightly continue on its merry, mucky, and beautiful path.

The famous *Blackadder* characterisation of Johnson is nicely perceptive about the impossibility of harnessing a language. The episode, 'Ink and Incapability', begins with Blackadder's master, Prince George – a young man apparently 'as thick as a whale omelette' – weighing up the merits of becoming Johnson's patron. He invites the great wordsmith to show him his handiwork. There follows a farcical sketch in which Blackadder delights in undermining Dr Johnson's claim that 'this book contains every word in our beloved language', and offering his own version of English. I give here a representation of Blackadder's words in the TV episode, rather than the original script.

I hope you will not object if I also offer the Doctor my most enthusiastic . . . contrafibularities. *[Johnson looks perturbed.]* Contrafibularities, sir? It is a common word down our way . . . Oh, I'm sorry, sir. I am anaseptic, phrasmotic, even compunctuous to have caused you such pericombobulation.

If its fidelity to history is a little limited (it presents Jane Austen as Johnson's contemporary, sporting 'a beard like a rhododendron'), the episode is loved by all lexicographers who know, as Johnson himself beautifully put it, that to try to 'enchain syllables' is as futile as 'lashing the wind'.

Meanwhile, 'contrafibularities' has slipped into the lexicon of at least one lexicographer as a byword for congratulations that are entirely insincere.

$$\boxed{\textbf{16 April}}$$

PASQUINADE

In April 1970, the first issue of the US satirical magazine *National Lampoon* hit the shelves. Its parodic style and surreal approach influenced American comedy for decades.

To lampoon someone today is of course to ridicule them, but its original applications were all about the booze. The seventeenth-century French cry *Lampons!*, 'Let us drink!', was most often associated with bawdy drinking songs containing salacious stories and mocking tales in a fashion not dissimilar to today's comedy roasts.

A lesser-used synonym for such mockery is 'pasquinade', a word that harks back to a worthy predecessor of the *National Lampoon* franchise. Used for an anonymous satirical comment that ridicules a contemporary individual or event, its inspiration was a statue in the city of Rome unearthed in the early sixteenth century, whose torso became the posting place for bitingly critical squibs and snubs. The statue was named the Pasquino, apparently after a local tradesman who loved nothing better than to exchange cynical inside gossip concerning the Vatican. Other monuments generated a similar focus, and the 'talking statues' of Rome became stone pinboards on which citizens attached anonymous criticisms of the church or state, in the scathing fashion of the infamous Mr Pasquino.

17 April

CANTER

Geoffrey Chaucer's *Canterbury Tales*, besides being rollicking narratives in themselves, marked a hugely significant move towards writing literature in English as opposed to Norman French. The centuries following the arrival of the conquerors saw French dominate the language of those in power. While others had made literary efforts in English before, Chaucer's *Tales* were among the most widely circulated stories of their day, featuring the dialect and slang from all corners of England that few had attempted to chart. On this day in 1397, the author himself recited some of his stories at the court of Richard II, marking not only the start of one of the most famous pilgrimages in history, but making English vernacular and dialect acceptable to an audience of the elite.

The *Tales* are presented as part of a story-telling contest held by a group of pilgrims as they travel together on horseback from London to Canterbury. Their destination is the shrine of St Thomas Becket at Canterbury Cathedral, and the winner's prize a free meal on their return at the Tabard Inn in Southwark.

The pilgrims are a crowd in holiday mood, exchanging gossip and stories to while away the hours. To make their entertainment audible, and to spare their horses for the long journey, they travel at a comfortable pace, known at the time as a 'Canterbury trot'. By the seventeenth century this had been shortened to 'Canterbury', and eventually to 'canter'.

┌─────────────────┐
18 April
└─────────────────┘

RHUBARB

Were it not for the glut of unlikely stories produced to fill virtual and paper columns, many of us would long for a slow news day. On 18 April 1930 – Good Friday – families gathered around the wireless for their daily news round-up from the BBC, only to be told 'there is no news'. The remainder of the segment was played out with innocuous piano music.

In the theatre, any uncomfortable silence might be filled by the hushed mouthing of the word 'rhubarb': the traditional formula repeated by performers imitating background conversation.

The combination of syllables apparently closely replicates a real human exchange. But the name of the plant, which comes into season in April, is linked with another, far weightier, word from ancient times – one that is also linked with unintelligible chatter.

To the ancient Greeks, all foreigners made strange noises that sounded to their ears a little like 'bah bah bah'. Such non-natives were generally seen as untrustworthy heathens, and it is from their indecipherable chatter that 'barbarian' was born. Rhubarb, meanwhile, was an exotic, 'foreign' fruit; the second part of its name comes again from the same Greek *barbaros*, 'foreign', making the pink-fleshed plant an unlikely sibling of 'barbarian'.

Such innate distrust for the foreigner is a recurrent feature in English etymology. The first meaning of 'strange' was 'from another country', while 'outlandish' was a very literal term for someone from the 'outlands'. Not for nothing can 'alien' mean both 'from elsewhere' and 'distasteful'.

It's clear that history has never delivered much cheer for foreigners, and language, as always, has followed suit.

19 April

GHETTO

Today is the anniversary of one of the most memorable acts of Jewish resistance against the Nazis. The Warsaw Ghetto Uprising in 1943 was, according to a commander of the Jewish Combat Organisation, Marek Edelman, a fight to 'pick the time and place of our deaths'. The uprising was in protest against the Nazis' effort to transport the remaining occupants of the ghetto to Treblinka and Majdanek. Those who resisted knew survival was unlikely – over 13,000 died in the destruction of the ghetto.

The cruel oppression of the Jewish people is at the heart of the word 'ghetto' itself, which dates from centuries before Nazi annihilation. The insistence by authorities that Jewish communities must live in segregation resulted, in 1516, in an enclave in Venice, and many European cities followed suit.

This Jewish section in Venice was established on the site of a former iron foundry, for which the Italian is *getto*. This may well be the origin of the modern term, although others believe its roots lie in *borghetto*, a diminutive of *borgo*, 'suburb'. The last to go, before the Nazis revived the term for their own horrific ends, was that of Rome in 1870. Today, 'ghetto' has broadened in reference to encompass any minority group that is isolated from mainstream society and acceptance. But its anti-Semitic foundations will never be forgotten.

20 April

MUMPSIMUS

'Mumpsimus' is a word that fills such a gap in our language that you may wonder how you ever lived without it. It is a five-hundred-year-old epithet for someone who insists that they are right, despite clear and incontrovertible evidence that they are not.

The term originated in a much-told story about a poorly literate Catholic priest, who consistently tripped up while reciting the post-communion prayer. The prayer includes the line *Quod ore sumpsimus, Domine* ('What we have received in the mouth, Lord'), but the priest substituted the non-existent word *mumpsimus* for *sumpsimus*. He was swiftly corrected on more than one occasion, but consistently gave the stubborn response that he would not change his old *mumpsimus* for his critic's new *sumpsimus*.

The story was told by Desiderius Erasmus (1466–1536) in a letter he wrote in August 1516 to Henry Bullock, in which he complained of the belligerent incompetence of those who resisted his edition of the Greek New Testament. It was subsequently picked up by many in the sixteenth century as an epithet for anyone who refused to accept reality. In his *Practice of Prelates*, from 1530, William Tyndale complained that those instructed by Cardinal Wolsey to find reasons for annulling the marriage of Catherine of Aragon and Henry VIII were 'all lawyers, and other doctors, mumpsimuses of divinity'.

Today's potential applications are surely even broader.

21 April

RED-LETTER DAY

The Roman calendar is calculated from this day in 753 BC, the traditional date given for the founding of Rome by Romulus and Remus.

Particularly significant days in the Roman calendar were *rubricated*, i.e. written in red. Inks containing red ochre or vermilion were particularly prized and reserved for writing of significance – the titles and prefaces to books, for example – while an extremely expensive red-coloured ink was used by the emperor for writing his edicts, written on an *album* or white table.

By the fourteenth century, red ink was used for individual characters or words in a manuscript that contained particularly significant information. On ecclesiastical calendars, red indicated a saint's day or another Christian festival; all other days were written in black. These became known as 'red-letter days', and many modern calendars continue the practice. The meaning of the expression has broadened to describe any day that is pleasantly noteworthy, or memorable.

The red ink of classical times inspired a handful of other words in English. The *rubrica terra* – the red earth or ochre used as a writing material – gave us the word 'rubric', a heading on a document or a set of instructions and rules. The Latin for vermilion meanwhile was *minium*. When monks and scribes decorated the initial letters of chapters in illuminated manuscripts in the strong red pigment, they often painted small images within them called *miniatura*. Over time, the word lost its connection with red and referred instead to those small pictures, which by the sixteenth century had become known as 'miniatures'.

22 April

HEIST

On an otherwise uneventful day in 1981, at a suburban Tucson branch of the First National Bank of Arizona, a daring heist by heavily armed robbers wearing grotesque Halloween masks resulted in the theft of more than $3.3 million – at the time the largest bank haul in American history.

'Heist' has a long heritage. It is a variation on 'hoist', originally used for shoplifting, and seems to have been first used in print by Carl Panzram, an American serial killer who recalled how in 1911, while carrying out a mugging (a term dating right back to the early 1800s), 'I was figuring when to pull out my hog-leg [a large pistol] and heist 'em up.' During Prohibition, to 'heist' meant to 'hijack a liquor shipment' and took on an element of glamour; today, that sense of filmic derring-do remains. For all their frequent brutality, 'heist' still suggests a distinct, if sneaky, admiration, much like 'caper'.

The language of crime was in fact the first category of slang to be collected, in the printer Robert Copland's wonderfully titled *Hye Way to the Spyttel-house* (c. 1535; a 'spittle house' is defined in the *Oxford English Dictionary* as 'a place . . . chiefly occupied by persons of a low class or afflicted with foul diseases'). This slang was properly known as 'cant', a word based on the Latin *cantare*, to sing, because of the sing-song tones of the criminal beggars who used it. Dictionaries such as these included terms for villains that could have come straight out of a Marvel comic. They feature, for example, 'the Ruffler', who pretended to be a war veteran and then robbed those who took pity on him, as well as the 'Counterfeit Crank'. The 'Bawdy Basket', meanwhile, was a female thief posing as a seller of pins and needles.

Of course, the dictionary bears the footprints of crimes committed centuries before these characters prowled the streets. Viking law distinguished between *morð*, which meant 'secret slaughter', and *vig*, or 'slaying'. The former crime involved concealment, such as killing a person while they were asleep: a heinous offence, punishable by death. *Vig*, as long as it was acknowledged, was less contentious, although families sinned against were perfectly entitled to take their revenge. It is *morð* that became the English 'murder'. 'Pain', meanwhile, originally meant 'punishment' – it came from the Greek *poine*, 'quit-money for spilled blood'. The original sense is retained in the phrase 'on pain of death'.

---

23 April

BARDOLATRY

Can there be such a thing as an *excessive* admiration for the works of William Shakespeare, whose birth and death both fell on this day? Given his contribution to English, it would take a brave soul to agree, and yet the word for such fervent worship exists in the form of 'bardolatry', first recorded in comments made by George Bernard Shaw in 1901. Shaw apparently took issue with the Bard for failing to engage with social issues as he himself did in his own work. Anyone who blindly followed him without question (an ipsedixit: *see* 10 March) was thus a 'bardolater', a synonym for the earlier and equally ungainly 'Shakespeareolater'.

Whatever you may think of Shaw's view, few scholars maintain that Shakespeare invented all 1,580 of the words and phrases for which he is credited as first user in the *Oxford English Dictionary*. He certainly was the master of new word combinations, but the popularity of his work almost certainly accounts for his reputation as a neologiser. But irrespective of who actually coined 'his' words, Shakespeare was undoubtedly key to their longevity. It is thanks to him and his actors that

a myriad of words entered the English stage and, most emphatically, never left it.

They were not universally applauded at the time. The word
'laughable', so natural to our tongues now, was roundly derided
by Shakespeare's critics: it should be 'laugh-at-able', they cried
(just as, a little later, 'reliable' was itself considered laughatable
– surely it should be 'rely-on-able', the nay-sayers complained).

Wordplay was undoubtedly Shakespeare's greatest art. The
playwright and poet loved turning the traditional functions
of words on their head, so that nouns became adjectives (such
as 'barefaced', 'bloodstained', and 'gloomy'), adjectives and
nouns became adverbs ('trippingly', 'rascally'), and, most
successfully of all, nouns became verbs.

Some of the neologisms that resulted from the Bard's verbing
are among his most powerful creations. Cassio doesn't tell
Othello to run off to a cave, but rather to 'encave' himself. In
Richard II, the Duke of York spittingly interrupts Bolingbroke's
'my gracious uncle' with 'grace me no grace, nor uncle me
no uncle'. They leave his audiences bedazzled – another
glorious adjective we owe to the Bard.

Such linguistic rebellion remains with us today. We verb
our way through life with similar exuberance – often to the
sounds of frequent disgust. Yet if Shakespeare was happy with
the idea of 'friending', some five centuries before social media
came along, then what use 'behowling' now?

For anyone protesting too much, the playwright even offers
an arsenal of insults with which to retort. 'Away, you starveling,
you elf-skin, you dried neat's-tongue, you bull's-pizzle, you
stock-fish!' is just one to offer any verbing pedant. And there
is always the argument-closing 'Villain, I have done thy
mother', a retort from *Titus Andronicus* of such eviscerating
wit that we still honour it today with jokes beginning with
'your mum'.

24 April

GHOST

Today is St Mark's Eve, a night when it is believed the ghosts of those who will die in the coming year can be seen gliding though the doors of the church. The superstition is first recorded in the seventeenth century, but probably goes back much further, to times when death loomed large in the imagination thanks to plagues such as the Black Death.

Such spectral incarnations of a living being are known as 'wraiths' or 'fetches'. A 'fetch-life' was the term for a supposed messenger of death sent to collect a living person. Both terms are listed as synonyms for 'ghost' in the dictionary, but ghost itself is a word with a fittingly invisible story to tell. It involves a different kind of ghoul to those appearing on St Mark's Eve, though for some it is just as grisly.

The silent 'h' of 'ghost' is the result of a historical hiccup dating back five centuries. The pioneering printer William Caxton, having learned his trade in Flanders, returned to England with a team of experienced Flemish typesetters for his new press. It was they – or more likely a single individual – who decided the Old English *gost* looked all wrong. As their native Flemish was *gheest*, they lobbed in an 'h' to make it more familiar. A ricochet effect meant that *agast* and *gastly* each inherited an extra letter too: all the result of a single decision by one hand, half a millennium ago.

25 April

GUILLOTINE

Before Anne Boleyn was beheaded with a stroke of a sword in 1536, she is said to have remarked with a note of gratitude that her neck was small. A French executioner, dubbed the Hangman of Calais but equally proficient with the sword, was allegedly sent for even before Anne was found guilty. For all his skills, Anne would have known that death by sword was often botched and messy, even while some claimed it was far kinder than the gallows generally preserved for the lower classes.

Two hundred and fifty years on, a doctor named Joseph-Ignace Guillotin decided that change was necessary. Troubled by the suffering endured by all victims no matter what the method of execution, Guillotin proposed to an assembly on legislative reform that, irrespective of social status, 'the punishment shall be the same ... Such punishment shall be decapitation, and the execution shall be carried out by a simple machine'. Guillotin would have been aware of prototype machines being used in Scotland, and he turned to a surgeon named Dr Antoine Louis for help. The machine they created was initially called the Louisette after its principal inventor, but was later given the eponym Guillotin thanks to its championing by the persistent physician. The first person to experience the new machine's efficacy was a highwayman, Nicholas J. Pelletier, who knelt beneath its blade on this day in 1792.

The word 'guillotine' was propelled into English in the year France's Reign of Terror began, when the machine was put to use for the systematic execution of thousands, including Louis XVI and Marie Antoinette. For something created to reduce the suffering of those unable to escape death, it, and Guillotin's name, became inextricably linked with cruelty and injustice.

---

26 April

KING'S EVIL

Even in the later Middle Ages, when advances in learning were changing the shape of science and medicine, superstitious convictions about physical and mental illness held firm. Sickness had distinct moral associations: certain diseases in particular were viewed as divine intervention and punishment for wrongs committed. Syphilis, for example, because of its sexual origins, was a particular taboo. Generally attributed to moral depravity, it went by many euphemistic names, including 'Cupid's measles', 'French marbles', and (by Shakespeare) 'Neapolitan bone-ache'. The stigma was such that each nation blamed it on another: for the Italians it was *Morbus Galus* (i.e. 'the French disease'); for the Germans *Franzosen boese Blattern* ('French bad blisters') – the French retaliated with *Mal de Naples*.

Some diseases were believed curable by the touch of a special hand – notably one belonging to the monarch. Scrofula, a chronic constitutional disease affecting the lymphatic glands, went by the name of the 'king's evil', as it was thought to be reversible only by the powers of the king or queen. This idea of magic stroking originated in legends of ancient gods performing miraculous cures with a single touch. In England the practice began with Edward the Confessor and continued right up until the reign of Queen Anne, who was encouraged to practise the art as a way of demonstrating the divine right of the Stuarts. The ceremony was held for the last time in England by Anne in this week of 1714, three months before her death and two years after Samuel Johnson – afflicted with scrofula as a very young child – himself travelled to London to receive the royal touch. Johnson was given a ribbon in memory of the event, which he claimed to have worn for the rest of his life. The ritual was ineffective, and Johnson went on to need an operation that was to leave him with permanent scarring.

---

27 April

PANDEMONIUM

The poet and polemicist John Milton, impoverished and blind, sold the rights on this day in 1667 to his magnum opus *Paradise Lost*, for the sum of £10.

The *Oxford English Dictionary* credits Milton with over six hundred neologisms, putting him ahead of co-patriots Ben Jonson and John Donne, and even, by some counts, Shakespeare, who is thought to have been as much a populariser as a neologiser. The early 1600s was a time when English was ripe for innovation, and when those with some education could freely borrow from other tongues and create new coinages themselves.

Among Milton's contributions are the adjectives 'stunning' and 'exhilarating' – which he simply extended from the verbs to 'stun' and 'exhilarate' – 'cherubic', a riff on 'cherubim', and compounds such as 'lovelorn' and 'arch-fiend'.

But it was with new creations that the poet came into his own. He was the first to use 'moonstruck', for someone dazed by an obsession or infatuation, and 'politicaster', for an inadequate or contemptible politician. Perhaps his most memorable, though, is the invention of the apocalyptic 'pandemonium'.

In Milton's epic poem *Paradise Lost*, Pandemonium is the capital of Hell, the 'citie and proud seate of Lucifer' where Satan presides over his council of malevolent spirits. Milton coined the term from two Greek words: *pan*, meaning 'all', and *daimon*, 'spirit' or 'devil'. A century later, his word had become a synonym for a centre of vice and a haunt of evil, before gradually loosening further to mean a state of utter chaos and confusion, which is where it remains today.

> ## 28 April

MAROON

On this day in 1789, Fletcher Christian led a mutiny on HMS *Bounty* against its captain, William Bligh, cutting short a mission to transport breadfruit plants from Tahiti to the West Indies as cheap food for plantation slaves. Bligh had served as Master aboard HMS *Resolution* under James Cook on his third and final voyage. This expedition completed a circumnavigation of the earth in the southern hemisphere.

The propagation of the breadfruit plants required a six-month stay in Tahiti, during which Bligh noticed with increasing concern examples of idleness and neglect among his crew. When they finally set sail to return, his intolerance became such that he decided to cut food and rum rations by half. Christian and his fellow mutineers set Bligh and his allies adrift in an open boat; their subsequent voyage to safety was to encompass some 4,000 miles.

The word 'mutiny' comes from the French for a violent uprising. To 'maroon' someone, meanwhile – the fate, deserved or not, of Captain Bligh – has another story to tell. The Maroons were descendants of runaway slaves who lived in the mountains and forests of Suriname and the West Indies. Their name came from the Spanish *cimarrón*, meaning 'wild' or 'feral'. The early Maroons are celebrated for their resistance to European plantation owners, and for their fortitude and capacity to survive in remote and inhospitable regions. By the early eighteenth century, just a few decades before the *Bounty* set sail, to maroon someone was to irrevocably abandon them on a desolate island.

The colour maroon is an altogether different word – this

comes from the French *marron*, 'chestnut', referring to the lustrous reddish-brown nut. The noise of a chestnut bursting in a fire inspired the use of 'maroon' for a firework used as a signal or warning – one which explodes with a loud bang and a bright flash of light.

29 April

THESAURUS

In 1852, Peter Mark Roget, a doctor of medicine, saw the fruition of a lifetime's cataloguing and classifying of words according to their meaning. This day marks the anniversary of the publication of the *Thesaurus of English Words and Phrases, Classified and Arranged so as to Facilitate the Expression of Ideas.*

Founded as much upon intuition as upon strict lexicographical principles, Roget saw twenty-eight editions of his work published in his own lifetime. The *Thesaurus* is less a collection of synonyms and antonyms, and more a reverse dictionary, in which words are presented as part of a spectrum belonging to a particular idea. Just as his hero, the father of taxonomy Carl Linnaeus, had divided animals into six classes, so Roget divided his catalogue into six broad and stylistic concepts, from Abstract Relations to Space and Matter. This, he thought, reflected the human brain's method of word association, as opposed to the more artificial strictly alphabetical approach. Most importantly, he thought that everyone – no matter their education or social status – was deserving of some help when it came to writing with eloquence. Whether or not he achieved that – many of his words are resolutely highbrow – Roget was to become one of the lasting eponyms of our language and, fittingly, a synonym for 'thesaurus'.

Roget will have known the etymology of the word he chose for his work. In the early nineteenth century, archaeologists had begun to borrow it from ancient Greek (via Latin), where it meant a 'treasure' or 'storehouse', or even a 'temple'. The meaning was soon extended to a book containing a 'treasury' of words or information about a particular field. It was thanks to Roget that the definition narrowed to define exclusively a book of words and their synonyms – or, as Roget might like to add, their 'poecilonyms'.

30 April

THE NAKED TRUTH

Today is Honesty Day, established in the 1990s as an antithesis to the perceived lies and fake news of modern life, particularly within politics.

The day was the idea of M. Hirsch Goldberg, a former press secretary and novelist who devised it while researching a book on the most deceitful and seismic lies in history. His chosen date is the tail end of a month that began with April Fool's Day, traditionally associated with all manner of fibs and pranks, as well as the anniversary of the inauguration of George Washington who, according to (unsupported) legend, owned up to damaging his father's prized cherry tree with the words 'I cannot tell a lie'.

The expression 'the naked truth' has at its heart a fable little known today, which featured in the Roman poet Horace's *Odes* and in several other stories from classical antiquity. It is the tale of 'Truth and Falsehood', and the decisions of each during a bathing trip. Falsehood, who emerges from the water first, decides to steal Truth's clothes. True to her nature, Truth prefers to go naked rather than be seen in anything belonging to Falsehood.

The retelling of the story through the ensuing centuries ensured that, by the Middle Ages, the expression 'naked truth' was well established. Today's 'the skinny' became the more modern riff in the 1930s.

MAY

1 May

MAYDAY

Most of us recognise Mayday as the universal on-air radio protocol for persons in distress, but linguistically speaking it has nothing to do with the month of May.

The term is believed to have originated in the early 1920s at Croydon airport, England's only international airport at the time. One story relates how a senior radio officer named Frederick Stanley Mockford had been asked to devise a simple word that would indicate a plane was in trouble and in urgent need of assistance. The time-honoured Morse equivalent SOS could not be used, as its dual sibilants were too difficult to distinguish over the airwaves. It is said that he came up with 'mayday' from the French *Venez m'aider* ('Come and help me'), largely because so much of Croydon's traffic went to and from Le Bourget airport in Paris. In 1927 the phrase was ratified at the International Radiotelegraph Convention of Washington as the official radio distress call, and it is still in use today. Note, however, that a distress call for a less serious incident is known as a 'pan-pan'. This comes from another French word *panne* (breakdown).

The Morse SOS doesn't, as is popularly believed, stand for Save Our Souls. It was chosen because it is one of the simplest and easily recognised in Morse code.

2 May

MAY

May takes its name from the Latin *Maius mensis*, 'month of the goddess Maia'. In Greek mythology, Maia was one of seven daughters of the Titan Atlas, while the Romans identified her with Maia Majesta, goddess of spring and of fertility.

May is also the name given to the beautiful hawthorn blossom, which flowers in this month and which blooms in hedges up and down the British countryside ('haw' derives from *hage*, the Old English for 'hedge'). It is found in the Old English May Day rhyme 'Here we go gathering nuts in May', in which the mention of nuts, scarcely available before the autumn, may seem curious. In fact its use here is thought to be a corruption of 'knots of May', and to refer to tied posies of May blossom. The hawthorn may also be the inspiration for Shakespeare's 'darling buds of May'.

But in the long-standing warning 'Ne'er cast a clout till May be out', recorded as an 'old proverb' even in the 1500s, it is the month not the hawthorn that is being referred to, as another version makes clear:

> Button to chin, till May be in,
> Cast not a clout, till May be out.

'Clout' here is an old dialect word meaning 'clothing'. The chill of May can persist, the proverb tells us, so hold on to your woollies until summer is truly bedded in.

---

3 May

MACHIAVELLIAN

It is better to be feared than loved, if you cannot have both.

Never attempt to win by force what can be won by deception.

These are two of the aphorisms attributed to writer and statesman Niccolò di Bernardo dei Machiavelli, who was born on this day in 1469.

Best known for his 1513 political treatise on statecraft *Il Principe*, whose focus is the acquisition and retention of power, the Italian's name has long been synonymous with political opportunism, duplicity, and manipulation. *The Prince*, as the text is known in the English-speaking world, paints a picture of human nature that is as controversial as it is pessimistic. For centuries Machiavelli has divided scholars; some believe his teachings bordered on evil, while others see him as an early exponent of realpolitik, and a man able to distinguish between the practicalities of ruling, and virtuous idealism.

Soon after the publication of the treatise in English, to be described as Machiavellian was to be someone who acted on the principles espoused by its author. It didn't take long before the term was applied more widely to an amoral pursuer of political power, an intriguer or schemer willing to use any means to achieve their goal. The epithet has lasted nearly half a millennium, and to this day there are very few synonyms for the prioritising of expediency over morality.

4 May

JEDI

Today, famously, is Star Wars Day (May the Fourth be with you). It is observed by disciples of a franchise that is said to have changed, if not the world, then at least the world of film, pioneering the use of computer-generated special effects and capturing the imagination of millions for generations.

It also captured the language. The *Oxford English Dictionary* gives *Star Wars* credit for the words 'droid', 'jedi', 'lightsaber', and 'Padawan', as well as for a new sense of 'Force'. Most have acquired a wider sense, showing how comfortably they now sit in the lexicon. A Jedi, who in *Star Wars* is a member of an order of heroic, skilled warrior monks able to harness the mystical power of the Force, can today also be someone credited with great skill or preternatural powers. Droid, a term in the films for any robotic entity, is now more likely to be a personality-devoid human automaton. Padawan, meanwhile, has moved beyond its status as an apprentice Jedi and come to embrace, by extension, a youthful, untrained, or naive individual.

The film even found its way into politics. 'Star Wars' itself became a nickname for the Strategic Defense Initiative, a military defence strategy proposed by Ronald Reagan in 1983 for destroying, in space, incoming Soviet missiles.

Some forty years after George Lucas's creation, the story of triumph over evil, and of a hero's fall and subsequent redemption, remains for most of us a fundamental part of our cultural knowledge.

5 May

CAVALIER

The English Civil War claimed the lives of 200,000 people and shook the foundations of British society. It brought military rule, and the arrest and execution of an anointed sovereign. It was on this day in 1646 that Charles I surrendered in Scotland, and was handed over to the English Parliament.

If today's epithets of abuse tend to focus on money and social status (chavs, pikeys, and neds, to name just a few), those during the Civil War focused on alliances and beliefs. The name 'Roundhead', initially one intended to ridicule members of Cromwell's parliamentary party, was a reference to the custom among Puritan men to wear their hair cut close. For their part, the Roundheads despised the flamboyant appearance of their opponents, with their long curling locks, and lace collars and cuffs.

By 1641, Parliament had taken to calling the royalists 'Cavaliers', a relatively new term that had crossed into English from French. Its origin is the Latin *caballus*, 'horse', which came to English via the Italian *cavaliere*, also the root of chivalry and first used of chivalrous knights on horseback. At first 'cavalier' retained those echoes of courtly behaviour and all that was honourable and gallant, but it gradually took on overtones of swagger and bluster – perfect, the Roundheads thought, for Charles I and his followers. Once again, however, the epithet was embraced by those it was used against, and became a badge of pride for the swashbucklers on the king's side. Both insults have left a legacy in modern English – a cavalier attitude today is haughty and offhand, while to be puritanical and censorious is arguably the harsher slight.

Beyond the main parties of Protestants and Catholics, other religious societies flourished at this time, and here too conflict was linguistically apparent. Such groups were frequently given disparaging names to reflect their perceived unorthodox practices. The clergyman Thomas Hall offered a striking inventory of some of the religious societies of the time: 'We have many Sects now abroad; Ranters, Seekers, Shakers, Quakers, and now Creepers.'

Most of these names were meant as disapproving summaries of the groups' behaviour, such as the loud and vehement preaching that the 'Ranters' were said to indulge in. But once again some were appropriated; the Quakers came to embrace a name originally used to ridicule their 'trembling' at the word of the Lord.

---

6 May

MILE

On a blustery and wet afternoon of 6 May 1954, a medical student at St Mary's Hospital in London finished his shift and took a train to Oxford. The next few hours would radically reshape the future and history of running.

Roger Bannister followed in the footsteps of his father – a successful runner at school who, Bannister was later to recall, was prone to fainting afterwards 'as so many runners did in those days'. Bannister himself learned running in different circumstances – not only for fun, but also as a scramble to the nearest air-raid shelter during the Blitz; he would imagine bombs raining on him if he didn't quicken his step.

By 1953, Bannister was running for his country, and a year later, on that inclement May evening, he broke the four-minute mile in front of a crowd of 1,200 spectators. The *New York Times* declared his achievement as 'one of man's hitherto unattainable goals'. His record didn't last particularly long – just weeks later, his rival John Landy was to cut it by a second – but for the elite athletes in our lifetime he remains an icon. This was a man who, as another one-time record-holder for the mile, Sebastian Coe, has pointed out, was running both with heavy spikes and 'on tracks at which speedway riders would turn up their noses'. For Bannister himself, 'the arms of the world were waiting to receive me, if only I reached the tape without slackening my speed'.

A mile was always configured as a long distance in the mind's eye. For the Romans, one thousand paces marched by disciplined troops became a fixed and useful unit of measurement. In Latin this was *mille passus*, 'one thousand paces', later shortened to simple *mille*. A *stade*, meanwhile, measured one-eighth of a mile; the name was borrowed from the Greeks as the distance covered by footraces at the Olympic games, and was eventually transferred to the 'stadia' or venues where such races took place – including the one at Iffley Road, Oxford, where Bannister was given the embrace he so craved.

---

7 May

WHITE ELEPHANT

On this day in 1865, an elephant named Old Hannibal died after a life of sad captivity in an American menagerie. In his prime, his weight was ascertained to be over 15,000 pounds, or roughly six and a half tons. Isaac A. Van Amburgh's travelling circus covered on average 3,000 miles a year: according to one obituary, Old Hannibal became 'the greatest curiosity ever exhibited to the wondering millions'.

An elephant's life in Siam, now Thailand, was probably not a much happier lot, unless, that is, it was white. Pale elephants were highly revered and, when born or found, became the immediate property of the king. Such was the animal's significance that a picture of a white elephant was the emblem of the Siamese flag until 1917 when, it is said, the monarch ordered a symmetrical design that worked at any angle, having seen the original flipped on its head by the wind.

White elephants may have been highly prized, but they were also, from one point of view, completely worthless. Their special status meant they were not allowed to become working animals; they furthermore required a high level of maintenance and expense. And so legend holds that successive kings of Siam would make a gift of a white elephant to any individual who had displeased them. They did this in the full knowledge that the animal's upkeep might eventually bankrupt the recipient. To this day, a 'white elephant' is any burdensome or useless endeavour that is far more trouble than it's worth.

8 May

GROAK

A longside the *Oxford English Dictionary*, the *English Dialect Dictionary* is compelling bedtime reading, if a little on the large side. Begun by Joseph Wright, a philologist at Oxford University, the six-volume collection of regional vocabulary is still the standard in its field, and in 2019 plans were announced to renew his work and continue with the survey that informed it, taking in the words, phrases, and accents that define our local landscapes.

The *EDD* contains so many familiar and entirely forgotten treasures that it's nigh impossible to choose its greatest hits. On anybody's list, however, surely one word should always feature, and that is the verb to 'groak'.

Wright defines this as a Scottish and Irish term that can variously mean to 'cast a suspicious eye' over something, or to 'whimper and whine'. Combine those two ideas and you get Wright's third definition, which is to watch someone eating in the hope that they might share their food. In other words, dogs are continuously groaking, as are humans whenever they eye someone eating a plate of chips.

Wright lists this particular meaning of groaking as 'obsolete', with his last record dating from 1892. If the efforts of those who relish this word have met with any success, we can hope that the *Survey of English Dialects* will record a renewed uptake of a verb you never thought you needed, but might now never leave behind.

---
9 May

HUGGER-MUGGER

On 9 May 1941, during the Second World War, the Royal Navy captured the German U-boat *U-110* in the North Atlantic as part of Operation Primrose. On board they recovered an Enigma machine, its cipher keys, and code books that allowed the Allies to decipher German signal traffic. The code-breakers at the top-secret headquarters in England's Bletchley Park managed to systematically crack a system that the Germans had considered impenetrable. The boat was scuppered the next day, leaving the Germans with the comfortable assumption that their ciphers had sunk with it.

The word 'enigma' first described something that is kept deliberately obscure as a test of ingenuity. In other words, it is a secret riddle: the word is based on the Greek *ainissesthai*, 'to speak allusively'.

Secrecy rings through another expression that the code-breakers of Bletchley Park would have been familiar with. To do something 'hugger-mugger' is to do it clandestinely, while a 'hugger-mugger' (sadly not a huggerer-muggerer) was once a miser, who hoarded things on the quiet. Born for its sound, the term combines the sense of huddling together in conspiracy with an old sense of 'mucker', meaning to conceal. It is what is known to linguists as a reduplicated compound, a broad category that includes some of the most colourful phrases in our language, among them helter-skelter, higgledy-piggledy, and willy-nilly (*see* 9 January).

10 May

NICOTINE

In the course of his first voyage, the Genoese sailor Christopher Columbus observed a custom among the Taino people of the Caribbean of making a rough roll of dried leaves, lighting the end, and breathing in the smoke. Columbus was convinced this was an entirely new form of drug, although we know today that the same practice originated with the Mayans, over a millennium and a half earlier. Columbus and his crew duly brought cuttings of the plant back to Spain, for which they borrowed the Taino word *tabaco*.

In 1561, a young French ambassador named Jean Nicot de Villemain dined at a friend's house during his diplomatic stint in Lisbon, and was shown the same plant. It was believed by many, including those at the dinner that night, that its leaves held incredible healing properties. Upon his return to Paris, Nicot sent some pulverised tobacco to the Queen Consort and Regent of France, Catherine de' Medici, urging her to give it to her son for his insufferable migraines. Whether they cured him or not, the popularity of tobacco soon spread around Paris, and from there to the rest of Europe.

The French gave the tobacco plant the Latin name *herba nicotiana* in honour of the diplomat. When the alkaloid obtained from the plant was identified, it too took his name. 'Nicotine' was borrowed by the English in the early part of the nineteenth century, and has wielded its power ever since.

11 May

ZUGZWANG

On 11 May 1997, chess grandmaster Garry Kasparov was defeated by the IBM supercomputer Deep Blue. Although since downplayed, this historic rematch marked the first time a reigning grandmaster had been beaten by a machine under strict tournament conditions. The event was billed as a giant leap forward in the development of artificial intelligence, and the beginning of the end for the human race.

'Zugzwang' is a chess term borrowed directly from the German *Zug*, meaning 'move', and *Zwang*, a 'compulsion' or 'urge'. It's used to apply to a state of play in which any move will have a detrimental effect: in short, it is a no-win situation. If both players are in Zugzwang, it may be called a *trébuchet*, named after the powerful siege engine of the Middle Ages.

Chess has a lexicon all of its own, incorporating such gloriously named moves and scenarios as 'blind pigs', the 'coffeehouse', the 'Maróczy Bind', the 'vacating sacrifice', and the shade-throwing 'wood-pusher', used to describe a particularly poor player who knows only how to push the pieces and for whom a Zugzwang is simply something unpronounceable.

12 May

BARRICADE

For a period of thirty-six years, from 1562 to 1598, the stability of France was blighted by the Wars of Religion. The Huguenots, who subscribed to the branch of Protestantism known as Calvinism, demanded the same religious freedom as Catholics, a move strongly contested by the House of Guise, a highly influential French noble family who championed the Catholic cause.

In 1576 the French king, Henri III, signed a peace treaty that accorded the Huguenots full religious liberty. On 12 May 1588, the Duke of Guise and other strict Catholics entered Paris, where they were welcomed by thousands who rose up against the king and his decision. To deter any countermove by the king's loyal subjects, they erected barriers of huge barrels, weighted with earth and paving stones, to block the streets. The event and its isolation of the king became known as *la journeé des barricades* – 'the day of the barricades'. Barricade is from the French *barrique*, 'barrel'.

Those same barrels have informed other words in English too, including 'barrier' and also 'bar', referring to the staves from which the casks were constructed. Bars themselves lie hidden inside 'embarrassment', which comes from a French verb meaning to impede or obstruct, just as those wine and beer barrels did so effectively all those centuries ago.

13 May

SWEAR

Winston Churchill occupies many columns in the *Oxford Dictionary of Quotations*. His eloquence and fondness for wordplay have ensured the longevity of such remarks as 'Politics is more dangerous than war, for in war you are only killed once', and 'The English never draw a line without blurring it'.

Among his most famous speeches is the one in which he declared 'I have nothing to offer but blood, toil, tears, and sweat'. This was Churchill's first speech as prime minister to the House of Commons, delivered on 13 May 1940, four days after the so-called Phoney War had become devastatingly real with the invasion by Germany of France, Belgium, and Holland. A day later, the news from the front was equally grim: the Germans had broken through the French defences at Sedan. Churchill wrote that 'the weight and the fury of the German attack was overwhelming'.

In his speech, Churchill swore to fight for 'victory, victory at all costs, victory in spite of all terror, victory, however long and hard the road may be; for without victory, there is no survival'. This sense of swearing – of pledging allegiance to a person or cause – is the earliest meaning of the word. 'Swear' comes from the Old English *swerian* (of which the past tense was *swor*, and the past participle *sworen*), meaning to make a solemn oath. It is a sibling of 'answer', which was originally a sworn statement that rebutted a charge.

Collateral always helps, and those making their oaths would often swear on their lives or upon their honour. Eventually, they might swear to God, a very serious promise that carried the heaviest conviction of all. Today's primary use of swearing to mean profanity descends from the belief in the Middle Ages that the over-liberal invoking of God's name was highly blasphemous.

---

14 May

MEDICINE MAN

In 1607, an expedition led by Captain Christopher Newport arrived at Jamestown, Virginia. The passengers went ashore the next day and that chosen spot went on to become the first permanent English colony in North America. Thirteen years later, the Pilgrim Fathers aboard the *Mayflower* became the second.

The families on board that second sailing were, for the most part, people of high literacy as well as high courage. When they and their predecessors in Jamestown set foot upon the new shores, they were, of course, far from the first to do so. Native Americans had occupied the land for thousands of years, speaking an enormous number of different languages. You might, as a result, expect an almighty clash between these languages and the English of the settlers. And there may well have been one, had it not been for one man called Squanto.

Squanto was a Native American who had been kidnapped by English sailors some fifteen years before the arrival of the *Mayflower*, and was subsequently taken to London, where he was trained as an interpreter before making his escape by hiding on a ship bound for his homeland.

Squanto was to witness the fear among the Pilgrims when they arrived in their new country, one that to them seemed hostile and forlorn, full of 'wild beasts and wild men'. Cold, sick, and starving, unsure how to feed themselves in this new environment, over half of the 144 people who had set sail had died. One day, Squanto, himself a 'wild man' – but in reality a highly skilled linguist – approached them and delivered the simple word 'Welcome'. For the next weeks and months he would be their guide, showing the settlers how to grow native crops, vital for food in those early days when the seeds they had brought with them failed to thrive. Such was Squanto's contribution that a considerable mythology has grown up around him – many maintain that it is thanks to him that English is spoken on American soil today.

But, of course, that language was never going to be enough. It had never encountered 'raccoons', 'moose', 'skunks', or 'terrapins'; 'wigwams', 'moccasins', or 'tomahawks'. And so the Pilgrims either borrowed from the local languages, or simply took old words and applied them to the new phenomena. They formulated new combinations of words to fill the linguistic gaps they encountered – 'rattle snake', 'medicine man', 'war path', and 'bull frog'. Perhaps it was the comfort of the familiar that made them reach for their own words – certainly they did so with place names, with choices such as New England, Cambridge, Plymouth, Dartmouth, and Boston.

The beauty of the indigenous languages spoken by those such as Squanto was not lost upon some of the new settlers.

William Penn, founder of Pennsylvania, remarked: 'I know not a language spoken in Europe that hath words of more sweetness and greatness, in Accent and Emphasis, than theirs.'

American English began as an amazing hybrid of the old and new, the native and the foreign, the homespun and the earthily exotic. It would be churlish to resist a language with such adventures in its making.

15 May

VOLCANO

On 15 May 1844, Charles Goodyear received his patent for the process of vulcanisation, intended for use in the manufacture and strengthening of rubber. At the heart of the term is a Roman myth featuring a deity of fire, and blacksmith to the gods. It tells how Vulcan, the son of Jupiter and Juno who had been disfigured as a child, is thrown off Mount Olympus by his mother, but survives the great fall and is raised in secret by the sea-nymphs, gradually honing his skills as a blacksmith until he is without equal in his craft.

Following his survival, Vulcan later takes revenge on his neglectful mother. Rejecting her demands that he return to the gods on Mount Olympus, he crafts for her a beautifully ornate throne instead – in reality a trap that binds her fast for three days and nights. Jupiter intervenes and promises Vulcan the hand of the beautiful Venus if he will only release Juno. Vulcan gladly accepts his new wife, and returns to Mount Olympus to live in what will, in the end, be rather unhappy matrimony.

The ancient Romans associated Vulcan with the power of fire, both as a destroyer and creator. Their belief in this might can be seen in the English journey of their word for a 'hearth', the all-important *focus*. They also believed Mount Etna to be the forge of the god, hence the term 'volcano'. Whenever Mount

Etna would show signs of activity, it was said to be Vulcan beating his great sheets of iron in anger at his wife's infidelity.

16 May

DIEHARD

We use 'diehard' today as an adjective to describe a person who is utterly unshakable in their beliefs. But this is a word that wears its heart on its sleeve – a bloody sleeve, it turns out, for 'diehard' has a grisly and far more literal beginning.

In the eighteenth century, the term was used for any execution victim who struggled against the hangman's noose. Subsequent execution methods would 'advance' so that the condemned would be dropped through the gallows, ensuring (usually) a clean break and therefore a quick death. Nonetheless, the phrase 'die hard' persisted in the public imagination until over a century later, when it was romanticised during the Peninsular War, at the Battle of Albuera on this day in 1811. Here, Lieutenant Colonel William Inglis, of the 57th (West Middlesex) Regiment, while facing heavy attack from the French and himself suffering grievous wounds, rallied his men with the cry 'Die hard, the 57th, die hard!' His regiment would later take 'The Die-hards' as their official soubriquet.

17 May

BAH

Some twenty-five years before Ebenezer Scrooge – the 'squeezing, wrenching, grasping, scraping, clutching, covetous old sinner' of *A Christmas Carol* – delivered his first 'Bah, humbug!', the poet and peer Lord Byron gave us the first recorded use of that 'bah' as an expression of contempt. It comes in his lengthy poem *Beppo*, written while in exile from Britain amid concern he might be sued for perversion.

Beppo is in many ways an exhortation to take pleasure in life. Its story involves an Italian woman who believes her husband to be lost at sea, and who takes on a 'vice-husband', known simply as 'the Count'. In the poem's implicit comparison of Italian and English morals, the British come off worse in their hypocritical squeamishness towards adultery.

The Count is a fashionable, cultured man, with a discernment that strikes fear in any musical performer's heart:

> The fiddlers trembled as he look'd around,
>   For fear of some false note's detected flaw;
> The 'prima donna's' tuneful heart would bound,
>   Dreading the deep damnation of his 'bah!'

'Bah' is one of several terms introduced or popularised by Byron, among them – appropriately for one who sent his female fans into an erotic frenzy – 'beddable' and *carpe diem*. But another, 'miscreator' – someone who creates or performs something objectionable – links to this day in 1824, when what has been called the greatest crime in literary history was committed, at the offices of the publisher John Murray in London.

Five years earlier, Byron had entrusted a manuscript, apparently containing his memoirs, to his friend and fellow poet Thomas Moore, with the insistence that its contents should only be published after his death. To another friend, Thomas Medwin, he promised that 'when you read my Memoirs you will learn the evils, moral and physical, of true dissipation. I can assure you my life is very entertaining and very instructive.'

The world would never be in a position to judge the truth of Byron's words. It is said that three of his closest friends gathered on 17 May 1824, a month after the poet's death, and agreed that his memoirs were so unsuitable for public consumption that they should be ripped up and destroyed.

Which they duly were – tossed into the fire in the offices of John Murray.

Whatever the contents of the pages burned in 50 Albemarle Street that day, Byron remains the template of the Romantic hero, a genius with tragic flaws who was ultimately denied burial in Westminster Abbey on account of his 'questionable morality'. 'Bah' seems an unlikely response to a man who invited such extreme emotions, an early celebrity and provocateur who was the very first to be described – by his lover Lady Caroline Lamb – as 'mad, bad, and dangerous to know'.

18 May

VAMP

Any woman described as a 'vamp' can take some heart from the term's description in the *Oxford English Dictionary*, which includes 'adventuress' as well as 'Jezebel'. But then a term that derives from 'vampire' was never going to sparkle as a compliment.

On this day in 1897, Bram Stoker's second novel *Dracula* was published by Archibald Constable and Co. The Irish author was better known in his lifetime as the manager of London's Lyceum Theatre, owned by Henry Irving, for whom Stoker also worked as an assistant and who, it is said, provided the inspiration for Count Dracula. Irving's relationship with Stoker was an unequal one – the author was said to idolise his boss, but to be frequently wounded by the fickleness of his attentions. In the words of the historian Louis S. Warren, 'Bram Stoker internalized the fear and animosity his employer inspired in him, making them the foundations of his gothic fiction.' Others maintain it was Vlad the Impaler, aka Draculea, who was the real prototype for Dracula – a plausible suggestion given the ruthless prince's continued hold over the popular imagination; in modern Romanian, *drac* has moved from its original meaning of 'dragon' to encompass the Devil himself.

As for the word 'vampire', English took this, via French, from the Hungarian *vampir*, and ultimately from the Turkish *uber*, a witch. While Stoker nailed the image of the blood-sucking creature, he followed in the footsteps of John William Polidori's *The Vampyre*, a book which had a dramatic impact on contemporary sensibilities. By this time, vampires had been part of folklore for centuries. In early European tales, they were shroud-wearing, bloated figures of the undead. It is down to Polidori and Stoker that we see them as the gaunt, pale, conflicted beings of today's vampire mythology.

As for the vamp, while they may not drink the blood of their victims, their history means they will forever be those who entrance, seduce, and then ruthlessly exploit. Not a term, or individual, to be handled lightly.

19 May

GOODBYE

In a letter of 1575, the author and scholar Gabriel Harvey promised a correspondent that, 'to requite your gallonde of godbwyes, I regive you a pottle of howedyes'. With this he gave us the first records not just of 'howedyes' – a greeting 'how do ye [fare]?' that eventually morphed into 'howdy' – but also of 'godbwye', a contraction of 'God be with ye' and a salutation on parting that was to become our modern 'goodbye'. In its religious convictions the term sits alongside the more formal 'adieu', taken from the French 'to God', yet the hope of divine fellowship has left scarcely a footprint on today's breezy 'bye'.

Many more of our greetings and farewells, for all their modern appearance, are rooted in medieval tradition. Even 'wotcha', the hello of choice for many of us in the 1980s and 1990s, disguises a greeting that would have customarily tripped off the lips of Henry VI. 'What cheer' was once the traditional expression upon meeting an acquaintance; an enquiry after their health or state of mind – its 'cheer' was a synonym for 'face', because our facial expressions mirror our soul. 'What cheer' was eventually mangled to the archetypal cockney 'wotcha'.

Such long histories are not restricted to English. The Italian farewell, *ciao*, is an alteration of an Italian dialect word *schiavo*, meaning 'I am your slave'.

20 May

ATLAS

The *Theatrum Orbis Terrarum*, printed in Antwerp on this day in 1570 by cartographer Abraham Ortelius, is widely considered to be the first true modern 'atlas', even though it did not officially carry the name. We owe one of the first uses of the term to the notable Flemish geographer Gerhardus Mercator, whose collection of maps displays the familiar Hellenic image of the kneeling Titan carrying the globe on its front cover. The title offers Mercator's definition of an atlas as *Atlas Sive Cosmographicae Meditationes de Fabrica Mundi et Fabricati Figura*, translated as 'Atlas or cosmographical meditations upon the fabric of the world, and the universe as created'.

Mercator's collection was published posthumously in 1595, but the mythology surrounding Atlas goes at least as far back as the eighth century BC. The Greek poet Hesiod's epic *Theogony* offers ancient Greece's only surviving account of what is known as the Titanomachy, the mythological series of wars between the old gods, the Titans, and the new gods, known as the Olympians. Zeus is the powerful leader of the Olympians, who with his brothers rises in insurrection against their tyrannical father, Cronos, and the Titans loyal to him. According to Hesiod, Zeus is at last victorious, and banishes the majority of the Titans to Tartarus, a primordial predecessor of hell. The Titan Atlas, however, is forced to bear the weight of the heavens on his shoulders for eternity as punishment for his opposition. He later features briefly in the Twelve Labours of Hercules, in an episode in which Atlas is duped by the mighty son of Zeus, Hercules. The myth tells how he is finally turned to stone by the hero Perseus, using the petrifying head of Medusa, and thereafter forever transformed into the Atlas mountains in Africa.

21 May

NUTMEG

On this day in 1904, the cumbersomely titled Fédération Internationale de Football Association was founded in the rear of the headquarters of the Union des Sociétés Françaises de Sports Athlétiques, on 229 Rue Saint Honoré in Paris. The aim of FIFA, as it inevitably became known, was to oversee international competition between national associations. Today, it represents the highest authority in football.

Among the thousands of terms in the game for moves, successes, defeats, goals, and players both poor and glorious, is the curious 'nutmeg', used of an attacking player who kicks the ball through their opponent's legs and reclaims it on the other side. But why define it in terms of an exotic spice?

Our best bet is that it derives from the use of 'nuts' as slang for testicles – the ball passes between the player's legs, after all. Others look to the cockney rhyming slang – 'nutmeg' = 'leg'. But there are some who believe that the term goes further back than that. In the 1870s, nutmeg was a highly prized and valuable commodity, frequently traded between England and North America. It's said that less scrupulous merchants would add worthless shavings of wood into their sacks to increase their weight in order to deceive the purchaser, a practice that became known as 'nutmegging' – anyone who had been swindled in this way could be said to have been nutmegged.

For now, it's the testicle link that prevails. Nutmegs were a euphemism for a man's bollocks (*see* 14 August) as early as the 1600s. In the ballad 'Kentish Dick or The Lusty Coach-Man of Westminster', you can find the uncomfortable line: ' "We'll geld him," says one, "of nutmegs we'll free him." ' For all the humiliation of being nutmegged with a ball, nothing in the beautiful game can, thankfully, compare to that.

22 May

ABSQUATULATE

If an event or party, even a conversation in the street, is not to our liking, many of us will take the earliest opportunity to make a swift but polite exit. Others may be a little more obvious in their distaste and simply 'absquatulate'. This word is a playful invention from 1830s America for leaving somewhere abruptly, part of a fad at the time for creating preposterous or comical words and expressions. In this case, the coinage is a mishmash of Latin with a bit of everyday English thrown in.

Other fanciful concoctions from this time of frenzied word-play are 'discombobulate' and 'skedaddle', which need no explanation. Some sadly fell by the wayside – to be 'goshbus-tified' is to be excessively pleased, while 'dumfungled' pitches the perfect image of feeling utterly used up and exhausted. And any bombastic braggart might, in this time of linguistic merriment, have been accused of 'blustrification', or even of trying to 'hornswoggle' the opposition by means of 'humbug-gery' and 'bamboozlement'.

---

23 May

PICNIC

The first version of the computer programming language Java was released on 23 May 1995, designed by a team led by the developer James Gosling, who realised the elusive goal of extending network computing to general human activity. Today, Java is the invisible engine within many of the devices that power our everyday lives.

The language was initially called 'Oak', after an oak tree that stood outside Gosling's office. As that trademark was already taken, it is said that the team proposed a variety of short, punchy names that reflected the ethos of the technology, including 'Silk', 'Jolt', 'Dynamic', and 'Java'. Perhaps because many of its creators were fuelled by coffee, Java, the name of a coffee bean from Indonesia, won the day.

The apparent arbitrariness behind the choice of name is fairly typical of the technology lexicon. This is a lingo of inventive nicknames, slick acronyms, references from literature, and shortcuts that really aren't shortcuts at all ('WWW' famously takes longer to say than 'World Wide Web'). 'Google' is said to have been a spur-of-the-moment riff on 'googol', a fanciful term for 10 raised to the 100th power and an allusion to the volume of information contained on the Net. 'Bluetooth' was gloriously named for King Blåtand (real name Harald Gormsson) who ruled over Scandinavia in the tenth century and who apparently had a conspicuously dead, blue-tinged tooth. Whatever his dental arrangements, Harald was credited with uniting Denmark and Norway, and so seemed a fitting choice for a technology that unifies the telecommunications and computing industries.

Named after the Heisenberg principle in quantum physics, a Heisenbug is a software bug that alters its behaviour or disappears entirely upon any attempt to examine it. This should not be confused with the morbidly named Hindenbug, given to one that causes enormous damage to a system.

A Jenga code quite predictably falls apart as soon as one line of data is changed, while a Yoda code, describing anything that has been entered in a roundabout or backwards manner, gives a nod to the distinctive speech pattern of the diminutive Jedi master of *Star Wars*.

As for acronyms, these are usually determined by a distinct 'us and them' mentality. NATO is a technician's code for 'No action; talk only' – a means of appeasing a frustrated office worker – while PICNIC is secret slang among technical support staff for 'repeat offenders', i.e. users who repeatedly ask for help with problems whose solutions are clearly explained in the documentation, if they'd only read it (RTFM = 'read the fucking manual'). Put simply, PICNIC on a job sheet will tell the rest of the IT crew: 'problem in chair, not in computer'.

---

24 May

GYLDENBOLLOCKES

In South Korea, some 20 million people share just five surnames. Every one of Denmark's top twenty surnames ends in *sen*, meaning 'son of', a pattern that is replicated across Scandinavia. By contrast, British and American surnames have never favoured this degree of neatness; while we may have lost such delightfully chewy names as Crackpot, Crookbones, and Sweteinbede, the average city will still provide its Slys, Haythornthwaites, and McGillikuddys.

In the seventeenth century, under the influence of the Puritans, the practice arose of baptising children with scriptural or pious phrases annexed to their last name. There are church records of such names as Preserved Fish, Thankful Thorpe, Repentance Water, Kill-Sin Pimple, and Humiliation Hinde. Conversely, other surnames of the period offer unflinchingly pithy descriptions of the condition of the bearer, including Blackinthemouth, Blubber, Mad, Measle, Peckcheese, and Hatechrist.

Many such examples would have begun as nicknames, a significant category in the origin of surnames. Gyldenbollockes was one such epithet on the streets of medieval England, centuries before David Beckham, while others such as Thynne and Belcher speak for themselves. Not all of these can be taken at face value: the ancestors of anyone called Brown today may have traditionally worn brown cloth, but they may also have been of dark-skinned complexion; similarly, the surname Stout may have begun as the result of a medieval joke at the expense of someone notably skinny.

Nonetheless, the importance of such nicknames must not be underestimated: not only are they the source of a great number of British surnames, they also provide dictionary-makers with important evidence of a word's early use. While the first quotation in the *Oxford English Dictionary*'s entry for 'bilberry' is dated 1584, the Court Roll of Nottingham offers evidence of one 'Adam *Bilberylyp*' who lived some two centuries earlier (presumably with vividly purple lips).

---

25 May

PANIC

Today is Towel Day: the annual celebration of Douglas Adams's *The Hitchhiker's Guide to the Galaxy*, whose fans conspicuously carry a towel with them in honour of the great writer – because, as the book tells us, a towel 'is the most massively useful thing an interstellar hitchhiker can have'. Besides, 'any man who can hitch the length and breadth of the galaxy, rough it, slum it, struggle against terrible odds, win through, and still knows where his towel is, is clearly a man to be reckoned with'.

The *Hitchhiker's Guide* is also a book that proudly bore the legend DON'T PANIC on its front, thereby uniting a paranoid android of the future with a mischievous ancient god. That god is, of course, Pan, inventor of panpipes and a lover addicted to the pursuit of revelry and romance. He was also, depending on which account you favour, a player of pranks or a figure inclined to great anger – either way, his reputation is said to have instilled fear in anyone who encountered him.

Pan possessed a stentorian voice that helped the gods vanquish a horde of giants; mischievously he liked to test it out in lonely places, such as deep caves and dark forests. As a consequence, any loud or eerie noises emanating from the unknown were, in the frightened imagination of travellers, entirely down to him.

Such was the strength of the myth, and of Pan's reputation, that the terms 'Panic frights' and 'Panic fear' moved into English idiom in the sixteenth century. Eventually the eponymous associations slipped away, and 'panic' stretched to embrace extreme anxiety and the frenzied irritation of running late for work. Or, perhaps, of finding yourself without a towel.

---

26 May

COCKNEY

The beautiful church of St Mary-le-Bow is an oasis in Cheapside, within the City of London. Founded in around 1080 as the London headquarters for the Archbishop of Canterbury, its history is as formidable as its architecture – devastated by the Great Fire of London in 1666, it was rebuilt by Sir Christopher Wren, only to be destroyed once more in this month in 1941 by German bombs during the Blitz. It was rebuilt and reconsecrated in 1964.

For all its majesty, it is perhaps the bells of the church that have settled most firmly in the imagination. For a true cockney is one who, it is famously said, was born within their sound. Which is further than you might think – one study from 2000 estimated that they were audible six miles to the east, five to the north, three to the south, and four to the west, an area that covers Bethnal Green, Whitechapel, Spitalfields, Stepney, Wapping, Limehouse, Poplar, Millwall, Hackney, Hoxton, Shoreditch, Bow, and Mile End, as well as Bermondsey, south of the River Thames.

The word 'cockney' has for centuries resisted any simple etymology. The first record discovered to date is from 1362, when it clearly meant a 'cock's egg' – a physical impossibility and hence a byword for a rotten or defective one. But Chaucer used it in a different way, to mean a 'cockered' or spoilt child, and, by extension, a weak or overindulged man. It seems that cockney was consequently picked up by chippy countrymen as an insult for any mollycoddled townsfolk who had no clue about the hardships of the countryside (a revenge perhaps for all those disparagements thrown the other way by urban/urbane town-dwellers, such as 'bumpkin', or 'yokel').

Eventually, cockney was applied not just to a Londoner, but specifically those born near St Mary-le-Bow, until it embraced their local dialect, too. Shakespeare was said to have been a speaker of it, although his cockneyisms are in the form of pronunciation rather than vocabulary.

But if there is a single expectation of what the world sees as 'typically cockney', it is rhyming slang, a code that may have begun as a tribal banter among early nineteenth-century costermongers. Like all slang, it was meant to baffle outsiders, including the authorities. The original versions often relied on the omission of the rhyming element, whether it was 'Barnet fair' – 'hair' – 'barnet' in the 1850s, or 'Sweeney Todd' – 'Flying Squad' – 'the Sweeney', a century later.

Rhyming slang has survived, but inevitably it has changed. 'Mockney' relies on riffs on well-known names, in which Posh and Becks (Victoria and David Beckham) represent sex, and poor Pete Tong is a synonym for everything going wrong.

Social implications have almost vanished as the patois is picked up by millennials who enjoy the wordplay. Meanwhile multi-ethnic London English has also emerged, a dialect that reflects the city's multicultural make-up, blending terms from slang, Caribbean, and American rap, as well as London's own cockney.

Whatever its future, 'apples and pears' (stairs), 'not having a Scooby' (Scooby Doo: clue), and 'going down the West End for a ruby' (Ruby Murray: curry) are still very much part of the British lexicon, and the idea, if not the reality, of the born-and-bred cockney will remain on London's tourist map, the linguistic equivalent of Routemaster buses and black cabs.

27 May

FUCK

Today is St Augustine's Day, the troubled saint famous for saying 'God give me chastity and continence, but not yet'.

Augustine is said to have confessed that he was a slave to lust. Many centuries later, it seems that others of the cloth found it equally hard to resist. One of the earliest records of the word 'fuck' in the *Oxford English Dictionary*, from 1500, tells us that a certain number of monks 'are not in heaven because they fuck the wives of Ely'.

Today, almost every post-watershed comedy or panel show is studded with instances of the F-bomb. It has been used publicly by a future prime minister, and no Oscar winner's speech is complete without one. And yet, for all its ubiquity, it is a word that still holds its own, with a sting that has endured for over half a millennium.

Ask any linguist for a list of the most versatile words in English, and 'fuck' will be near the top of the list. It can be inserted into almost any part of a sentence in countless ways.

How many other words can act as a noun (he doesn't give a fuck), adjective (not a fucking clue), verb (I fucked up), intensifier (it's all gone fucking mad) and an everyday filler (abso-fucking-lutely)? But that's far from all. Today's arsenal might also include a fuck-off hat or fuck-me shoes. You might have a fuck face, know fuck all, be fucked up, fucked over by a right fucker, scare the fuck out of someone, cause a clusterfuck, be a total fuckwit, fuck about, and even cry 'fuck a duck!' in astonishment.

A common myth is that 'fuck' is an acronym for 'Fornication Under Command of the King', and that it comes from a time when the population had been so decimated by plague that the Crown ordered everyone to go forward and procreate. They were instructed to hang a sign with F.U.C.K. on their doors, to show others that they were on important business, and should not be disturbed by royal decree. Lovely story as it is, it is also (literally) fucking nonsense.

For lexicographers, however, the answer is far from simple. To date, the evidence points to an origin far more sinister than the joy of sex. Ultimately, the word may be a much-altered sibling of the Latin *pugnus*, 'fist', which means that 'fuck' and 'pugnacious' may be related.

And that's how we originally understood fucking – not as having sex, but hitting. Some of fuck's earliest outings were in surnames: a Mr Fuckbeggere (Mr Beggar-hitter), for example, was clearly a violent citizen of the thirteenth century. Around the same time, a 'wyndfucker' was another word for a kestrel: a bird that strikes or hits the wind with its wings.

But as time went on, fuck took on a different meaning. In 1475 the Scottish poet William Dunbar wrote about a young man attempting to enter a girl's 'crowdie mowdie' (an old word for 'vagina'). In 1528 an anonymous monk wrote 'O D fuckin Abbot' in the margin of a book on moral conduct. No one knows if he was accusing the abbot of having too much sex, or if he was simply using the word as a strong exclamation; what matters most is that he was happy to deface a holy book with the word, yet couldn't bear to write out the term 'damned' (which is what the D stood for). For him 'damnation' was the real obscenity.

Fuck really hit its stride in the seventeenth century as a popular word for sex. In 1663 a man called, rather impossibly, Richard Head, wrote: 'I did creep in . . . and there I did see him putting the great fuck upon my weef.' By the 1700s, if the word was printed at all, it was always as f—k. These dashes and asterisks continued until relatively recently in an attempt to avoid any charge of obscenity. Relaxation only came after the unsuccessful prosecution in 1960 of Penguin Books for the publication of *Lady Chatterley's Lover*, considered to be obscene in the extreme: the prosecution counsel urged the jury to hold 'hidden from your wives and servants' a book that contained '30 fucks or fuckings, 14 cunts, 13 balls, 6 each of shit and arse, 4 cocks, and 3 piss'.

For a word that has been taboo, to varying degrees, for six centuries or more, fuck still holds most of the power in the swearing game.

28 May

COLLIESHANGIE

The fearsome 130-ship-strong Spanish Armada set sail for war on 28 May 1588: a reminder of the bitter enmity towards Elizabeth I at a time when England and Spain were at loggerheads.

In the sixteenth century, a 'logger' was a heavy block of wood that would be tied to a horse in order to prevent it from wandering too far. Figuratively, a 'logger-head' was a foolish person, someone 'wooden headed', but by the seventeenth century it had come to describe a heavy iron tool used in shipbuilding for making pitch – a potentially lethal weapon in a fight, hence, it's believed, the expression 'at loggerheads'.

English has a useful range of synonyms for a wrangling or competitive kerfuffle, ranging from the more cuddly 'argy-bargy' to Scotland's bloodier 'stramash'. The *Oxford English Dictionary* provides terms such as 'rippit' and 'hubbleshubble' from the sixteenth century, and 'rumpus', 'bobbery', and 'foofaraw' from the nineteenth.

'Collieshangie', from Victorian times, is one of the more unusual. It may come from *callaidh*, Gaelic for an 'outcry', but is more likely to refer to the sheepdog, with the sense of either a noisy quarrel of dogs, or the racket made by a dog when a 'shangie', or 'encumbrance', is tied to its tail.

As for the French 'brouhaha', rarely used in English without some sense of comedy or irony, its beginnings are far darker: it was originally seen as the utterance of the Devil, designed to inspire terror in all who heard it.

---

29 May

TAKING THE BISCUIT

World Biscuit Day traditionally prompts the annual discussion as to which of the myriad biscuity wonders available should be crowned queen. Like the correct pronunciation of 'scone' (*see* 30 June), it is a not a debate that is easily settled.

Given our love affair with these staples of the Western diet, it seems a little curious that a person or thing that 'takes the biscuit' is a cause of irritation rather than celebration. It signals, to riff on a similar foody expression, the icing on an already overloaded cake.

The phrase is thought to have originated in America, as an extension of 'take the cake'. This in turn is thought to hark back to nineteenth-century African American dance competitions, where those displaying the most accomplished steps, and cutting the finest figures, would be awarded a delicious slice of cake. Such entertainment became known as the 'cake-walk'. Such events frequently took place in black slave plantations in the southern states; perhaps it was in their offering of a necessary distraction that the answer to the modern use of 'cakewalk' lies – as a metaphor for anything that is considered easy or, as the expression has now become, a 'piece of cake' .

As for those biscuits, they take their name from the French for 'twice-cooked'. Before refrigeration, one way of keeping food from spoiling was to preserve flat loaves of bread by baking them a second time in order to dry them out. In early French, this bread was called *pain bescuit* or 'bread twice-cooked'. Later the term was shortened to *besquit*, and the term came to embrace the sweet and savoury delights we adore today, and that are very likely to be the cause of a 'snaccident' (*see* 21 February).

---

30 May

FOBBED OFF

The Peasants' Revolt began on this day in 1381, when the tax collector John Brampton, under the authority of the teenage King Richard II, rode into the Essex village of Fobbing to collect the poll tax of 3 groats from each of the local inhabitants. Frustrated and impoverished, the village folk are said to have gathered together in protest, sending Brampton off empty-handed. Their descendants today will tell you that this is how 'fobbed off' came about.

Tourist guides are a common source of colourful stories regarding the origin of certain words and phrases. The truth, more often, is far less entertaining. Ironically, in this case, it is the village of Fobbing that is, albeit in good faith, doing the fobbing off.

A consultation of the *Oxford English Dictionary* will tell you that 'fob' as a verb began to appear in the late sixteenth century, centuries after the events in Essex. Its meaning was, as it is now, to 'deceive or delude', and its heritage takes us to the German *foppen*, meaning the same thing.

The English playwright Robert Greene used the term in his prose romance *Mamillia: A Mirrour or looking-glasse for the Ladies of Englande* (1583): 'I will not . . . fobbe you with fayre wordes, and foule deedes.'

Greene is best known for the pamphlet *Greenes Groats-Worth of Witte*, seen by many as a veiled attack upon the writings of Shakespeare. That notwithstanding, the Bard himself used 'fubbed' in *Henry IV, Part Two*, where Mistress Quickly protests that 'I have borne, and borne, and borne, and have been fubbed off, and fubbed off, and fubbed off, from this day to that day, that it is a shame to be thought on.'

Fob as a noun followed the same idea of a fraud or imposter. By the mid-seventeenth century, it denoted a pocket in the waistband of a pair of breeches, used for a watch or other valuables. This pocket was hidden, and perhaps eluded the pickpockets who skulked along the streets of London. Which means that 'fob' was still entwined with the thread of deception.

---

31 May

CLEPSYDRA

On this day in 1859, the clock tower at the Houses of Parliament in London first began to keep time, although the infamous counterpart bell colloquially known as Big Ben would not be heard by the public until July of the same year.

Back in the sixteenth century BC, time-keeping was somewhat less complex than the gargantuan clockwork vanity projects of the Victorian era. The ancient Egyptians have been credited with the invention of the water-clock, a device that essentially kept time by measuring the uniform rate of water flowing from one container into another. It was later advanced by the Greeks to improve its accuracy, who gave it the name *clepsydra*, from the Greek words *kleptein*, meaning 'to steal', and *hydor*, meaning 'water'.

Kleptein also gave us 'kleptomania', the compulsion to steal, but its horological use extends further still; using the same metaphor of stealing time, a 'clepsammia' is an archaic word for a sand-timer or hourglass.

JUNE

FEISTY

If ever there was a job title that deserves to be reinstated in the books of the career office, it's that of the 'flatulist': a professional farter, who entertains crowds with the sole exercise of their windy skills. Born on this day in 1857, Joseph Pujol, under the stage name of Le Pétomane, became the most celebrated flatulist of all time, a performer who drew record crowds to the Moulin Rouge in Paris.

Pujol's anatomy allowed him to suck air into his rectum, which he would then control through use of his sphincter muscles ('sphincter' being a sibling of the Sphinx, who would strangle passers-by if they failed to answer her riddle: both get their name from the Greek for 'draw tight'). While serving in the army, Pujol entertained his fellow soldiers by demonstrating his unusual skills. Such was the reception that he decided to try his luck on stage. The rest is noisy history.

English has a bit of a love affair with farts. They escape in all sorts of unexpected ways. The verb to 'fizzle', for example, once meant to 'break wind quietly', while the same French *péter* that inspired Le Pétomane also gave us the expression 'hoisted by his own petard'. The petard in question was a small bomb that exploded with a sound not unlike a 'windipop', 'fowkin', 'poot', 'parp', or act of 'ventosity' (as listed in the *Oxford English Dictionary*). The name of the partridge is also founded upon that same *péter*, apparently because the chirring noise of the bird's wings, when taking flight, is fairly fart-like.

Another unlikely harbourer of farts is the word 'feisty', which began as a 'fisting hound' – a small and no doubt slightly snarling lapdog, but also one rather prone to wind.

2 June

CHERUBIMICAL

English has over three thousand words for being drunk, from 'schnockered' to 'spifflicated', 'befuggered' to 'woofled', and 'phalanxed' to 'liquorish'.

Benjamin Franklin famously published a *Drinkers' Dictionary*, for which he collected two hundred or more synonyms for a slathered state, including 'he's taken off his considering cap', 'been to France', 'contended with Pharaoh', 'smelt of an onion', and 'been too free with Sir Richard'.

One that might well fill a gap in the language today is 'cherubimical' – a descriptor for the happy drunk who goes around hugging everyone.

The Elizabethan Thomas Nashe approached the lexicon of befuddlement slightly differently. He described the various states through which one might progress as the alcohol finds its momentum. Someone who is 'ape-drunk' leaps and yells like an ape; one who is 'lion drunk' roars and fights; he is 'fox drunk' when crafty; 'swine drunk' when heavy and lethargic; 'sheep drunk' when unable to speak; and 'goat drunk' when, specifically, 'he hath no minde but on Lecherie'.

3 June

CHIPS

The first Friday in June brings us National Fish and Chips Day, which, beyond the usual salivation, might bring to mind the peculiar idiom 'to have a chip on one's shoulder'. Predictably, the phrase has nothing to do with savoury potatoes. Rather it refers to anyone with a grievance or sense of imposed inferiority.

The first written use of the phrase depicts something quite literal, involving the dockworkers of the eighteenth century. Shipwrights in the late 1730s were able to take home any offcuts of timber after work, and would carry these 'chips' on their shoulders for inspection before leaving. A subsequent order some years later would reduce the number of offcuts permitted for removal to that which could be carried under one arm (aka an 'oxterful'). Unhappy dockworkers recorded as strikers in a 1756 letter from Chatham dockyard were said to have 'pushed on with their chips on their shoulders', giving us our first example of the term used in an agitative sense.

At this point the phrase was not yet used as a metaphor for a grudge. For that, we need to jump to the 1830s, when reference begins to be made to children spoiling for a fight, who would place a chip of wood on their shoulder and challenge anyone to knock it off, if they so dared. By 1840, a typical use runs: 'Jonathan's blood is "pretty considerable riz" anyhow, and it wouldn't take so much as knocking a chip off a boy's shoulder to make it a darnationed sight riz-er' ('riz' here is a regional variation on 'risen').

As for other, edible, kinds of chip, these are first recorded in English in a manual for the 'experienced housekeeper' from 1769, when they referred to slices of orange. It was Charles Dickens who, in *A Tale of Two Cities*, gives us our first written record of 'husky chips of potato, fried with some reluctant drops of oil'. Today the oil flows in abundance, but our love remains undiminished (*see* 'French fries', 4 December).

---

4 June

HACKNEYED

In June 1654, the first ordinance was passed by Cromwell's Parliament regulating hackney carriages. Unfortunately, some may say, there is no such law governing the other kind of hacks – the journalistic kind.

Over the centuries, journalists have gone by many names, including 'diurnaller' (1600s, meaning 'a day-time writer'), 'couranteer' (1700s), 'pressman' (1800s), and 'Bigfoot' (1980s, 'a prominent reporter'). Surely the most enduring epithet, however, is that of the hack. But what links a writer of everyday news with one of the most iconic symbols of a capital city?

Hackney today lies north-east of the City of London. In the year 1300, it was the name of a small village that lay on the west side of the River Lea in the middle of pleasant and open countryside. The area became famous for the horses bred and pastured there; these were riding horses, or what were known as 'ambling horses', as opposed to the 'destriers' that were the war or draught animals (which took their name from the Latin *dextra*, 'right hand', because they were led by the squire with his right hand). Horses bred for strength rather than looks and pedigree were known by the term 'Hackney'.

These riding horses were often made available for hire, and so 'hackney' came to apply both to them and to the vehicles they pulled. 'Hackney carriage' became the usual term for a vehicle that plied for hire – London's black taxis, and those in other cities, are still formally referred to in legislation by that title.

Hackney horses were both widely available and visible on most streets of the city – used to such an extent that they became both commonplace and unremarkable. The animals were also often so overworked that they were positively jaded through fatigue (a 'jade' being a worn-out, 'knackered' horse). It's down to this that 'hackneyed' evolved to mean something used so frequently and indiscriminately that it loses its fresh-ness and interest: in other words something old, unoriginal, and worthy only of being chip-paper. Modern hack journal-ists continue to carry this legacy with them – though, like so many epithets used against a group of people, it is now worn by many journalists as the self-deprecatory badge of the tribe.

5 June

PACIFIC

Every year on 5 June, World Environment Day is celebrated as part of a multinational campaign to raise awareness of a diverse array of environmental issues and, in particular, to draw focus to the climate crisis. The oceans of the world are likely to experience an enormous detrimental impact.

The word 'ocean' comes to us through the Greek *okeanos*, meaning 'great river', although modern etymologists have theorised that its origins may be even older. The ancient Greeks believed in a disc-shaped earth, and envisaged the ocean as a single great river running around the giant landmass.

When distinctions began to be made between the different bodies of water, naming was inspired by varying cultural and personal impulses. The Indian Ocean is simply based on its topography; 'India' itself comes to us via Greek from the Sanskrit word *Sindhu*, the name for the Indus River. The Atlantic Ocean was named after the Atlas mountain range in Northern Africa, which was in turn named after the powerful Titan who supported the heavens (*see* 20 May).

The Pacific Ocean owes its title to the explorer Ferdinand Magellan, who, in 1520, was searching for a route through the New World to the Spice Islands. Magellan was to find a stretch of water that would become eponymously known as the 'Straits of Magellan', where he and his fleet experienced unpredictable winds and currents. They eventually passed into the open waters of what was known at the time as 'the Sea of the South', so-named by the explorer and conquistador Vasco Núñez de Balboa when he sighted it from land in Panama. Magellan's crossing of the ocean might have been long, but he was struck by its calmness and serenity, leading him to name it *Mar Pacifico*, the 'tranquil sea'.

6 June

SNOUTFAIR

'Hot', 'fit', 'hench', 'dench': the lexicon of words for attractive is smaller than you might think, while that of terms for ugly is positively bulging at the seams. Perhaps it's because we're a pessimistic lot, and a gossipy one at that, that we like nothing more than commenting on others' faults and being all-round 'smellfungi' (those who consistently find faults in others). But a historical dictionary can help provide a few choice adjectives from the past that, though they might initially elicit a few odd looks, may help you win the heart you're seeking.

'Snoutfair' is a now-obsolete term from the 1600s for someone who 'has a fair countenance', or who is 'fair-faced, comely, handsome'. Even this, when it began, had a disparaging, envious feel to it ('I knowe a snowt-faire, selfe-conceited asse', 1616), but it soon settled into an adjective of approbation for a person admired and desired.

If this is too nose-focused for you, there are alternatives, though not as many as you might think. They include 'seemly', 'comely', 'pulchrous', and the slightly risky 'glorious skinny' (from the 1400s no less). Some adjectives took a tumble from their original meaning of simply 'beautiful' and embraced wantonness instead – among them 'smicker' and 'lusty'. As for describing a beautiful woman, you could always call her a 'bellibone', a mangling of the French *belle et bonne*, but tread carefully. When it comes to attractiveness, envy is clearly the enemy of the dictionary.

7 June

TREACLE

On 7 June 1654, Louis XIV was crowned King of France. His reign, at 72 years and 110 days, was to be the longest of any monarch in European history. His system of absolute rule was to last up until the French Revolution. It was marked by many reforms, wars, and hugely-augmented French influence across the world. It also included a murder and witchcraft scandal that rocked the aristocracy and royal circles, and which led to the execution of thirty-six individuals. Madame de Brinvilliers, found guilty of poisoning her father and two brothers in order to inherit their estate, was forced to drink sixteen pints of water (the so-called 'water cure') before she was burned at the stake.

The case struck fear in the population, who began to see instances of poisoning in even the most innocent of deaths; the king himself feared for his life and began to mistrust those around him. Authorities arrested a number of fortune-tellers and alchemists who were suspected of selling not only medicinal potions, but also 'inheritance powders' (a euphemism for toxins). Confessions were extracted under torture, and some gave up the names of clients who had allegedly bought poison to murder their spouses or rivals in the royal court.

The perils of poison are embedded in our language, silently hidden behind many ordinary words. The power of the 'potion', a word that originally meant a draught of poisoned liquid, informs the most surprising of words.

Almost every advanced biochemical weapon known today had an ancient prototype. Toxic projectiles, medicinal compounds, venomous insects and animals – all date back centuries. And the wealth of recipes in early medical texts for remedies and antidotes, often alchemically produced, demonstrate the extent of the desire to assassinate. Treacle is the result of one such remedy. The sticky, syrupy confection would seem as far as you might get from murderous intent, and yet the ancestry of its name lies in the Greek *therion*, a venomous wild beast whose bite was thought curable only with a unique antidote called the *theriake*. It is said to have tasted foul, digestible only with the counterbalance of something sweet. *Theriake*, which was to become 'treacle' in English, was later transferred from the anti-venom to the very syrup that made it more palatable. By the end of the seventeenth century, treacle was not only a medicinal remedy but also a sugary syrup of molasses.

Quite what the *theriake* cure consisted of we're not sure. One recipe in an old herbal begins 'Take of Myrrh, Saffron, Agarick, Ginger, Cinnamon, Frankincense, Treacle' and goes on to list forty-one more ingredients, many of them extremely rare – some Roman recipes are said to have included opium and the flesh of a viper. It's a far cry from treacle pudding.

---

8 June

NEWSPEAK

Misinformation, disinformation, fake news – these are among the defining preoccupations of the century. Key to each is a protest against any authority's ability to define what constitutes the truth. The debate, of course, is nothing new, not least to readers of George Orwell's *Nineteen Eighty-Four*, published on this day in 1949.

Orwell had much to say about language. He witnessed, he believed, such a degeneration that dialogue was rendered impossible: double-talk, cliché, and pseudoscience created a vacuum in which authority could thrive unchallenged. 'Bad' language is about concealment: the good kind allows for opposition and clarity.

In his fight against linguistic decadence, Orwell's writing

gave us its own additions to our vocabulary, including 'Orwellian' itself, a marker of dystopia, repression, and totalitarianism. His book *Nineteen Eighty-Four* also pushed the phrase 'Big Brother' into popular currency, although it has represented various kinds of supervision since the middle of the nineteenth century. Decades later, it must have seemed the perfect choice of name for a TV series in which viewers become both the watchers and the controllers. Similarly, Orwell took the idea of 'thought-crime' and sealed its place in the language – it was, he wrote, 'the essential crime that contained all others in itself'.

But he was a creator too. Orwell was the first to give us the 'unperson', one who is deemed not to have existed and who is therefore erased from all public records; it evolved to signify one considered of no political or social importance. He formulated the idea of doublethink, whose labyrinthine world is defined in *Nineteen-Eighty-Four* as 'to know and not to know, to be conscious of complete truthfulness while telling carefully constructed lies . . . to use logic against logic, to repudiate morality while laying claim to it, to believe that democracy was impossible and that the Party was the guardian of democracy'.

In the same novel, 'Newspeak' is a highly controlled, artificial language that is created exclusively for purposes of propaganda – one whose vocabulary is ever diminishing in order to stifle free speech. 'Newspeak' has often been interpreted as 'news-speak', as opposed to Orwell's use of it as the antithesis of Oldspeak (though he may well have intended the ambiguity). Today's fears over the vast reach of misinformation presented as 'news' have given the term fresh resonance. Social media, allowing us all to publish our every thought, have flooded our screens with digital falsehoods.

This blurring of the lines is useful to some. Donald Trump in recent years has liberally handed out the accusation of 'fake news' against the 'fake media' he perceives as critical of his presidency. The questioning of hard facts, or lack of them, has dominated his time in office – his critics lampooned a phrase used by his team when they were challenged over the claim that thousands more had attended his inauguration than that of Obama; they were, one spokesperson for the president said, simply citing 'alternative facts'. The phrase evoked a word introduced a decade earlier to American vocabulary by the satirical US show *The Colbert Report*: 'truthiness', used for facts as we would like them to be rather than as they actually are (*see* 'ipsedixitism', 10 March).

Today, a statue of Orwell, created by the sculptor Martin Jennings, stands outside the BBC (whose conference room is said to have inspired the name of a torture chamber in *Nineteen Eighty-Four* known as 'Room 101'). Behind him the wall bears a quote from that same work: 'If liberty means anything at all, it means the right to tell people what they do not want to hear.'

Liberty, not truthiness.

9 June

DUTCH FEAST

John Camden Hotten was one of the first and best lexicographers of slang. He gathered and documented what he himself described as 'that evanescent, vulgar language, ever changing with fashion and taste . . . spoken by persons in every grade of life, rich and poor, honest and dishonest'. One result of his indefatigable quest for the language of 'fast, high, and low life' was the publication, in 1859, of *A Dictionary of Modern Slang, Cant, and Vulgar Words*. On the day Hotten died in 1873 (of brain fever, or a surfeit of pork chops, depending on which historian you ask) he was still revising his work.

Among the back slang and rhyming slang, and the patter from sailors and shopkeepers, are such expressions as a 'Dutch uncle', defined by the author as 'a person often introduced in conversation, but exceedingly difficult to describe'. A 'Dutch concert' is one in which 'each performer plays a different tune', and 'Dutch consolation' is simply 'Thank God it's no worse'.

These less well-known Dutch formulae sit alongside those that have endured to this day: 'Dutch courage', namely false courage garnered through drinking; 'double Dutch', i.e. gibberish; and 'going Dutch', where everyone splits the bill and thus risks the suggestion of miserliness. But why Dutch?

In the seventeenth century, the Dutch and British were at loggerheads (*see* 28 May). Both sought maritime superiority, and not least the control of the sea routes that carried exotic cargo from the rich Spice Islands of the East Indies. The result of such vying for supremacy was three naval wars between the years 1652 and 1674. On 9 June 1667, the Dutch sailed up the Medway, sank multiple British ships, and blockaded the Thames. The ensuing bitterness on the part of the British resulted in 'Dutch' becoming synonymous with such unappealing qualities as cowardice and stinginess.

Today, even while most prejudice towards our friends in the Netherlands has long since vanished, a couple of contemporary examples might occasionally feel useful. A 'Dutch reckoning' is a bill that is presented without any details and which only gets bigger if you question it, while a 'Dutch feast' is one at which the host 'gets drunk before the guests'.

10 June

THEIST

You might think that a 'theist' is one who holds a fundamental kinship with God. And that is indeed its first recorded sense back in the late seventeenth century. But the word has a secondary sense, one that might be more familiar in modern life. In this case the object of worship is not a divine deity, but rather a cup of something hot. Theism appears in only a single record in the *Oxford English Dictionary*, but for some of us that is enough reason to adopt it with immediate effect. There it is defined as 'a person addicted to tea-drinking', and is recorded as a label fondly used of himself by the poet Percy Bysshe Shelley, a noted lover of tea.

For those who refuse to perform anything other than drinking tea while lounging in bed (*see* 'hurkle durkle', 27 July), another recent word may be of use: 'prioriteasing'. And for coffee-lovers ('caffeists'?), there is always 'procaffeinating', a more widely known verb for delaying anything productive until you've had *at least* one cup of coffee.

---

11 June

ALCATRAZ

On this day in 1962, brothers John and Clarence Anglin, together with a fellow inmate Frank Morris, escaped from Alcatraz Federal Penitentiary. They were among only five to ever have done so.

The brothers constructed a makeshift raft from inmates' raincoats for transporting themselves across the water and away from the island. What happened to them is not known. Fifteen years later, the FBI closed the investigation on the assumption that they had drowned in the icy waters of San Francisco Bay; nevertheless, the escapees remain on their wanted list.

Behind the name of Alcatraz itself lies the story of a bird associated with both the pelican and the albatross. In Arabic, an *al-gattos* was a sea eagle. The term passed into Spanish as *alcatraz* where it denoted various kinds of pelican. The change from a *g* to a *c* may have come from a folk association with the Spanish *alcaduz*, meaning a 'water bucket' and a term that also came from Arabic – this word may have seemed particularly appropriate for the pelican because of the prominent pouch under its bill, used to capture and hold fish but also, according to legend, for drawing up water to carry to its young in the desert.

The island in San Francisco Bay was home to hundreds of the birds, and so the name was simply transferred to the prison for which it became notorious. It also inspired the naming of the 'albatross', which was given the same name but which was altered to reflect the Latin *albus*, white.

---

12 June

DOOLALLY

As we yearn for the holidays, and anticipate some serious summer heat, some of us might feel we are going more than a little 'doolally'.

Heat plays a role in the history of this curious-looking word. At the height of the British Empire, the British army established a military sanatorium in Deolali, north-east of Bombay, which also doubled as a transit camp where soldiers who were considered to be 'time-expired' would await their boat home at the end of their tour of duty. Boats left only between November and March, with the result that some soldiers waited for many months under either the scorching Indian sun or the deluges of the monsoon season. Others contracted venereal disease and were confined to hospital. The resulting boredom and restlessness ensured that behaviour soon began to deteriorate.

The men were described as going 'doolally tap': 'doolally' being the Englishman's pronunciation of Deolali, and *tap* being an Urdu word for 'malarial fever'. In other words, they had 'camp fever'. The *tap* was soon dropped, and 'doolally' slipped over from army slang into the mainstream, where it has stayed at the friendlier end of the 'madness' lexicon ever since.

13 June

CLATTERFART

At the height of the Second World War, a now-famous poster urged British officers and other servicemen and women to 'keep mum', lest confidential information fall into the hands of the enemy through idle chatter and gossip. The full slogan read 'Keep mum; she's not so dumb!', below a picture of a gorgeous reclining woman surrounded by men in uniform, with the implication that she was not only a seductress, but also a spy.

In this case the assumption was that it would usually be men indulging in careless gossip – probably because it was they who were entrusted with the 'important' things of war. Traditionally, of course, tittle-tattle has been seen as the sole preserve of women. Even the word 'gossip' comes from 'godsib', an old word for godmother, who attended at a friend's birth and, it seems, lingered as a chatty companion for quite a while after. The godsib was therefore considered to be a prolific 'clatterfart', 'bablatrice', 'prattle-basket', 'chat-termag' and 'jangleress': all words applied to female gossips over the years.

Some evidence suggests that the word 'girl' is linked to 'garrulous', suggesting, once again, a chatterbox. But do women really talk a lot more than men? A recent study says that both sexes use an equal number of words per day. In its results, men accounted for both ends of the scale: the speaker of the fewest words, and the most loquacious (a whopping 47,000 words per day).

What do you call someone who, on the other hand, keeps the confidences of others without reaching into the prattle-basket? The answer would once have been a secretary, who, in the 1400s, was typically a male confidant, someone privy to secrets. Fast forward to the twentieth century, and the stereotype of most secretaries would be a woman, and probably a gossipy one at that.

14 June

SANGUINE

This day, 14 June, is World Blood Donor Day, a thank you to all those who have given life-saving blood to others. Unsurprisingly, the fundamental liquid of life runs through the veins of the English language, too.

It is there in 'sanguine', for example, often used to describe an individual who is positive, cheerful, and confident. The word arrived in English through the Latin *sanguineus*, meaning 'of blood': sanguine can still refer to a deep red colour, especially in heraldry. The link between this body fluid and positivity is rooted in ancient belief and superstition.

For almost two thousand years, good bodily health was inextricably bound to the four 'humours' espoused by the teachings of Hippocrates (and later Aristotle). They postulated that four bodily fluids – blood, yellow bile, black bile, and phlegm – needed to be kept in strict balance to avoid sickness. An excess of yellow bile, for example, would make one irritable, bilious, or choleric. Too much black bile caused unease and sadness – the word 'melancholy' comes directly from the Greek words for 'black' and 'bile'. An excess of phlegm, on the other hand, was a sure route to total apathy; when we say someone is phlegmatic today, we mean they are laid-back and calm.

And so to the blood of sanguine, of which a predomination was thought to lead to an optimistic and cheery disposition – as well as a florid complexion, although that might be down to a 'grogblossom' or two (*see* 1 January).

15 June

CHARTER

When William the Conqueror became King of England on Christmas Day, 1066, his coronation ceremony was conducted in English and Latin. William himself, however, recited his lines in French. For the next three centuries, a varied French lexicon, and its Latin roots, threatened to topple English as the dominant tongue.

After the conquest, educated people were required to become adept at moving between French, Latin, and English. The pressure of French was irresistible, and direct replacement of native terms with the Norman French equivalent was commonplace. The Old English *rood*, for example, denoting a large crucifix in a church, survives only in terms such as 'rood-screen' and the place name 'Holyrood'. After the Conquest, the Old French *crois* was propelled into English and eventually standardised as 'cross'.

William's *Charter for London*, dated 1066, detailed the rights and privileges available to every man. The name, given to it retrospectively by later historians, is of suitably French origin. 'Charter' is from the Old French *cartle*, meaning a small leaf of paper, and itself a diminutive of the Latin *carta*. A legal document or deed delivered by the sovereign or legislature was usually written on a single sheet of paper.

As was the Great Charter, or *Magna Carta*, to which King John gave his seal on this day in 1215 in Runnymede, a meadow by the Thames. In essence, this was a medieval peace treaty designed to avert civil war and appease outraged nobles by providing a leash with which to curtail arbitrary royal power: the majority of its sixty-three clauses address grievances over the king's rule. But the document also guaranteed all 'free men' the right to justice and a fair trial, and as such was primarily a deal for those who already held power in society.

The charter is written entirely in Latin; those English-speaking serfs, whose lives it circumscribed, could understand little of it, if anything at all.

What was to become one of the significant documents in constitutional history was not only ratified by the man who is generally viewed as the worst king of England; it was also largely unenforceable – John himself applied to the Pope for its annulment. After many revisions, during which it both halved in size and acquired the name we know today, it granted some modest rights to the wider masses. But many historians maintain it doesn't quite deserve the legacy it enjoys – it owes much of its fame to its later adoption as a rallying cry for liberty both in England and in the US. As the writer Jill Lepore puts it: 'Claiming a French-speaking king's short-lived promise to his noblemen as the foundation of English liberty and, later, of American democracy, took a lot of work.' As, in fact, did the language of the conquering elite.

16 June

UXORIOUS

Today is Bloomsday: a day of celebrating everything to do with novelist James Joyce and his strange and brilliant novel *Ulysses*. Joyce was a prolific neologiser, a filler of gaps in the language to suit his writing needs. Among them are unexpected combinations like 'poppysmic' (in relation to the smacking of lips when 'liplapping loudly') and the supercilious 'smilesmirk', while the dictionary of drunkards definitely deserves the word 'peloothered' for being hopelessly plastered. Few have survived beyond Joyce's work and most would make the spellchecker bristle, but all have undeniable verve.

Ulysses takes place on 16 June, the date upon which, in 1904, Joyce himself had his first outing with Nora Barnacle, the woman who was later to become his wife. The couple did not officially marry until 1931, but the relationship was passionate to the end – for Joyce, Nora remained, notoriously, his 'dirty little fuckbird'. (In this, perhaps he was fulfilling another of his neologisms, and being a little 'pornosophical'.)

The word 'uxorious' describes a husband who dotes on his wife obsessively, and Joyce's relationship with Nora seems to have fitted the bill. The term is a straight borrowing from Latin, in which *uxor* means 'wife'. It is not entirely neutral: the poet John Milton gives us a taste of the judgement with which the word tended to be used: 'Effeminate and Uxorious Magistrates . . . being themselves govern'd and overswaid at home under a Feminine usurpation'.

As usual in English, it was the male viewpoint which took priority. There is a single, isolated instance in 1607 of a word describing the reverse: a woman excessively fond of her husband ('Dames maritorious, ne're were meritorious'), which was not picked up again for some three centuries, and which never quite took off. 'Maritorious' comes from the Latin *maritum*, husband.

As ever, Joyce expressed things far more eloquently, and in his own idiosyncratic style: in the end, what truly matters is that 'love loves to love love'.

---

17 June

ULTRACREPIDARIAN

Most of us know at least one person who loves to talk at length on a subject they know nothing about. One word for this kind of presumptuous critic is an 'ultracrepidarian', a term that has travelled across centuries thanks to a classical story of a man who dared to pass comment on matters far beyond his area of expertise.

That man was an unnamed cobbler from ancient Greece who, while observing a painting by the renowned artist Apelles, apparently criticised the rendering of a sandal in the picture, which had one loop too few. It was said that Apelles liked to eavesdrop on those who came to see his paintings, in order to hear their views of his artistry. In this case, the cobbler proceeded to criticise not just the shoe, but the subject's leg too. To this Apelles is said to have retorted that the cobbler should judge nothing but the shoes, which were his only sphere of knowledge. The Latin tag *ne ultra crepidam* means 'not beyond the sandal' – from this was formed 'ultracrepidarian': one who gives opinions of matters quite beyond their understanding or knowledge.

---

18 June

BUMF

Today is Waterloo Day, the anniversary of the Battle of Waterloo in 1815.

Popular belief holds that the traditional euphemism for the toilet, 'loo', pays (not-so-silent) homage to the name of the battle. James Joyce, for example, brought together the words Waterloo and water closet in a line in *Ulysses*: 'O yes, mon loup. How much cost? Waterloo. Water closet.'

And yet 'loo' has long been a word in search of an etymology. Another suggested derivation is that it derives from the phrase *gardyloo* (a mangling of the French *Regardez l'eau!* – 'Watch the water!'), which was shouted by servants in some cities in the seventeenth century before they emptied the contents of a chamber pot onto the streets below. But there is too long a gap between such use of the word and the first appearances of 'loo' in the early twentieth century. An alternative French origin points to *lieu d'aisance*, 'place of ease', similar to the American 'rest room'.

For now, the true origin of 'loo' remains a mystery. It endures as a fig leaf for those who can't bring themselves to say 'toilet', and sits alongside an entire lexicon of less well-known euphemisms. At the formal end is the 'phrontistery', a place for solitary contemplation, but few are quite so poetic. In the 1800s, those caught short would 'play arse music', 'visit the Spice Islands', use the 'thunder-jug', or even 'strain the potatoes', while in the last hundred years we've turned to 'releasing a hostage', 'emptying the anaconda', or 'draining the lizard'.

Among the best of them is 'visiting the doughnut in granny's greenhouse', a circumlocution taken from a sketch by Michael Palin and the late Terry Jones that featured an embarrassed man who, although in dire need, feels he must avoid being blunt at all costs. The pay-off was a phrase so good it even became an album title.

For any trip to the Spice Islands you will of course need the 'bumf', short for 'bumfodder' or toilet paper, and a term extended to anything that is essentially throwaway. Other names for loo-paper over the centuries should surely never have been flushed away: they include 'arsewisp', 'tail-timber', 'wipe-breeches' and 'bungwad'.

---

19 June

G-STRING

This was the day, in 1935, when Coopers Inc. of Chicago sold what is thought to be a world first: men's briefs, which their creator Arthur Kneibler named 'Jockeys'. It was, by all accounts, a nervous launch in a downtown department store during a blizzard. Its management thought the day far too cold for a display of such skimpy items, and promptly ordered it to be removed – but before their instruction could be acted upon, some six hundred pairs of the briefs were swept up by excited customers. As news spread, so did the Jockeys. Before long, Simpsons in London's Piccadilly was selling 3,000 pairs a week.

Until that day, the only serious rival to the traditional long johns had been the boxer short, launched a decade earlier as a nod to the swathes of silk sported in the boxing ring. For all their apparent glamour, they failed to provide sufficient 'leverage' for some. The jockey or jockstrap was to change all that. Their name reflects the support that jockstraps traditionally give athletes, as well perhaps as the 'jockeys', or riders, of penny-farthings, for whom they were originally designed.

It turns out we've been preoccupied with undies for a very long time. King Tutankhamun's tomb contained no fewer than 145 pairs of spare underpants in the shape of triangular nappies that fastened at the hips. In the centuries that followed, our 'underfugs', as they were once called, have embraced everything from long and baggy drawers to the faint-inducing bodices that gave us the adjective 'strait-laced'.

They have also swapped genders. Corsets were once worn by men, as were brassieres. Both words come from French and were parts of body armour: a *bracière* was a protective covering for the arm, while the corset, meaning 'little body', shielded the chest. 'Bodice' was a seventeenth-century sanitised version of 'bodies', a garment covering the trunk of both men and women, while the 'basque' began as a doublet or waistcoat worn slightly below the belt, in the style of Basque countrymen.

Bloomers were named after the US civil rights and temperance campaigner Mrs Amelia Jenks Bloomer, who favoured wearing a pair of knickerbockers or loose trousers in place of a skirt. Ebenezer Cobham Brewer, author of *Brewer's Dictionary of Phrase and Fable*, wrote in 1894 that 'Bloomerism' was 'becoming enough to young ladies in their teens, but ridiculous for the fat and forty'. 'Knickers', meanwhile, are short for 'knickerbockers'; in 1809, Washington Irving, using the pseudonym Diedrich Knickerbocker, published his satirical *History of New York* with illustrations of Knickerbocker men, descendants of New York's Dutch settlers, wearing loose breeches gathered at the knee. Men liked to wear knickerbockers as sportswear until women commandeered them as a style for underwear and called them 'knickers' for short, even though, in those days, they were anything but short.

Today's knickerbockers are 'pants', named after Pantalone, a type of clown who wore garish trousers, or 'pantaloons', in Italian comedy. At the opposite extreme sits (barely) the G-string, originally a loincloth worn by Native Americans. Some suggest the name is a grinning nod to the thinness of the G-string on a violin.

20 June

SHARK BISCUIT

Today is International Surfing Day. Ironically, it is also the anniversary of the release, in 1975, of the film *Jaws*. The two themes come together nicely in 'shark biscuit', slang in the tribe for a newbie or inexperienced surfer, or their wobbly board.

When it comes to surfer language, we tend to take stereotyping to a whole new level. Few of us look beyond the 'cowabunga', 'totally radical, duuude!' or 'most triumphant!' of Bill and Ted. But while bodacious adjectives still rule on the beaches of Malibu and Hawaii, most surf geeks and freaks prefer a lexicon equal to the proper challenges of their sport, albeit with a good smattering of 'surfari' humour thrown in. Types of wave, move, and board are all distinguished in minute detail, and the characters riding them are equally delineated.

Fellow surfers are usually 'brahs' or dudes; as opposed to the 'barnie' or grom/grommet, who, like the shark biscuit, is very new to the art. A 'frube' is a surfer who fails to catch a single wave, while a 'paddle-puss' is one who stays in the white water close to the beach. A 'shubie' is instantly recognisable: someone who buys all the gear, often the most expensive kind, but never actually goes in the water. At the other extreme is the 'hellman' – an extreme surfer and king of the waves (also known as a 'hotdogger').

And then there are those who in the surfer's mind don't belong anywhere near them: the 'kayakers', aka 'goat-boaters'; the 'hodad', a non-surfing beach bum; and the 'eggbeater', a surfer who somehow never fails to get in the way while you're trying to catch a wave.

---

21 June

SCARPER

'Scarper' is a word with its heart in London's Ealing comedies or reports of diamond heists. Yet it has been in the English language for longer than you might think, reaching us through a secret nineteenth-century dialect known as Polari (*see* 16 December).

'Scarper' probably originated from the Italian word *scappare*, meaning to 'escape'. In the language of Polari, to 'scarper the Letty' was to make a quick exit from your board and lodgings. The *Swell's Night Guide* from 1893 offers another example: 'He must *hook it* before daylight does appear, and then scarper by the back door.'

But that wasn't the end of 'scarper's' journey through English. A few decades later, it was given a different impetus. Scapa Flow in the Orkney Islands was a major British naval base, and in 1919 it hosted a highly dramatic post-war event. In order to prevent the Allies from claiming the defeated German fleet as spoils of war, German Rear Admiral Ludwig von Reuter gave the order to scuttle the fleet. A grand total of fifty-three warships were sunk that day, and the time and place were etched into the public imagination. As a result, Scapa Flow became a handy rhyme for 'go', usually in order to escape a spot of bother.

22 June

BOGUS

On 22 June 1986, Diego Maradona created one of the most controversial events in the history of the World Cup. A clear handball resulted in a goal for Argentina against England during the quarter-final match at the Azteca Stadium in Mexico City. Argentina went on to win both the quarter-final and the whole tournament. After the match, Maradona stated that the goal was scored 'a little with my head, and a little with the Hand of God'. In other words, and as England fans have never forgotten, his goal was entirely bogus.

The earliest evidence we have for the word 'bogus' is in reference to a machine for making counterfeit coins. In 1827, an Ohio newspaper related the discovery of such a device in the hands of a gang of coiners in Painesville, Ohio. The newspaper reports that it was a mysterious-looking object, which someone in the crowd called a 'bogus'. The term was then adopted by the *Painesville Telegraph* and reprinted in many of its next editions.

Many stories have been created to account for the origin of the word, most of which are probably bogus themselves. It may have been inspired by a dialect word from Vermont, where a 'tantrabogus' was once the equivalent of today's 'thingamajig', applied to any strange-looking object. That word may have been brought over by early colonists hailing from Devon, where local dialect included 'tantarrob', a nickname for the Devil. Who is also of course the bogey in 'bogeyman', which leads us right back to Maradona.

If this story is correct, then 'bogus' is a sibling of an appellation for the Devil. For most England fans, even today, the 'Hand of the Devil' goal would seem far more appropriate.

---

23 June

IDDY-UMPTY

On this day in 1868, a patent was granted for what is widely seen as the first modern typewriter. It was given to US newspaper editor Christopher Latham Sholes, who sought to perfect what many before him had already attempted.

Sholes's first machine had a few teething problems. Anyone typing at speed experienced the frustration of seeing the metal arms of various letters become hopelessly entangled. The typewriter's keyboard also presented an unexpected challenge. Having arranged letters alphabetically, as seemed logical, Sholes and his colleagues soon realised that language is far less orderly and predictable, and that an organisation was needed that reflected the frequency of letter distribution, rather than its formal sequence in the alphabet. It also separated the most common sequence of letters, avoiding the stickiest jams. The team's efforts resulted in the qwerty keyboard, which Sholes himself described as a 'blessing to mankind'.

The relative frequency of letters was also crucial for Samuel Morse, inventor of Morse code. In order to give the simplest codes to the letters used most often, he drew up a chart by counting the numbers of letters in sets of printers' types. This put E at the top of the list, and Z, unsurprisingly, at the bottom – positions that are largely true to this day.

Morse would have studied umpteen types to arrive at his conclusions, and 'umpteen' is itself a word that has its roots in the code he invented in 1836, which was known facetiously as 'iddy-umpty' thanks to the stuttering sounds of its *dits* and *dahs*. A 'dash' became an 'umpty', leading to its use for an unspecified or impossibly large number. 'Umpteen' was a natural further spin-off.

24 June

CHOREOMANIA

Choreomania is the compulsion to dance. This bizarre phenomenon has been recorded a number of times in the past, and one notable outbreak occurred in the town of Aachen in Germany on this day in 1374. According to some historians, citizens there congregated en masse and began to 'dance' uncontrollably, often to the point of near-total exhaustion.

Possible explanations given at the time ranged from evil spirits inspiring mass hysteria, to the accidental consumption of hallucinogenic fungi in a condition known as 'ergotism', or 'St Anthony's fire', after the monks of the Order of St Anthony who were said to be particularly skilful at curing the dreaded disease.

A similar historical phenomenon is 'tarantism', a manifestation that occurred primarily in Italy during the sixteenth and seventeenth centuries. Superstition held that a bite from the tarantula wolf spider (so named from its habitat in the seaport of Taranto, Italy) would result in hysteric and convulsive behaviour that could only be cured by the patient engaging – at length – in a frenzied, whirling dance known as a *tarantella*. The belief persisted for centuries – Samuel Johnson included it in his *Dictionary of the English Language* where a tarantula is defined as 'an insect whose bite is only cured by musick'.

25 June

JUGGERNAUT

Depending on the day you're having, a juggernaut might be either an unstoppable force, a gigantic truck, or a villainous foil for the *X-Men*. Its origin is one of the most unlikely in the English language, involving the meeting of two vastly different worlds and cultures.

'Juggernaut' entered the English language in the early nineteenth century as colonial Britons in India witnessed the Hindu ritual of Rath Yatra. In this festival, wooden forms of the gods are ceremonially placed on immense chariots and pulled through the streets by worshippers in processions attended by thousands of devotees. One of the gods is Jagganath, which in Sanskrit means 'Lord of the Universe', a fitting name for a deity worshipped in regional traditions of Buddhism and Hinduism and most often depicted as one of the ten incarnations, or avatars, of Vishnu. (Vishnu, 'The Preserver', is one of the *trimurti* in the Hindu religion, the three most powerful gods; the other two being Brahma 'The Creator', and Shiva 'The Destroyer'.)

When the British encountered Jagannath and his chariot, they tried to make sense of what they were seeing. Some of the earliest accounts present the festival as violent and foolhardy, recording the frequent sacrifice of worshippers who would leap under the giant wheels of the chariot. Western visitors would write about a barbarous and unstoppable 'Juggernaut' that would crush everything in its path.

This dangerous image of the Rath Yatra festival persisted, to the extent that, in Georgian and then Victorian Britain, 'juggernaut' was used as a metaphor for the vices of alcohol, or any practice to which people blindly devoted themselves, or were ruthlessly sacrificed. This was the beginning of the separation of the word from the name of the Indian deity, and 'juggernaut' took on an entirely different meaning, though always with the sense of a powerful, giant, and unstoppable force.

26 June

TENNIS

This is the time of Wimbledon, and once the strawberries and cream have been politely demolished, it's traditional to unpick some tennis terminology.

The word 'tennis' itself comes from the imperative form of the French verb *tener* meaning 'to hold, receive, or take'. While few records exist, it's assumed that in earlier incarnations of the game, players would shout '*Tenez!*', 'Receive!', to their opponents as they served the ball.

The 'racquet', or 'racket' (the official spelling of the International Tennis Federation), had not been adopted at this early stage; instead the ball was struck with the palm of the hand. This makes sense of the tennis racket's probable origin, which is the French *rachasser*, 'to strike back', although one outlying theory goes back to the Arabic *rahat al-yad*, literally translated as 'palm of hand'.

'Deuce' is a simple anglicism from the French *à deux*, 'at two', because each player, drawn at 40–all, is two points away from the win.

The greatest bemuser of them all, however, is surely *love*. On the face of it, it seems a rather unusual way of describing 'no points' between two competitors fiercely pitched against each other. Nevertheless, the *Oxford English Dictionary* suggests it may derive from the phrase 'for love', implying the game was simply being played for the love of it, with no silverware or financial reward at stake. A more popular theory is that *love* is a corruption of the French word for an egg, *l'oeuf*, due to its resemblance to the '0' displayed on the scoreboard. If evidence for this is lacking, it would bring things into line with the cricketing 'duck', a batsman's score of 0 and short for duck's egg.

---

27 June

BONK

This is the time of year for one of cycling's three grand tours, and surely the most iconic – the Tour de France. Whether you're a MAMIL (middle-aged man in Lycra) or a professional roadie, the appeal of the bicycle is both timeless and utterly of the moment.

'Cycle tracks will abound in Utopia', wrote H. G. Wells in 1905, when the Tour was just two years old. Cycling at that time was of the gentle-paced and sit-up variety, with an abundance of breeks (tucked-in suit trousers) for the men and, for the women, perilously long skirts and highly elaborate hats. One advertisement of the time offers 'serges, tweeds, shrink-naught twills, homespuns, etc. eminently adapted for cyclists' use'. Such resplendent fashion could be witnessed in its full collective glory in Hyde Park, London, where spectators would gather to watch the bustle (and bustles, if a woman was particularly daring) on two wheels. At the same time, 'Elliman's Universal Embrocation' offered relief from saddle-soreness, euphemistically declaring its use for 'aches, pains, and bruises'. Other riders, particularly those on older boneshakers, resorted to sitting on a raw steak, which would be fully tenderised by the end of the ride.

Today's serious riders suffer similar irritations – a chafing of the undercarriage that can only be soothed by chamois cream and vitamin I (aka ibuprofen). Far worse an end, however, is the infamous 'bonk', a four-letter encapsulation of the fate everyone wishes to avoid. To bonk, in cycling parlance, means something very different to its more common use in English slang. It means, ironically enough, to be devoid of any energy whatsoever, when the body's glucose reserves fall so low that the rider hits a wall of exhaustion beyond which pedalling and almost any other human activity becomes impossible. In cycling, 'if you're hungry, it's too late' is a mantra to live by. Bonking on a bike is never fun.

28 June

ANSERINE

Charles V was elected Holy Roman Emperor on 28 June 1519. He ruled over a vast empire, extending from the German Low Countries to Spain, Italy, and new territories in Central and South America. He is famously said to have preferred to speak Spanish to God, German to soldiers, French to diplomats, and Italian to women. English, it seems, he spoke little – allegedly only to converse with geese.

Animal-based adjectives abound in the dictionary. Feline, canine, equine, and bovine are all well known, but there are many more. Someone with a noticeably hooked nose might be described as aquiline (eagle-like), or they might sport a leonine (lion-like) mane of hair. They may be vulpine (fox-like) in their stealth, or leporine (hare-like) in speed. A murine (mouse-like) disposition is a timid one, as opposed to the strutting pavonine (peacock) kind. The serpentine river is snake-like, the Great Bear constellation ursine (hence *Ursa Major*), and cancer cancrine (crab-like), thanks to the swollen veins surrounding a tumour that were thought by early medics to resemble the limbs of the crustacean.

As for those with whom Charles V conversed? They were 'anserine', from the Latin *anser*, 'goose'.

29 June

CERULEAN

Koreans have a word that distinguishes yellow-green from regular green; Russians have different words for light and dark blue; in German, it is yellow rather than green that's associated with envy, while for the Koreans green means anger. In Lithuanian, rage is expressed not with a single colour, but with varying colours for different levels: white (controlled anger), red (normal anger), blue (intense anger), and black (extreme anger).

Each culture's perceptions of, and associations with, colour are so different that the picture is perplexingly inconsistent. Moreover, some colours were named far earlier than others – beginning with black, white and red, and ending with pink and orange (which was only named after the fruit began to be imported in the Middle Ages).

'Blue' has very distinct associations in English. It takes its name from an ancient root that meant 'shining', as of the colour of the sky or deep sea on a clear day. It is variously used for melancholy, the obscene (thanks to the traditional blue ink of the censors, and the once-enforced wearing by prostitutes of blue gowns in prison), and clarity. It's in this last bracket that 'cerulean' falls – a word that we all yearn to use, for the deep blue or azure of a cloudless sky, or a calm and ripple-less ocean.

30 June

SCONE

National Cream Day takes place traditionally in the last week in June. Every year, the event sparks two inevitable debates. Is it jam or cream first? And what *is* the correct pronunciation of 'scone'?

It's generally recognised that the answer to the first depends on where you live. For those in Cornwall, it's always jam first of course, while hard and fast Devonians will splutteringly tell you that the cream is the foundation of everything.

The first record we have of the word 'scone' is from the sixteenth century, when it slipped into English from the German *Schönbrot*, 'fine bread'. Such an innocent word seems an unlikely provocateur of fiercely divided opinion some five hundred years later, but the pronunciation of 'scone' is still hotly contested.

It may be a source of bitter disappointment to learn that, if you look up 'scone' in the *Oxford English Dictionary*, it will tell you that it can happily rhyme either with 'gone', or with 'cone', and that both are equally standard. In other words, everyone is right. Where once it was perhaps a matter of class (the 'gone' sound is said to be more middle class), it is now much more about your personal geography. 'Sk-on' is the version that's overwhelmingly picked in Scotland, Northern Ireland, and northern England. In many parts of the Midlands, and in southern Ireland, the 'cone' sound has the upper hand. Those in the south embrace both, though each party is insistent that theirs is correct.

In the end, fittingly, it's all a matter of taste.

JULY

1 July

CWTCH

In defiance of all those who raise an eyebrow at the news of another curious 'Day' in the calendar, July is otherwise known as International Free Hugs month. A movement that was started in 2004 by an Australian known by the pseudonym Juan Mann, it celebrates the positive mental effects of embracing complete strangers.

The origins of the word 'hug' are a little mysterious. It may be a legacy of the Vikings and their word *hygga*, to 'comfort' – a cosy exception to their otherwise dark lexicon of such words as 'dagger', 'ransack', 'berserk', and 'slaughter'. After their initial marauding, the Norse warriors worked alongside Britain's indigenous population, so perhaps this was when embraces began to flow. Others, however, believe the word to have begun with the Germanic word *hegen*, meaning to cherish – or alternatively to surround with a hedge, just as you might encircle your huggee with your arms.

Welsh offers a joyful synonym in *cwtch*, pronounced *kutch*. Like 'snug' and 'snuggle', the noun can be used to mean a small cubbyhole, but when used as a verb it means to cuddle up or hug.

That Old Norse *hygga*, incidentally, also gave us a word of the noughties: the Danish *hygge*, which came into English to define a lifestyle based on cosiness and conviviality that simply hugs the senses.

---
2 July

SUFFRAGE

In July 1858, Emmeline Pankhurst was born. Were you to ask any man at the time what 'suffrage' meant, they would have been aghast at the notion it included voting rights for women.

Suffering is not at the etymological heart of the word 'suffrage', even if some of those men would later say it meant suffering a late dinner while their wives were distracted. The Latin *suffragium* signified 'support', specifically prayers or pleas made on behalf of a departed soul; the sense meaning 'a right to vote' was consolidated in the United States Constitution of 1787. A suffragette, then, was simply a female campaigner for suffrage.

But that doesn't tell the whole tale. The -ette is a diminutive, a borrowing from French to mark things that are either smaller than usual – a cigarette is a small cigar; a maisonette a small house – or, like hackette and leatherette, seen as imitative, inferior, or simply female.

So when, at the turn of the century, newspapers detected a militant shift in the women's movement, one that moved away from quiet petitions and towards breaking windows or physical protest, the '-ette' suffix was reignited to mock the new wave of what one newspaper described as 'hysterical' female agitators and 'violent cranks'. Postcards were printed of shrieking babies with the legend 'I want my vote!', or of a red-faced campaigner named 'Miss Ortobee Spankdfirst'.

The *London Daily Mail* was among the first to use the term 'suffragette' as one of derision, frequently putting the word inside 'sneer' quotes. It was used exclusively of women, and particularly those who engaged in what was regarded as mutinous and wildly indecorous behaviour, including, on one occasion, taking an axe to a picture in the National Gallery of Venus admiring herself in a mirror.

Those same women decided, as another act of rebellion, to embrace the term instead of the more neutral 'suffragist'. The Women's Social and Political Union, which Emmeline Pankhurst helped to found, named their own journal *The Suffragette*, publishing this explanation in 1914: 'We have all heard of the girl who asked what was the difference between a Suffragist and a Suffragette, and the answer made to her was that the "Suffragist just wants the vote, while the Suffragette means to get it".'

This they did: on 2 July 1928, Parliament gave women equal voting rights to men, thanks in no small part to the efforts of Pankhurst and those she inspired, even though she herself did not live to see her wish fulfilled.

---

3 July

PENGUIN

On 3 July 1844, a group of foolish fishermen killed the last pair of great auks on Iceland's Eldey island. The reduction to a single surviving pair of these flightless birds, natives of the North Atlantic, is astonishing given that the bird's population once numbered millions. But a taste for their meat and their use as bait, together with misguided efforts by museums to preserve their skins, ensured that they were ultimately hunted to death. It is the only British bird made extinct in recorded history.

The great auk was the largest species in the auk family, standing some 85 centimetres tall and weighing around 5 kilograms. Contrary to popular belief, their name is not thought to be a sibling of 'awkward', a word built upon the Vikings' 'awk' meaning 'the wrong way round'. It comes instead from the Old Norse *álka*, 'razorbill', but its story involves another, unexpected, bird altogether.

One of very few Welsh words in the dictionary (along with

'corgi', Welsh for 'dwarf dog') is 'penguin'. It's thought to come from *pen gwyn*, 'white head', and was originally applied to the great auk itself. It seems that sailors confused the flight-less black and white birds for auks, or perhaps simply used the same word for both. Eventually, 'penguin' settled on the waddling creature we know today, and the name replaced an older term in the ornithological lexicon for the much-loved bird: 'arsefoot'.

4 July

CHIASMUS

The Declaration of Independence, which bears the date of 4 July 1776, enshrined in US law each citizen's un-alienable right to 'Life, Liberty, and the pursuit of Happiness'. These are the sentiments, and words, that are best remembered on Independence Day, but the document that is arguably the most important in US history contains many other examples of stylistic artistry that are worthy of attention.

The authors of the Declaration, including Thomas Jefferson, did not hold back. In their proclamation they speak of the 'absolute Despotism' of the British crown, whose citizens are 'deaf to the voices of justice and consanguinity'. Their vocabulary is emotive: they speak of the 'swarms of officers' sent 'to harass our people, and eat out their substance', while the king 'has plundered our seas, ravaged our coasts, burnt our towns, and destroyed lives'. The 'necessity', consequently, of independence, means the American people would hold the British 'as we hold the rest of mankind, Enemies in war, in Peace friends'.

If the reader trips up over those last three words, expecting the matching phraseology 'friends in peace', this may have been Jefferson's intention. This reversed repetition is known rhetorically as 'chiasmus', a word from Greek indicating a change in direction. More literally, the word suggests a cross-wise arrangement based on its first element *chi*, the twenty-second letter of the Greek alphabet that was originally pronounced as a K and which is represented in modern English by an X (it is, incidentally, the same *chi* that gave us the abbreviation 'Xmas', in which the X represents the initial *chi* of *Khristos*, Christ).

The purpose of the chiasmus in the Declaration, perhaps, is to slow the text, forcing its audience to focus on this decisive hope that, though enemies then, the two nations would become friends again. The final words of the Declaration are about trust, both in 'divine providence', and in the loyalty of compatriots, to whom they 'pledge each other our Lives, our Fortunes, and our sacred Honor'.

Years later, another US politican employed chiasmus to unforgettable effect. John F. Kennedy, in his inaugural address of 1961, issued the hope, 'Let us never negotiate out of fear, but let us never fear to negotiate.'

---

5 July

JUMBO

On this day in 1810, the American business and circus promoter P. T. Barnum was born. While his name lives on in film and in legend, he built much of his success upon hoaxes. He offered his visitors the chance, for example, to see the 161-year-old nurse who had raised George Washington, and 'displayed' the legendary 'Feejee mermaid' which turned out to be a monkey stitched to a fish. Barnum traded upon such 'curiosities' and 'freaks', which he delivered to a hungry audience in the form of mass entertainment. It was, as Barnum was himself to admit, 'humbug', but humbug that he saw as being entirely justified. He mixed up the fake and the real with ease, realising how much his audience enjoyed being deceived. 'Nobody', he mused 'ever lost a dollar by under-estimating the taste of the American public'.

For all his dubious business practices, the marketing skills of the man dubbed as the 'greatest showman' are undeniable. One of his most famous stunts gave us a word that has become largely untethered from its dubious beginnings,

Jumbo was an enormous, 4-metre-tall African elephant born in the 1860s. His name may be from the Swahili *jumbe*, meaning 'chief': a likely reference to the animal's size. Barnum, with his unwavering eye for a spectacle and 'living curiosity', bought the poor creature for $10,000 and shipped him from London Zoo to the United States, despite pleas from thousands in Britain who feared an enormous loss to the British Empire.

The elephant's death was to be as tragic as his life – Jumbo was hit by a train on his way back to his boxcar after a 'performance'. Barnum seized the chance to earn yet more money by stuffing the animal and putting him on display.

Such was the fame of the elephant in life and in death that Disney reworked his name in the film *Dumbo*. Today, our use of 'Jumbo' for anything from sausages to planes hides a sad and sorry history.

---

6 July

UTOPIA

On this day in 1535, one of Henry VIII's most trusted servants, and the erstwhile Chancellor of England, was executed by beheading.

Thomas More was a passionate defender of the orthodox Catholic Church. When Henry established the Anglican Church, allowing him to divorce Catherine of Aragon, More resigned his chancellorship. He continued to argue vociferously against the king's divorce and his split from Catholicism, and was tried for treason for his dissent.

More is largely remembered today for having written *Utopia*, a satire set on a fictional island that he presents as the perfect world, one that relies on a shared community and culture, and a fair moral and spiritual framework. Utopia is the gateway to happiness.

More was not the idealist the story suggests. The name of this illusory, idyllic land implies that in reality it exists 'nowhere': it combines the Greek *ou*, 'not', with *topos*, 'place'. A century later, other writers reinterpreted it for other imaginary places where everything is perfect. Inevitably, the opposite soon followed: dystopia is a place where everything is as bad as it's possible to be; the word was formed in the late eighteenth century from Greek *dus* – 'bad' – perhaps on the mistaken assumption that More had formed his word from the Greek *eu*, meaning 'good'. For More, there was to be no 'eu-catastrophe', J. R. R. Tolkien's word for a happy ending.

---

7 July

SCOTCH MIST

This day in 1814 saw the publication of Sir Walter Scott's *Waverley*. Published anonymously, this was Scott's first novel, a departure from the poetry that had gained him world-wide attention. The novel, too, was well received, and not for the first time Scott was compared to Shakespeare for the scope of his fictional world and its characters.

Scott also left a legacy in language, leaving us with such words as the Gaelic *cailleach*, an old Highland woman; 'misguggle' (pronounced 'mis-google'), to handle something roughly; 'rintherout', a tearaway or vagabond, and 'Scotch mist', an already-established term but one to which Scott gave a new energy.

A Scotch mist is, literally, a kind of thick mist characteristic of the Highlands, and it is mentioned as far back as the mid-seventeenth century. In *Waverley*, the hero's aunt was said to have charged her nephew to 'beware of Scotch mists, which, she had heard, would wet an Englishman through and through . . . and, above all, to wear flannel next to his skin'.

From these literal beginnings the term also came to be used allusively, to denote something insubstantial or unreal, or that someone has imagined or not properly understood. Such a state might well be induced by the third sense of 'Scotch mist': a drink of whisky served with a twist of lemon.

8 July

FOO FIGHTERS

On 8 July 1947, the first reports began to circulate of what would soon be known as the infamous Roswell Incident in New Mexico. To this day, conspiracy theories abound as to the veracity of the events as described by the US military – that an Air Forces balloon had crashed near a ranch in Roswell, New Mexico. Gainsayers claim that the balloon was in fact an alien spacecraft, and that its occupants had also been recovered by the military and subsequently covered up.

A few years earlier, Allied airmen in the Second World War had reported unidentified flying entities that would eventually become known as 'foo fighters'. The term sprang from a 1930s Bill Holman cartoon strip *Smokey Stover*, whose firefighting protagonist's catchphrase was 'Where there's foo there's fire'. Holman had apparently seen the word 'Foo' on the bottom of a jade figurine in San Francisco's Chinatown some years earlier, most likely a translation of the Chinese *fu* symbol 福, meaning 'good fortune'. Many of his comics were peppered with nonsense terminology and further plays on the word *foo*.

According to some, the first military use of 'foo fighter' to refer to a UFO came in a 415th Night Fighter Squadron mission debrief on 27 November 1944. Avid *Smokey Stover* reader and radar operator Donald Meiers is said to have coined the term in a state of agitation following the sighting of a fireball that appeared to closely follow an Allied aircraft. When explaining the phenomenon to his unit's Intelligence Officer, he pulled a copy of the comic out of his pocket and exclaimed, 'It was one of them fuckin' foo fighters!' The term became popular among airmen, and stuck in the public imagination for years to come – albeit expurgated for profanity – before it was reignited in the name of the hugely successful rock band Foo Fighters.

---

9 July

GERONIMO!

A popular story attached to this gusto version of 'Here we go!' is that it's an alteration of *San Jerónimo*, the Spanish name for St Jerome. Evidence suggests, though, that the exclamation is less the invocation of a saint, and more that of a Native American medicine man.

The earliest user of the phrase in the modern sense is said to have been by Private Aubrey Eberhardt, of the US Army's parachute test corps, at Fort Benning, Georgia, in July 1940. The corps were due to make their first group jump the following morning and, as a nerve-soother, members of the platoon went to see the 1939 western *Geronimo*, in which the film's namesake is the famous Apache chief whose warriors battled the American colonisers. (His real name was in fact Goyahkla, which was understandably unpronounceable and perhaps garbled to Geronimo, but other stories suggest he acquired his nickname from terrified Mexican soldiers who called out the name of the Catholic St Jerome when facing Goyahkla in battle.) Over beers, Eberhardt is said to have responded to teasing from his crewmembers that he would back out from the jump with the words 'All right, dammit! I tell you jokers what I'm gonna do! To prove to you that I'm not scared out of my wits when I jump, I'm gonna yell "Geronimo" loud as hell when I go out that door tomorrow!'

This he duly did, and a new exclamation for bravery and fearlessness was born. Ironically for an expression exuding bravado and daring, the Apache chief's real name translates as 'he who yawns'.

---

10 July

LACONIC

On 10 July 1925, Indian spiritual leader and teacher Meher Baba began a forty-four-year silence that he would observe until his death in 1969. With a wide-reaching legacy that inspired numerous songs and slogans, even today his devotees will observe Silence Day in his honour.

The word *laconic* describes an individual who, if not entirely silent, is terse or verbally economical. It derives from the martially astute Spartans, who hailed from a region of ancient Greece known as Laconia, and who were also notoriously frugal with their words. One infamous interchange came in the form of a threat from Philip II of Macedonia, who had recently invaded southern Greece and subjugated a number of other key city-states. He is said to have sent a messenger declaring his intent that 'If I should enter Laconia, I will destroy your farms, slay your people and raze your city.' The Spartan reply consisted of one word: 'If.'

---

11 July

BULLDOZER

This day in 1960 saw the publication by J. B. Lippincott & Co. of Harper Lee's *To Kill a Mockingbird*. The story was to become a classic of modern American literature thanks to its author's searing portrayal of racial prejudice in 1930s Alabama. The plot revolves around the attempts of a lawyer, Atticus Finch, to prove the innocence of Tom Robinson, a black man charged with the rape of a white woman. One of its many lessons is that, to truly understand someone, you must experience what it's like to be in their skin.

This was also the day, fifty-five years earlier, when W. E. B. Dubois and a group of African American activists established the Niagara Movement, founded upon the principle of black equality and freedom. Their protest against discrimination brought attention to such activities as lynching and what was known as 'bulldozing'. The early bulldozer was a bully who intimidated others, but its beginnings are far more literal. The term, also spelled 'bulldose', referred to a heavy 'dose' of flogging with a 'bull' or bullwhip: an enormous whip with a long heavy lash for driving cattle.

Bulldosing became widely known during the US presidential election of 1876, arguably the most hard-fought, corrupt, and rigged in the history of the United States, during which supporters in the Southern states attempted to stop black voters from favouring the Republicans with such shouts as 'Give me the whip and let me give him a bull-dose'. A newspaper from the same year reported that '"Bull-dozers" mounted on the best horses in the state scoured the country in squads by night, threatening colored men, and warning them that if they attempted to vote for the republican ticket they would be killed'.

Just decades later, the word had moved to describe heavy and forceful devices used for pushing objects, rather than people, out of the way. But the fight for black freedom was far from finished. As Atticus Finch describes to his son Jem: 'I wanted you to see what real courage is, instead of getting the idea that courage is a man with a gun in his hand. It's when you know you're licked before you begin, but you begin anyway and see it through no matter what. You rarely win, but sometimes you do.'

12 July

LACKADAISICAL

Apathy and lethargy trickle through the veins of anyone described as lackadaisical. Strange, then, that it started out as something so much stronger. 'Alack-a-day!' meaning 'Reproach to the day [that it should have brought this upon me]!' was once a common and heartfelt exclamation of regret, surprise, or lament, which by the eighteenth century had turned into a rather flabby lackadaisy. This was probably under the influence of 'ups/whoops-a-daisy', still said today in various forms when a child falls or when something is inadvertently knocked over. Curiously, in neither expression is a flower involved – as so often in English, sound rather than sense shifted the word in a slightly illogical direction.

Someone inclined to shout 'lack-a-day' or 'lack-a-daisy', even at the most minor of upsets, was quickly seen as being irritatingly sentimental, and it's here that the rot set in. Through a strange but consistently worsening series of moves, 'lacka-daisical' shifted from meaning anyone who, in the words of one dictionary, was 'sentimentally woebegone', to one who had little energy but to mop their brow in indulgent self-pity – with a dash of ineffectual floppiness for good measure.

---
13 July

SOLD DOWN THE RIVER

On this day in 1832, the source of the Mississippi River was discovered by American geographer Henry Schoolcraft. For all its associations with showboats and anthems, the river was a bloodstream for many Native American peoples, who depended upon it for their livelihood. The history of the river, whose name means 'Father of the Waters' in the indigenous language of Algonquian, encompasses many dark chapters in American history, from battles for supremacy against European colonisers, to Civil War and the slave trade. Linguistically, too, it has left its mark.

To 'sell someone down the river' is a metaphor for betraying them deeply. The beginnings of the expression are anything but figurative. For much of the early half of the nineteenth century, Louisville in Kentucky was one of the largest slave-trading posts in the country. Slaves, usually men, would be taken there to be sold on to cotton plantations further south, where they would be taken using the Mississippi or Ohio rivers. What awaited them was brutal labour and ferocious hardship – for many, this was the worst fate of all. Some took their own lives before they arrived. In Harriet Beecher Stowe's *Uncle Tom's Cabin*, the book's protagonist embarks on such a journey, having been sold by his 'owners' to a particularly sadistic plantation owner.

The sense of profound betrayal we associate today with being sold down the river came only later, after the slave trade had been abolished. But human treachery runs through the phrase still, if only just.

14 July

KAKISTOCRACY

The word 'despot', meaning an absolute ruler, had been just faintly pejorative in Greek, before it became attached to the management style of various Roman emperors. Its meaning was to become fully damning with the French Revolution, where it was applied to Louis XVI, considered both a tyrant and an oppressor of the people. On this day in 1789, those storming the Bastille in Paris were the vanguard of a revolution that was to overthrow the monarchy and establish the French Republic, where 14 July remains a national holiday.

A few days after an angry mob attacked the state prison, for them the symbol of authoritarian rule, the English newspaper *The World* described the event:

A national Revolution, brought about in a period so short, has had no parallel in the history of the World. The popular tumult spreads far and wide, but the triumph of the PARTY is now complete . . . Here CAPTIVITY regained its *freedom*, and DESPAIR found instant *consolation!*

This was the spark that emboldened the people of Paris, who had been suffering both from extreme food poverty and the weight of taxes used to pay off Louis XVI's debts. Their aim was to overthrow what they viewed as a despotic government that operated by arbitrary rule – what was, in other words, a 'kakistocracy', a term coined some fifty years after the completion of the French Revolution and that was modelled on the Greek *kakistos,* 'worst', and *–cracy,* 'rule'. A kakistocracy is government by the worst of citizens – even when those citizens are kings.

15 July

MEME

This day in 2006 saw the creation of Twitter. With over 320 million active monthly members, the 140-character limit (doubled to 280 in 2017) catalysed a lexicon of its own. The most singular characteristic of the new spoken-written language of most social media is brevity. This is a land where vowels are dropped, phrases reduced to acronyms, sounds reduced to numbers, and most punctuation forgotten. All of these require a re-engineering of the conventions of normal conversation.

So integral are such language conventions to online and digital communication that Mark Zuckerberg, founder of Facebook, even defines what his service does in terms couched in linguistics. It began, he has explained, with a 'limited vocabulary', before 'nouns' were added with the introduction of the Open Graph, so 'you could like anything you wanted'. The latest addition, he announced, was 'verbs': 'We're going to make it so you can connect to anything in any way you want.'

To connection we could add replication: the idea of things going 'viral' like highly infectious agents began to emerge in the 1980s, a decade after the evolutionary biologist Richard Dawkins had coined the word 'meme' for a cultural element or behavioural trait whose transmission, imitation, and consequent persistence in a population is similar to the inheritance of a gene. The word is a shortening of the ancient Greek *mimema*, 'imitated thing'. To the cynics and selfie-shunners however, it is also an unhappy reminder that social media is ultimately all 'me-me'.

16 July

ADDER

Today is World Snake Day.

The much-maligned common or northern viper has had a bad rap from the start. Its name was once a generic one for any venomous, dangerous, or repulsive snake or serpent, including the snake in the Garden of Eden, the very manifestation of the Devil himself. Unsurprisingly, 'viper' went on to become a byword for any treacherous, deceitful, or venomous individual. Such associations notwithstanding, the flesh of the viper was thought to have great nutritive and restorative properties, and was a key ingredient in medicine.

'Viper' is from the Latin *vipera*, a shortening of *vivipara*, 'giving birth alive', reflecting the fact that the snake's eggs hatch inside the female and their yolks nourish the young before they are born. Superstition once held that the embryonic snakes, impatient to be born, would eat their way out of the mother's side at birth, killing her in the process.

Originally the common name for this snake was not 'adder', but 'nadder'. Its change, by a process called metanalysis or rebracketing, is a good example of how spoken English holds sway over the written form. The word is a sibling of the German *Natter*, a grass snake. In medieval times it was known as a 'nadder', but at some point during the fourteenth or fifteenth century the word managed to lose its initial *n*, as people heard 'a nadder' and misinterpreted it as 'an adder'.

In the same way, an 'eke-name' was an additional name given to someone ('eke' meaning a supplement or add-on), but the 'an' and 'eke', barely distinguishable when spoken, were gradually blended together to produce 'nick'. An apron was a 'napron', from the French *nappe*, 'table cloth', and an umpire was a 'noumpere': literally a 'non-peer': someone who is set apart from the other players.

---

17 July

FIRGUN

The Japanese apparently have a saying: 他人の不幸は蜜の味 (*tanin no fukou wa mitsu no aji*): 'the misfortune of others is sweet like honey'. The French know all about the *joie maligne*, and the Russians about *zloradstvo*. The Germans, famously, gave us *Schadenfreude*. All of these terms describe the smug pleasure we might feel in witnessing someone else's suffering.

The emotion is an ancient one – the Greeks knew it as *epichairekakia* (rejoicing over disgrace), and the Romans as *malevolentia* (the root of 'malevolence'). But very few languages have accommodated the feeling of the opposite, with *firgun* being an exception.

A relatively recent Hebrew word (1970s), *firgun* may derive from the Yiddish word *farginen*, itself a cousin of the German word *vergönnen*, meaning 'to grant'. The infinitive form of the word, *lefargen*, simply means to unselfishly make someone else feel good.

Firgun is a concept that is almost the total antithesis of *Schadenfreude*, signifying the altruistic joy one feels when another person succeeds. Another word with no literal English translation, it can mean both a generosity of spirit and a total absence of negativity. International Firgun Day, celebrated each year on 17 July, promotes the idea of giving compliments and praising others online without any ulterior motive or agenda. In other words, as one writer put it, firgun is 'the art of tooting someone else's horn' (*see* 'confelicity', 25 December).

18 July

GONZO

Gonzo journalism is a manic editorial style that is inextricably linked with American writer Hunter S.Thompson, born 18 July 1937. Best-remembered for his 1971 book (and subsequent movie) *Fear and Loathing in Las Vegas*, Thompson's typically subjective, first-person narrative carved out its own niche in the New Journalism style of the 1960s and 1970s, and is still widely imitated today. He supported the belief of writers such as William Faulkner that 'fiction is often the best fact'. In an era where newspaper editors prized objective, verified reporting, Thompson championed truth-telling through personality – and a great deal of profanity.

He also indirectly added a new term to the journalistic dictionary: one that designated a type of manic, subjective journalism, especially when written in an exaggerated rhetorical style. Picking up on a description of his work by the journalist Bill Cardoso, who praised one of Thompson's articles as 'pure Gonzo', Thompson wrote in *Rolling Stone* magazine:

> But what *was* the story? Nobody had bothered to say. So we would have to drum it up on our own. Free Enterprise. The American Dream. Horatio Alger gone mad on drugs in Las Vegas. Do it *now*: pure Gonzo journalism.

'Gonzo' may well be a blend of 'gone crazo', perhaps with an added riff on 'gung-ho'. Its meaning has broadened to describe anything bizarre, crazy, or far-fetched. In the slang of some US states, it is apparently also a term applied to the last man standing after a mammoth drinking session.

19 July

HYSTERICAL

On this day in 1848, the first Women's Rights Convention was held at Seneca Falls, New York. Its attendees vowed to fight for the civil, social, and religious rights of women and, above all, female suffrage. They launched a 'Declaration of Sentiments', inspired by the Declaration of Independence and listing nineteen 'abuses and usurpations' designed to destroy a woman's self-confidence and right to independence. While the convention was supported by many, there were inevitably those who publicly mocked their efforts and urged them to return to the home. For these reactionaries the women were clearly 'hysterical'.

Hysteria is defined in the *Oxford English Dictionary* as a 'morbidly excited condition'. Its linguistic origins show that it was once thought to be an exclusively female complaint. In ancient times, hysteria was thought to be caused by a disturbance of the uterus or womb; its very name comes from the Greek for 'womb', *hustera*, which is also the root of 'hysterectomy'. Not dissimilarly, the German term for hysteria was *Mutterweh*: maternal suffering. Even the first mentions of 'hysterical' in the sense of 'hilarious' were frequently gendered: a linguistic study from 1969 noted that, 'To describe something as really funny, a woman will use "hysterical".'

In ancient Greece, it was believed that a uterus could migrate around the female body, causing not only ailments but also immoral behaviour such as kleptomania (*see* 31 May) and even murder. The theory of the roaming uterus was supported in many classical texts, including those by Plato and the physician Aretaeus, who knew it as 'hysterical suffocation'. 'Cures' were curious to say the least: the offending organ had to be coaxed back into position by the placing of good smells near the vagina, and bad smells near the mouth. Sneezing was also believed to have a positive effect.

Not everyone agreed: the physician Galen believed that it was the retention of 'female seed' within the womb that caused hysteria, leading to anxiety, insomnia, depression, and – above all – fainting.

Hysteria became a popular diagnosis in the 1800s, when it was often mentioned alongside 'the vapours', so called because of the exhalations believed to come from the stomach, and almost exclusively ascribed to women.

Even today, few men are ever described as being 'hysterical' (or feisty, frumpy, bossy, emotional, frigid, or high maintenance). An erroneous belief that is over two millennia old persists in language still.

20 July

GORDIAN KNOT

A Gordian knot is a problematic situation that seems completely unsolvable until lateral thinking is brought into play. The metaphor can be traced back to an ancient legend involving the Macedonian king Alexander the Great, born 20 July 356 BC.

Some years before Alexander decided to invade Phrygia, an oracle foretold that the next man to enter the city driving an ox-cart should be declared the new ruler of the kingless realm. This honour fell to a farmer named Gordias, whose son Midas would later dedicate his ox-cart to the god Sabazios, tying it to a post in the palace of kings with an immensely intricate knot made of bark.

Another oracle subsequently predicted that the man able to untie the ox-cart's knot should become the ruler of all Asia. Enter Alexander and his army in 333 BC. After wrestling with the knot for a short time, according to one version of the tale, he simply cut the knot in two with one almighty stroke. Another version of the story has him pulling out the yoke's linchpin to expose the two ends and loosening the knot. Either way, 'Gordian knot' remains a literary allusion to an apparently intractable problem that is solved easily by, to mix a metaphor, thinking outside the box.

21 July

July sees the celebration of World Emoji Day, although for many of us every day is punctuated by the thumbnail images that are the lingua franca of the digital age.

In 1982, Scott Fahlman posted the world's first documented 'emoticons' on the Carnegie Mellon University bulletin board system, setting in motion a language that has split the rest of us into two distinct camps: those who embrace it 😃, and those who feel it is sending English to the dogs 🙁.

Those were the two emoticons that Fahlman produced, using simple ASCII characters from his keyboard. The character sequences sped across networks and quickly began to infiltrate computer network message boards at other institutions around the world. Within a few months a whole lexicon of different 'smileys' had emerged. The keyboard characters morphed into colour images, and the emoji was born, taking its name from the Japanese *e*, 'picture', and *moji*, 'character'.

In 2015, the team selecting Oxford Dictionaries' Word of the Year chose for the first time a pictogram, 😂, known as 'Face with Tears of Joy', to much controversy. Most of those who complained resented the replacement of 'standard' language with simple pictures. Yet emojis are the fastest-growing area of language because they serve the medium of digital communication so well. Whether or not they are considered 'words', they offer nuances that traditional language can't always convey. Some see them as the natural successors to ancient pictorial representations of language, such as Egyptian hieroglyphs. In the new era of 'written-spoken' language, in which we speak with our fingers, emojis are becoming highly versatile adjuncts to our communications.

In some cases, pictures and words combine when descriptions of the emojis occasionally creep into conversation: 'small aubergine' (or, in the United States, 'eggplant') has come to be a not-so-secret cipher for a penis. The emoji inspired a trend on Instagram and other social-media sites called #EggplantFriday, in which men posted explicit images of their 'aubergines'. Instagram later blocked both the emoji and references to it from its search functionality, prompting the inevitable campaign #FreetheEggplant, a riff on the earlier #FreetheNipple hashtag urging gender equality.

Today, emojis are the fastest-moving of language, with every update on our devices eagerly anticipated. Unlike language, however, no amount of facial expressions can ever convey true complexity of emotion. Our digital impulse may be to keep things light, but some psychologists believe emojis may be limiting our ability to express *exactly* how we feel. Smiles and tears are easy enough to select from the emoji lexicon, but they are always going to be one-dimensional. For true eloquence, the dictionary still reigns supreme.

As one character in *The Emoji Movie* puts it: 'It's not always easy being meh.'

---

22 July

ARSEROPES

In his *Etymological Dictionary of the English Language* of 1825, John Jamieson gives the pleasing term 'groozlins' for the intestines, with the example 'I had a grumbling about my groozlins; a curmurring in the guts'.

A few decades earlier, Samuel Johnson had included the verb 'wamble' in his own *Dictionary*, which he defined as 'to roll with nausea and sickness', thereby opening the potential for us to speak today of a 'wambling in the trollibags' for a similar complaint (trollibags being a synonym for 'trillibubs', entrails or intestines).

But if you need an even more descriptive term for your guts, look no further than the fourteenth century, when anatomy in particular was described in perfectly neutral, descriptive terms. These were the days when testicles were 'ballocks', and 'cunt' made a regular appearance in anatomy manuals. The guts, then, were your 'arseropes', first mentioned in Wycliffe's translation of the Bible: 'the arsroppis of hem goyng out stoonkyn' (his intestines came out stinking).

There's a lot to be said for saying it as it is.

23 July

FASCISM

On 23 July 1929, the Fascist government in Italy banned all uses of foreign words, with the aim of purging influences that might pose a threat to the purity and power of the state.

In strictly linguistic terms, this was the equivalent of Brexit supporters petitioning, in 2017, for a ban on all French words on the British passport, in ignorance of the fact that 'passport' itself comes from French. The chosen name of Mussolini's party also had its roots in another tongue.

For the Romans, *fasces* were bundles of elm or birch rods. They were chosen as the emblem of a magistrate's power, held in place by red leather ribbon and tied in a cylindrical shape, from which the blade of an axe emerged symbolising the authority borne by magistrates to punish and even execute transgressors of the law. The sticks themselves were intended to represent unity: individually they were breakable, while collectively they were strong.

The *fasces* survived as a symbol of authority for centuries. It appeared on US coins as well as the podium in the House of Representatives, and became a popular motif in heraldry. It was also the emblem of solidarity – union workers in nineteenth-century Sicily, for example, were known as *fasci siciliani* – and the term was subsequently appropriated by organisations of military veterans in the wake of the First World War. Over time, many such confederations spurned socialism and became highly nationalistic in outlook.

Benito Mussolini was both a veteran and former socialist, and so was well versed in the symbolism of the *fasces*. His followers selected the ancient symbol as their badge and the *Partito Nazionale Fascista* was born, one that exalted the status of the nation and the authority that presided over it.

Like all attempts to freeze language or protect it from corruption, Mussolini's attempt was misguided and ultimately unachievable. Language can never be artificially harnessed, and will always resist the totalitarian urge for control.

24 July

ZEPHYR

Surely one of the most mellifluous words in English, a 'zephyr' is a soft, gentle breeze, characteristic of slumberous spring and summer days.

In ancient Greek myth, the Anemoi were the wind gods, each named according to the direction of the winds within their charge. In many stories they are depicted as horses, kept in the stables of the storm god Aeolus. Zephyrus was the god of the west wind, considered the most clement in contrast to the cold north wind, Boreas.

On languorous summer days, when the mind wanders to a hammock below a canopy of trees, the word 'psithurism' might also waft into view. Psithurism is a direct borrowing from a Greek word meaning to whisper, and is often used to describe the murmur of leaves in a gentle breeze. Not too dissimilar is the beautiful 'susurrus', another word for 'whispering', this time from Latin, used for a soft, low sound like the murmuring of the waves or rustling of the trees.

---

25 July

LAUREL

On this day, just three days before the start of the First World War, W. G. Grace played his last day of club cricket, aged sixty-six, scoring sixty-nine runs. To this day he is regarded as one of the sport's greatest-ever players.

Grace's sport was the first to give us innumerable phrases, from 'slogging away' to 'sticky wicket' and 'upping sticks'. It also inspired the hat-trick. In 1858, H. H. Stephenson was awarded a cap, bought with the proceeds of a whip-round, for taking three wickets in three consecutive balls at Hyde Park cricket ground in Sheffield. The idea, and the term, was soon transferred to other games to denote three consecutive achievements.

Historically, the prize for sporting achievement was more symbolic. A laurel wreath, traditionally bestowed upon successful commanders of Greek and Roman battles, was also the prize for those who excelled in education and in athletic endeavour. The laurel was the emblem of victory, honour, and of peace. Such associations were rooted in Greek mythology and the story of Apollo and Daphne. As retribution for mocking Eros, the god of love, Apollo is shot with a golden arrow that causes him to fall hopelessly in love with the mortal Daphne. She in turn is shot with an arrow that causes her to reject love for ever. The anguished result is Apollo's relentless pursuit of a woman who will never accept him. Daphne, begging to be saved from this fate, is pitied by the gods who transform her into a laurel tree as a means of escape. From that day on, Apollo wears a laurel wreath made from the leaves of his beloved Daphne. And, in honour of Apollo, the victor at the gods' Pythian Games is crowned with a laurel wreath.

The branches of the laurel extend further still. The tree has an unlikely association with the baccalaureate, or university bachelor's degree. Originally from the medieval Latin *baccalarius*, itself meaning 'bachelor' (once a young or novice knight, and therefore the first degree sat by a university student), it was altered as a play on *bacca lauri*, 'laurel berry', because of the laurels traditionally awarded to scholars.

26 July

PAREIDOLIA

Every now and again a photograph emerges that captures the imagination of an entire generation: the first true image of a black hole in 2019, for example, or the stunning 'moonrise' photo, taken from Apollo 8 in 1968.

In late July 1976, the spacecraft *Viking 1* captured the infamous 'Face on Mars' photo. Within weeks there were dozens of theories as to how this 'human' face could have been etched upon the surface of another world. Further investigation revealed this to be nothing more than a phenomenon known as 'pareidolia'. Deriving from the Greek words *para*, meaning 'beside', and *eidōlon*, meaning 'shape' or 'form', it refers to the instinctive behaviour of the human brain to ascribe familiar concepts to random objects – shapes in clouds, hidden messages in audio tracks played backwards, images of Jesus Christ on a piece of burnt toast, etc.

Pareidolia is classified as a subcategory of 'apophenia', itself defined as the irrational perception of connections between unrelated occurrences. It is often linked to gambling, where a random outcome can appear to become less so by the preceding events. If three coin-tosses reveal three successive 'tails', it can seem more likely to the gambler that the next coin toss will reveal itself to be 'heads' despite bearing an unchanging 50 per cent statistical likelihood.

> ## 27 July

HURKLE-DURKLE

U *nikeonpäivä*, or National Sleepy Head Day, is an annual celebration in Finland that commemorates the Christian and Islamic myth of the Seven Sleepers of Ephesus, a group of youths who, in order to escape religious persecution, hole up in a cave where they fall asleep. The cave is sealed off by the authorities, but when it is reopened centuries later they are somehow found to be still asleep.

One legacy of the tale was the medieval superstition that the person in the household who slept late on this day would be lazy and non-productive for the rest of the year: the only solution was a cold bucket of water thrown unceremoniously over their sleeping body.

For the guilty ones amongst us today, there is always the old Scots phrase 'hurkle-durkle'. It appears in Jamieson's *Etymological Dictionary of the Scots Language* (1808), where it is broadly defined as to 'lie in bed, or lounge, long after it's time to get up'.

28 July

POTATO

In the sixteenth century, Western Europe was hungry for the luxuries of the Orient – notably spices and fabrics – which they had first begun to come across during the thirteenth century. As a result of the voyages taken in search of such goods, and the encounters they brought, the fifteenth and sixteenth centuries saw an influx into English of words borrowed from the native languages of the Americas. 'Tobacco', 'canoe', 'hammock', and 'hurricane' all feature in the records of sixteenth-century discoverers.

In 1565, John Hawkins's accounts of his voyages to Florida provided the first mention of the word 'potato'. He accorded them high praise: 'These potatoes be the most delicate rootes that may be eaten, and doe far exceed our passeneps or carets.' On 28 July 1586, the astronomer and navigator Sir Thomas Harriot introduced the delicacy to Europe on return to England from a venture funded by Sir Walter Raleigh, which had aimed to found the first permanent English settlement in North America.

The original Taino term for our favourite vegetable (technically a tuber) was 'batata', and the Spanish variant of it is 'patata'. Shakespeare was among those who believed it possessed aphrodisiacal qualities: in the *Merry Wives of Windsor*, Falstaff hopes to arouse the passions of Mistress Ford by beseeching the sky to 'rain potatoes'. The tomato, a native of tropical America and another discovery during this time of intense exploration, was similarly revered, to the extent that it became known as the 'love-apple' – a sixteenth-century herbal notes that 'there be two Kindes of Amorus or Raging Love-apples'. That's one way of adding linguistic pep to your salad.

29 July

PYRRHIC VICTORY

On 29 July 1693, the Battle of Landon became a fault line of the Nine Years' War between France and the allied forces of England, Scotland, and the Dutch republic. The numerically superior French forces eventually prevailed, but at such a heavy cost that they were unable to follow up their 'Pyrrhic victory'.

Pyrrhic victory describes an outcome that could be technically classed as a victory, but that incurs such losses that the win appears entirely pointless. The eponymous term can be attributed to King Pyrrhus of Epirus, whose armies 'defeated' the Romans in 280 BC at the Battle of Heraclea, and again at the Battle of Asculum the following year. When Pyrrhus was congratulated on his victory, he famously responded: 'Another such victory and we shall be utterly ruined.' Ultimately, even though the Epirotic forces prevailed, their losses were so significant that any semblance of victory became irrelevant.

That irrelevance might have been the Romans' 'parting shot', an expression that once looked quite different, when the shot in question was both live and dangerous. It looks back to the Parthians, an ancient people living in south-west Asia whose warriors demonstrated exceptionally clever battle tactics. Parthian horsemen would baffle their enemies with their rapid manoeuvres; the most deadly of which was to discharge missiles from their horses while apparently riding away from the fight.

The idea of delivering this final blow passed figuratively into the language in the seventeenth century. Over time, as fewer people understood the allusion, 'Parthian' was corrupted to the very plausible 'parting'. Happily, such a shot today is also a lot less lethal.

30 July

BEEFEATER

In 1485, Henry VII appointed the Yeomen of the Guard as the bodyguard of the sovereign, and as part of the royal train in banquets and other state occasions. They made their first appearance in public at his coronation on 30 October 1485, and were later to acquire the popular name 'Beefeater'.

By the time it was applied to royal servants, 'beef-eater' was already established as a fairly contemptuous term for a well-fed menial, a literal eater of beef; it harks back to a similar term, 'loaf-eater', applied to servants in Anglo-Saxon times. Furthermore, it was (and remains) an enduringly popular nickname among the French for the British. The reason behind the extension of the term to the Yeomen of the Guard is probably a straightforward one: records show that they were frequently paid in rations of good cuts of meat, including, on occasions, choice beef from the king's table.

But that might not be quite all. Some historians recount a specific event in history that prompted the appellation. According to an anecdote of Henry VIII, the king, fond of disguising himself and going incognito among his subjects, decided to dress up in the uniform of his Yeomen of the Guard while on a hunting expedition at Reading Abbey. He was invited to dine at the table of one Thomas Noke, an abbot who was also one of the king's retinue. The principal dish, it is said, was a large joint of beef, and the king partook heartily in the meal. The abbot, observing his evident enjoyment, addressed him, saying, 'Well fare thy Heart! And here in a cup of sack I remember the health of His Grace your master. I would give an hundred pounds if I could eat as heartily of beef as you.' When the abbot found himself, inexplicably, imprisoned in the Tower of London, his fare was limited to bread and water, until to his delight a joint of beef was put in front of him. Tucking in, the abbot was astonished to see the king enter the room and demand a hundred pounds from him for having restored his appetite for roast beef. The money was duly paid, and the prisoner released.

The tale is very probably an example of high jinks, as colourful as the uniform of the beefeaters themselves. Nonetheless, it might well have spread so far and wide that the japery popularised the term so proudly borne today. The official name for beefeaters of course is the Yeomen Warders of Her Majesty's Royal Palace and Fortress the Tower of London, in which 'yeoman' means 'young man', one who ranked between a sergeant and a groom.

31 July

PETRICHOR

In the course of the summer, many of us breathe in the distinctive smell of rain falling on dry, scorched earth. It is an elusive scent, hard to pin down in words – some describe it as musky, others as something 'primal'. However hard it is to define, there is at least a word for it, coined in the 1960s by two research scientists who named it 'petrichor'. In scientific terms, it comes from an oily, liquid mixture of organic compounds that collects in the ground. A key element is geosmin, a molecule made by bacteria from decaying organic matter. Raindrops that follow a prolonged period of dry weather release more geosmin into the air, and its scent is carried by the wind to alert others that rain is on its way. 'I can smell rain' has a firm basis in scientific fact.

Hard science apart, it's the name of the phenomenon that is almost as pleasing as the fragrance. Its first element is the prefix *petro*, used in words that are linked to rock and stone – words like 'petrified' ('turned to stone', figuratively or literally), and 'petroleum', a liquid that seeps out from rock formations. But it's the second part of 'petrichor' that surprises, steeped as it is in Greek mythology where 'ichor' was the ethereal fluid said to flow like blood in the veins of the gods.

In other words, petrichor is the 'true essence' of stone, one so powerful that parfumiers do their best to bottle it.

AUGUST

WAPENTAKE

The opening day of August is Yorkshire Day, first celebrated in 1975 by the Yorkshire Ridings Society.

Historically, Yorkshire was divided into three 'Ridings' and the Ainsty of York, thought necessary because of Yorkshire's large size compared with other British counties. The word 'riding' is part of the Viking legacy to the area, coming from the Old Norse *þriðjungr*, meaning 'third part', which became 'trithing' in Old English before 'riding', more familiar to the English-speaking tongue, gradually took over. The Ridings were abolished in 1974, and York, hitherto independent, was incorporated into the new county called North Yorkshire.

'Shire' had a specific sense in Anglo-Saxon England: it was an administrative district made up of a number of smaller districts, known as 'hundreds' because they house 100 families, or 'wapentakes'. Districts often received their names from some natural or artificial object (e.g. a barrow or a tree) that offered a suitable rallying place for open-air meetings. 'Wapentake' is from the Old Norse *vápnatak*, meaning the 'taking up of weapons': Vikings would brandish knives, spears, or axes to indicate assent during the vote of an assembly, and re-arm themselves as they left. In Old English, a wapentake was used for a subdivision of a shire and is recorded in Yorkshire, Derbyshire, Nottinghamshire, Lincolnshire, Northamptonshire, and Leicestershire: all shires where there was a large Danish element in the population.

2 August

TESTICULATING

On this day in 1865, the children's author Lewis Carroll wrote in his diary: 'Finally decided on the reprint of *Alice*, and that the first 2,000 should be sold as waste paper.' The author had rejected the first printing of *Alice in Wonderland* because of poor-quality illustrations. It was clear that the book had to be nothing short of perfect.

Carroll's story has inspired wonder in every generation since. His language, though always artfully creative, is characteristically childlike. He relished wordplay, and it's to him that we owe the name of today's most popular method of producing new words, the mash-up of existing words to create new ones. Carroll called the results 'portmanteaux', because two words can fold together just like the two sides of an old-fashioned travelling bag. He himself was a master, creating words that remain with us still and that have lost all signs of 'artificial' construction. 'Chortle', for example, was his mixture of 'chuckle' and 'snort'; 'mimsy' a confection of 'miserable' and 'flimsy; and 'galumph' a blend of gallop and triumph (even if today we tend to galumph ponderously to the kettle of a morning).

Recent examples fill gaps in our language for emotions that are difficult to capture. 'Probsolutely', for example, is the articulation of a definite maybe, while 'textpectation' is the constant checking of a phone for the message you're hoping will arrive. Even more recently, 'testiculating' is the act of waving your arms about and talking bollocks. None of these have quite made it into the dictionary yet, unlike 'hangry', a recent addition that describes the feeling of irritability resulting from a lack of food.

Even the Muppets may have embraced the portmanteau: if Jim Henson always maintained the name of his characters was arbitrary, the producers of the Wilkins Coffee commercials that first featured them clearly thought the name for the enduring characters was a riff on 'puppet', with a hint of 'marionette' thrown in.

The *Washington Post* famously runs a competition in which it asks readers to change just one letter of an existing word to produce a new one. Back have come some masterful blends, including 'skilljoy', the friend that's always better than you at everything; 'glibido', all talk and no action; and sarchasm: the gulf between the person delivering a sarcastic comment, and the recipient who just doesn't get it.

---

3 August

READ THE RIOT ACT

Since the early nineteenth century we have used the expression 'read the riot act' as a metaphor for bringing people into line. But had we been reading the act in 1715, we would have been serving the will of Parliament rather than settling a personal dispute. At that time, there was a literal Riot Act, which was required to be read in public.

The government of early eighteenth-century England was acutely aware that Jacobite mobs, supporters of the deposed Stuarts, were gathering in protest and rebellion with the intent to overthrow George I, the Hanoverian king. The 'Riot Act' duly came into force in the early weeks of August 1715. Formally, the legislation went by a much fuller description: 'An act for preventing tumults and riotous assemblies, and for the more speedy and effectual punishing of the rioters.' It demanded that any crowds of dissenters disperse and go peacefully home, ending with the four words 'God save the King'. Once read, those assembled had a grace period of an hour before punishment ensued, unless the gathering turned violent, in which case the officer of the law was entitled to enlist the support of bystanders to repel and arrest the rabble. The penalties for ignoring the Act were severe – penal servitude, imprisonment with hard labour, or even death. It achieved notoriety when, in 1819, half the population of Manchester gathered in St Peter's Field to call for parliamentary reform. Although the crowd was largely friendly and peaceful, troops were sent to disperse them; their tactics were so violent that eighteen people were killed and hundreds more injured. In the aftermath of what became known as the Peterloo Massacre, the authorities insisted they had read the Riot Act before going in – but if they did so, few would have heard it.

When the Hanoverians did eventually obtain power, the Riot Act became close to redundant, yet it remained on the UK statute for over a hundred and fifty years and wasn't formally repealed until 1973. Today, any rambunctious rebellion might well get a reading of a figurative riot act, even while its literal namesake has long since vanished.

---

4 August

CHAMPAGNE

At the age of just nineteen, Dom Pérignon entered the Benedictine order at the Abbey of Hautvillers near the town of Épernay in France, within the historical province of Champagne. He was to become the abbey's cellar master, the overseer of the abbey's extensive wine store. Pérignon pioneered many winemaking techniques, including the perfection of a white wine from black grapes, and the capture of bubbles within champagne wines by enhancing their sugar retention. He was also the first to introduce cork instead of wood to keep wine fresh, which was fastened to bottles by means of hemp string, avoiding the explosions that had become commonplace with sparkling wines.

Contrary to popular belief, Pérignon did not 'invent' champagne. The progression to sparkling wine was a long, evolutionary process, rather than the inspired work of a single hand. Nonetheless, legend tells how Pérignon first tasted his self-made nectar on 4 August 1693 and exclaimed to his fellow monks, 'Come quickly! I am drinking the stars!' It is a phrase that has been associated with the delights of champagne ever since.

The Champagne region takes its name from its wide-open countryside: it is a descendant of the Latin *campus*, 'level ground'. This makes it a sibling of some unlikely words in English: *champignons*, or mushrooms, are found wild in those fields, while the 'champions' of ancient Rome practised their military craft in open fields such as the *Campus Martius*. Least expectedly, champagne is also linked to the first 'scamps': those soldiers who 'decamped' and swiftly fled the battlefield.

---

5 August

CHIVVY

Whether you have a tendency to chivvy along your children, your team, or yourself, the origin of this strange-looking word may have passed you by. Once the hurrying and harrying are over, however, its story is well worth a linger.

It begins in the 1380s, during the protracted border feud between the Northumberland House of Percy and the Scottish House of Douglas. The conflict was marked by criminality and local feuds, as well as raids across the Cheviot Hills, locally known as the Chevy Hills. One skirmish in particular took a heavy toll, taking place on this day in 1388, when James, the 2nd Earl of Douglas, led a raid across the line. His men ravaged the countryside around Durham and Newcastle, prompting Henry Percy, the 1st Earl of Northumberland, to send his two sons, Henry (commonly known as Harry Hotspur) and Ralph, to engage the enemy. The resulting battle became known as the Battle of Otterburn, from which the Scots took a decisive victory; nearly 2,000 people died in the skirmish.

The conflict was a landmark battle in the history of medi-eval Scotland and England, and was honoured in several popular songs from the period. The 'Ballad of Chevy Chase' tells of a large hunting party led by Henry Percy across hunting ground (known as a chase) over the Cheviot Hills, provoking a clash similar in outcome to the Battle of Otterburn.

The ballad became a big hit. The Elizabethan poet and courtier Sir Philip Sidney wrote of it: 'I never heard the old song of Percy and Douglas that I found not my heart moved more than with a trumpet.' Its popularity pushed the word 'chevy' into English as a byword for harrying, harassing, attacking, or goading.

There is one more part to the word's story, which is equally bloody. The change in spelling to our modern form was probably influenced by a term from the seventeenth-cen-tury criminal underworld: namely 'chiv', meaning a knife, and its accomplice 'chivvy', to slash someone with a knife or razor.

---

6 August

HWYL

Every year, during the first week of August, the National Eisteddfod inspires a celebration of culture, language, and community. The Welsh festival has taken place every year since 1861, with the exceptions of 1914 and 2020, when the outbreak of the First World War and the global coronavirus pandemic necessitated its postponement. It is one of the nation's richest showcases of music, dance, performance, song, and visual art, and with it comes an emotion for which Welsh uniquely has a word: *hwyl*.

Hwyl is defined in the dictionary as 'an emotional quality that inspires and sustains impassioned eloquence', as well as 'the fervour of emotion characteristic of gatherings of Welsh people'. Certainly it's used this way in English – as a gateway to inspiration and articulacy that might otherwise have seemed impossible. But in Welsh the word more often refers to a complex and intangible quality, conveying a sense of belonging and home, of mood and of passion. In this it is akin to another near-untranslatable Welsh term: *hiraeth*, the longing for home, and all that belongs there.

The origins of *hwyl* are as poetic as the word itself: once a term for the sail of one's ship, it was transferred metaphorically to the course in life that we ourselves choose to navigate.

---

7 August

CONSPUE

On 7 August 1956, the slugger for the Boston Red Sox and one of baseball's greatest hitters, Ted 'The Kid' Williams, became spitting mad. With two outs in the second innings against the Yankees, Williams misjudged an opponent's arcing fly and dropped it. The crowd of some 35,000 spectators erupted in boos. Even when Williams made an outstanding catch just moments later the jeering did not let up. Williams, returning to the dugout, directed a jet of saliva towards the fans, and was promptly fined $5,000.

Had Williams or his accusers needed it, there is a rarely used word for spitting on someone with contempt: 'conspue'. The verb has inexplicably just one recorded use in the *Oxford English Dictionary*, dating from 1890.

---

8 August

DOLLAR

On this day in 1792, the US Congress unanimously chose the dollar as the official monetary unit of the United States. The history of the currency's name has unlikely geographical beginnings: in a small mountain town in north-western Bohemia, named Jáchymov, better known at the time by its German name, Sankt Joachimsthal, or 'Joachim's valley'.

At the turn of the sixteenth century, a member of one of the richest noble families in Bohemia, the Count of Schlick, began mining in Jáchymov. The silver coins extracted from its ore began to circulate in Europe under the names of *Schlickenthalers* or *Joachimthalers*, in which 'Thaler' meant something 'from the valley'. 'Thaler' eventually became 'daler' (the German *Thal* is in fact etymologically linked to the English 'dale'). By the middle of the sixteenth century, 'daler' was used for an increasing variety of coins from Europe and elsewhere. So it was that the 'dollar', as it eventually became known, settled into the language, eventually spawning a whole lexicon to itself, including 'bucks', 'bones', 'smackeroos', 'clams', and 'plunks' (oddly, however, no schlicks).

---

9 August

BARNACLE GOOSE

On this day in 1924, Norway and Denmark signed a treaty that protected their respective interests in Greenland, following long disputes over access and a protracted war of words that was not to end completely until 2009, when Greenland voted for self-determination.

The name Greenland was apparently chosen by Eric the Red, who was exiled from Iceland for murder. Sailing north-west, he came upon a dazzlingly white land which he chose for his new home, giving it the name Grfnland (Green-land). Some believe the name was intended to attract more settlers and stifle the fact that only a small percentage of the country's land is free of ice. But even if the story is true, Eric had no need to exaggerate: for Greenland, sparkling beneath the midnight sun, has beauty enough. Its fauna is part of its magic, from Arctic foxes and polar bears to eagles, lemmings, and the endangered Arctic wolf. It also offers any traveller a sight of a bird with a highly curious name: the barnacle goose.

The wild bird is notable not only for its white face and black neck, so striking in the Arctic tundra, but also for its mysterious breeding habits. It chooses remote, inaccessible spots – steep crags or narrow rock spars, or even perilous cliff edges. Few of these places would be obvious to humans, to the extent that, in the Middle Ages, when no apparent nest could be found, a fantastical story was created to account for the bird's reproduction.

For centuries, including Shakespeare's era, it was believed that the goose was produced from the fruit of a tree that grew by the seashore. When the fruits fell into the sea, they were said to become small shellfish that attached themselves to a floating object such as rotting timber. The long, feathery fila-ments produced from the shellfish were said to mark the emergence of the goose.

The name 'barnacle' first belonged to the goose before becoming fixed, albeit less literally, on the shellfish that were said to be the bird's creator.

---

10 August

THE FULL MONTY

In August 1943, General Bernard Montgomery was appointed Commander of the British Eighth Army, which was to be in the front line of the North African and Italian campaigns of the Second World War. Montgomery was one of the most prominent commanders of the war, credited for restoring his men's flagging morale and for ensuring they were properly equipped for battle. A flamboyant figure, known by the army as simply 'Monty', he famously named his two pet dogs Rommel and Hitler. The US General Dwight Eisenhower spoke of Montgomery's 'flair for showmanship': 'he loves the limelight but, in seeking it, it is possible that he does so only because of the effect upon his own soldiers, who are certainly devoted to him.'

It would be unsurprising if such a memorable figure left his mark upon language as well as history. It is often said that Montgomery would insist on a full English breakfast each morning, and that this, in turn, gave rise to the phrase 'the full monty', meaning 'the full works'. Although the chronology of the expression – which didn't surface in English slang until the 1980s – makes the suggestion unlikely, it remains one of the most popular theories as to its history. Nonetheless, it joins, at the last count, some seventeen other explanations for the phrase's origin.

Among the other suggestions is the gambling term 'monte', referring to a stockpile of cards left after each player has had their share. In Australia, a monty is a racehorse that's a safe bet, while 'for a monty' means 'certainly, for sure'.

And then there is Montague Burton, a highly successful tailor and founder of the clothing empire that still bears his name. Burton contributed significantly to both world war efforts by producing uniforms for nearly a quarter of the armed forces. In peacetime, he went on to produce popular made-to-measure suits. Burton's firm, in Chesterfield in Derbyshire, was said to offer a two-piece suit as the standard, and a waistcoat and spare pair of trousers for an additional cost. Thus, the theory goes, 'the full Montague Burton' meant the full set, eventually shortened to 'the full Monty' and applied to the total or whole of anything – including our birthday suits, as Peter Cattaneo's 1997 film, in which a group of Sheffield steel-workers become strippers after being made redundant, demonstrated. The showman in General Montgomery might have been tickled by that.

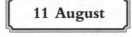

11 August

@

In 2010, New York's Museum of Modern Art introduced the @ symbol into its online collection. In doing so, it noted, it enabled curators to tag the world and acknowledge things that 'cannot be had'.

The origins of the symbol are similarly hard to capture. The punctuation we know only as the 'at symbol' is a foundation of social media and email, but where and how did it start? It is believed that medieval monks used a similar symbol to abbreviate the Latin *ad*, meaning 'toward', combining the *a* with the older ∂ form of the letter *d*. But its modern form began a century or so later, when Florentine merchants used it to denote an *amphora*, a terracotta vessel that had become a unit of measure for wine and other liquids. The symbol began to take on an important but specialised role in accounting, where @ meant 'at the price of'; the current Spanish word for @, *arroba*, has also denoted a liquid measure for centuries.

The @ symbol was consequently known as the 'commercial *a*' when it appeared on the keyboard of the American Underwood typewriter in 1885, and was used primarily in accounting and commercial invoices. From this relative obscurity, the symbol was propelled into the modern vernacular by a computer scientist looking for a way of connecting programmers with each other. Searching for a keyboard character that wouldn't get mistaken for anything else, Ray Tomlinson's eyes fell on @ on his Model 33 teletype. Using his naming system, he sent himself an email, which travelled from one teletype to another in his room. In that moment, a symbol that had once been restricted to a narrow sphere of human activity, became the very linchpin of connectivity and communication.

12 August

STITCHED UP

Isaac Singer patented the first sewing machine on this day in 1851, an invention that would revolutionise the manufacture of clothing.

The verb 'stitch up' was originally, in the sixteenth century, firmly tethered to the activity of sewing, where it also took on the sense of hasty or inferior work. It was another three centuries before the expression entered the criminal lexicon as a byword for manipulating someone and, more generally, bamboozling them out of money.

To be 'stitched up like a kipper' only added more emphasis. One theory suggests a reference to the kipper tie, created by fashion designer Michael Fish in the mid-to-late twentieth century (the kipper being both a play on his last name and a reference to its shape). The idea perhaps was of being left hanging, just like a tie.

In its early criminal use, a stitch-up often involved 'grassing' on someone to the authorities, a baffling phrase until you know that it began as cockney rhyming slang: 'grasshopper = shopper'. A 'shop', in the underworld patter of the seventeenth century, was a tribal word for a prison.

13 August

KIOSK

In 1889, William Gray created a piece of technology that would lead to one of the most iconic images of twentieth-century Britain. The inspiration for the first coin-operated payphone apparently came when the inventor's wife fell ill and he found himself unable to call a doctor. The first model of his creation was installed on the ground floor of a bank building at the corner of Main Street and Central Row in Hartford, United States, by the Southern New England Telephone Company.

The first standard public telephone kiosk to be introduced by the UK Post Office was produced in 1921 and was designated K1 (Kiosk No. 1). Today's much-loved, but increasingly scarce red telephone box, which was designed to commemorate the silver jubilee of King George V, is known as the K6.

For all the elegance of the British phone box, the first constructions to be called 'kiosks' were much grander affairs. The word designated an open pavilion or summerhouse, often supported by pillars and surrounded with a balustrade. They were common in Turkey and Iran, and subsequently imitated in gardens and parks across Western Europe. In the nineteenth century, the word was borrowed for light ornamental structures used for the sale of newspapers and other items before, in the 1920s, encompassing the public payphone. The word came into English via the French *kiosque*, but is ultimately from the Turkish *köşk* – 'pavilion', and the Persian *kuš*.

As for 'pavilion' itself, that is an alteration of the Latin *papilio*, a butterfly, because a large tent or summerhouse resembles the stretched wings of the insect. The eponymous character played by Steve McQueen in the film *Papillon* was so-called because of the butterfly tattoo on his chest.

14 August

THE DOG'S BOLLOCKS

For many of us, this is the time of year when we declare 'bollocks' to everything on our to-do list, and set off for sunnier, duty free (and duty-free) climes.

That word 'bollocks' has a long and distinguished history. As a noun, it is a straight-talking synonym for the testicles, which is how it all began. But today it can be used as a dismissal of nonsense as well as a multi-purpose expletive venting frustration, regret or annoyance.

'Bollocks' began its story in the 1300s when it was usually spelled 'ballocks' and was everyday vernacular for testicles, deriving from the Anglo-Saxon word *beallucas*. It is mentioned in an early translation of the Bible, while a surgeons' manual from 1541 describes the 'flesh of the ballocks' as being 'cruddy and kernely'.

At this point the word was not considered improper: even as late as the 1700s one military general was advising that 'kiss my arse is too vulgar' whereas 'kiss my ballocks' was *much* more acceptable. In poetry of the same period, you'll find references to 'the charms of the ballocks', while in horticulture, orchids (themselves named after the Greek *orchis*, testicle) come in varieties like ballockgrass, fool's ballocks, and sweet ballocks. For a while, it was even a term of affection, with friends introduced as 'bollock stones', another synonym for testicles.

As with 'shit', the meaning of 'bollocks' has shifted over the years from bad meaning bad, to bad meaning good. If something is 'top bollocks', for example, it's top drawer, top trumps, and top banana. The very pinnacle of greatness, however, is 'the dog's bollocks', a curious expression that originated in the book trade, where printers would jokingly use it to refer to a colon dash:— because that's exactly what the punctuation looked like. Like the bee's knees, cat's whiskers, and kipper's knickers, 'the dog's bollocks' quickly became a label of excellence.

In recent years, the BBC has placed 'bollocks' in eighth position on its obscenity list, in the — anatomically supremely accurate — place below 'prick' and above 'arsehole'.

---

15 August

BANG-A-BONK

What better way to spend a stifling summer's day than 'bang-a-bonking'? This perplexingly obsolete expression is recorded in the glossaries of Gloucestershire dialect as meaning, quite simply, lying on a riverbank and watching the world go by.

Sitting and observing activity on the water is behind another word in English, long espoused by those who love nothing better than to sit on the edge of a canal and idly observe passing boats and their crews. These are the 'gongoozlers', who take their name from a nineteenth-century verb of the Lake District, 'gongoozle', meaning to stare protractedly at anything uncommon. The word is a combination of two words in the same Cumbrian dialect: to 'gawn' is to gaze, either vacantly or with curiosity, while to 'goozen' follows the same theme: to gawp. An article in the *Nottingham Evening Post* from the summer of 1931 speaks of the gradual disappearance of the 'barge people' and their patter, including words like 'chalico' (a hot mixture of tar and horse manure, used for dressing barge timbers); 'jambling pole' (a pole projecting from the bow of some barges); 'gongoozler'; and 'loodel' (a staff used for steering).

Nowadays, gongoozling can be extended to mean staring vacantly at anything, including a cup of tea.

16 August

CORRIE-FISTED

Around this time every year falls International Lefthanders Day, a rare opportunity to celebrate what has linguistically long been viewed as an unfortunate, if not sinister, predicament, and involving a fair amount of paper smudging for those who want to see what it's like for those on 'the other side'.

For the Romans *sinister* meant 'left', as opposed to *dexter*, meaning 'right', the root of 'dextrous'. Throughout history, left-handers have had a particularly hard rap. Even the word 'awkward', from the Vikings' *awk*, 'the wrong way round', is said to have been a disparaging nod to those who were less than 'adroit' (from the French 'to the right').

Many terms for left-handers are locally specific. Depending on where you are in Britain, for example, you can be 'kay-pawed', 'cack-handed', and 'caggy-handed'. Further afield, you might find a 'cuddy-wifter', 'pally-duker', and, thanks to the game of baseball, a 'southpaw' (from the orientation of the diamond, which means the pitcher has their left hand on the 'south' side of their body).

Within a fourteen-mile radius in Scotland there are said to be fourteen different variations for being left-handed, and most are related to one particular family: the Kerrs, a family from Ferniehirst Castle in the Borders. 'Corrie-fisted' is one such term. According to local legend, the laird of the castle, Andrew Kerr, found his left-handedness to be a useful weapon in battle, allowing him to surprise the enemy with the unexpected direction of his sword. As a result, he only employed left-handed soldiers. The castle itself was built to maximise this advantage: unlike most castles where the staircases spiral clockwise, Ferniehirst has counter-clockwise ones, whose bends once gave a defender's left hand freedom to lunge.

$$\boxed{\textbf{17 August}}$$

RHOTACISM

This day in 1979 remains a seminal date for any fans of dead parrots, the Spanish Inquisition, elderberries, and the funniest joke in the world. Directed by Terry Jones, *Monty Python's Life of Brian* premiered after a funding crisis when the chairman of the film company EMI finally got around to reading the script and hated it. The film was saved by George Harrison, who remortgaged his house and called it 'the most expensive cinema ticket ever issued'. On the other hand, as he himself put it, how else was he going to get to view the comedy?

The film's troubles were far from over. Denounced for its religious blasphemy, it was banned by thirty-nine authorities in Britain, and by various countries including Ireland. The filmmakers' marketing campaign was later to bear the slogan: 'So funny, it was banned in Norway'. Today, the film is rarely far from the top of polls searching for the greatest comedy of all time.

The eponymous hero of *Monty Python's Life of Brian*, played by Graham Chapman, is born in a stable next door to Jesus. Later in life, by repeating some of Jesus's doctrines, he finds himself followed by those who believe he too can perform miracles. He is eventually captured and sentenced to death, but Pontius Pilate (Michael Palin) fears revolt and asks the assembled crowd which single person they would like to pardon. There is one problem: Pilate is unable to pronounce his 'r's. The crowd in mockery proceeds to shout out names containing the letter: 'Roger', 'Roderick', ('Are they wagging me?' Pilate asks), until eventually 'Brian' is mentioned. Pilate agrees and vows to '*welease Bwian*'.

The inability to correctly pronounce an 'r' sound is known as 'rhotacism'. Rhotic sounds are the last to be mastered by a child – those who are unable to get there produce what is known as a 'labiodental approximant': in other words, a sound that is close to a 'w'. Monty Python's Pontius Pilate is not alone in his rhotacizing: Elmer Fudd, the nemesis of Bugs Bunny, regularly urges others to be 'vewy, vewy quiet, I'm hunting wabbits'.

18 August

KAMIKAZE

The word 'kamikaze' found its way into the English language largely through the actions of the Japanese air force during the latter stages of the Second World War. The suicide-bombing flights made by the fearless pilots (or choice-less, or fuel-less, depending on which version of events you believe) have made *kamikaze* synonymous with self-sacrifice for what is believed to be the greater good. The original *kamikaze*, however, began not in the air, but on the seas.

Seven years after first attempting to invade Japan in 1274, Kublai Khan assembled what was said to be the largest naval invasion force in history (not surpassed until the twentieth century by the Normandy landings). In mid-August 1281, his fleet was hit by a typhoon, reportedly resulting in the loss of 70,000 soldiers, and ultimately the salvation of Japan. *Kamikaze* is the Japanese for 'divine wind'.

This sense of a divine intervention purging the enemy from the seas was taken up almost seven hundred years later in wartime propaganda as a metaphor to both spur on the kami-kaze pilots, and to keep the public onside.

19 August

ROGITATE

It is about this time in the summer holidays that parents begin to feel the rub of endless questions from their children. Which is where the word 'rogitate' comes in useful. An extension of the Latin *rogare*, 'to ask', it means to 'make frequent requests or entreaties'. It can also be used for endless repetitions of the same question, such as 'Are we there yet?'

20 August

HALCYON

Halcyon is surely one of the most beautiful words in our language. The days it describes are ones of tranquillity and happiness.

The term emerged from a poetic story from Greek mythology. The *alkuon* was a fabled bird identified with the kingfisher: the Greek word translates as 'sea-conceiving', and reflects the ancient belief that kingfishers bred their young in nests upon the sea. According to the legend, the goddess Alcyone, distraught at the drowning of her husband, casts herself into the sea. The gods, moved by her plight, bring her husband back to life, turning both him and Alcyone into kingfishers. Every year, Alcyone builds her nest on the sea, while her father Aeolus, the god of the winds, ensures that the waters are stormless and calm.

Kingfishers were said to breed during the seven days before and the seven days after the winter solstice. These were the original 'halcyon' or 'kingfisher' days, always peaceful and fair. Since the early 1500s the term has been extended to mean any period of quiet, unruffled happiness.

21 August

OXFORD COMMA

On 21 August 2019, the British Prime Minister Boris Johnson and the German Chancellor Angela Merkel met in Berlin to discuss the notorious 'backstop' that was becoming the gnarliest issue of the Brexit debate. Five months later, Britain officially left the EU, a historic break that was marked by the issue of yet another controversial move: the Brexit commemorative coin.

Inscribed on the back of the special 50-pence issue was the sentence: 'Peace, prosperity and friendship with all nations'. The writer Philip Pullman was not alone when he commented on social media: 'The "Brexit" 50p coin is missing an Oxford comma, and should be boycotted by all literate people.' Clearly there was more to this than met the eye, but what exactly is the Oxford comma?

This curious punctuation mark has, in the course of its lifetime, proved more controversial than the notorious split infinitive. Otherwise known as the 'serial comma', it is an optional comma added before the word 'and' at the end of a list. So 'we ate steak, green beans, and sautéed potatoes' includes an Oxford comma; without it the sentence would still make perfect sense and the punctuation mark is largely a matter of taste. In other cases, however, the comma is needed to avoid ambiguity, as in 'I'd like to dedicate this book to my parents, Sarah and God'. For many though, who were brought up to believe that a comma before 'and' is always wrong, the instinct is hard-set and even this last sentence would have them demurring.

The comma is embedded in the house style of Oxford University Press, hence its name. But its reach in Britain beyond the city of dreaming spires is limited, and it is almost a stranger in its own land. Widely used in the United States and Australia, the majority of people in the UK go without. It's hard to argue that the Brexit coin wouldn't be a little more elegant with a gentle breath after 'prosperity'. But perhaps it was fitting that a memento of one of the most divisive political processes in British history should cause such a grammatical brouhaha.

22 August

DOG DAYS

Traditionally, these are the motionless, breathless days of summer, when the sun is at its hottest and our bodies need to be fanned into any kind of action. They are, as the author Natalie Babbitt, described them, 'at the very top of summer . . . like the highest seat of a Ferris wheel before it pauses in its turning'. Others would describe these weeks as the 'dog days', a direct translation of the Latin *dies caniculares*. The term is used figuratively to describe a period marked by lethargy, inactivity, or indolence.

The dog days get their name not because dogs become lazy or mad when it's hot. Rather, as so often in English, we need to look to the stars. The phrase refers to Sirius, the Dog Star and the brightest in the constellation *Canis major* ('Big Dog'). Between early July and late August, the star rises and sets at about the same time as the sun.

For the ancients, this hottest time of the year could bring disease, or another catastrophe. In his *Iliad*, Homer refers to Sirius as Orion's dog that brings 'fever to wretched mortals'. Today, that fever is largely curable through the act of doing precisely nothing, and by swapping Sirius for shade. Only mad dogs – the real kind – and Englishmen go out in the midday sun.

23 August

MEANDER

The *meandros*, or *meander*, is an ornamental motif found throughout the art of ancient Greece, and particularly in sculpture and pottery. It is characterised by interlocking lines that form either a spiral or an intricate network of connected strokes. The form was viewed as a relative of the labyrinth, a similarly complex, branching pattern on ceramics and basketry that harks back to the myth of the maze that housed the Minotaur, from which Theseus escaped by using an unwinding ball of thread (a 'clew', the forerunner of our modern word 'clue').

The branches of the *meandros* design were seen by the Greeks as representing the eternal flow of the sea and, by extension, of life itself. The decorative style remains popular today on emblems and logos, such as the famous Versace 'Medusa' motif.

The *meandros* is named after the River Maiandros, the ancient Meander River which ran a twisting, winding course from the highlands of Phrygia into the Aegean Sea. Today, it is known as the Büyük Menderes River. To meander is, of course, to follow a winding, leisurely course, as one might on a summer stroll or lolling trip on the water.

24 August

WAYZGOOSE

Towards the close of August, as days slowly begin to draw in, printers would work the final hours of their shift by candlelight. To mark the change to what they knew as autumn working, and to brighten the prospect of increasing darkness, it was usual for the master printer to give his journeymen a feast around St Bartholomew's Day. This was called the *wayz-goose* or *way-goose*, one of the most curious-looking words in the dictionary.

The origin of the term is baffling. Some believe it to come from a dialect term 'wayz' meaning 'stubble', with the suggestion that a goose fattened upon the stubble of the harvest would be the main delicacy served at the feast. But this theory ignores the fact that most geese are still lean in the summer months; today's etymologists believe the name to have been part of some old joke, now lost, or a mangling of a phrase such as 'Away goes!'

Whatever its story, the term evolved to mean the annual summer dinner or outing held for the printers in a publishing house or newspaper office, also known as a 'beano' – a shortening of 'beanfeast' and defined in the dictionary as 'a festive entertainment frequently ending in rowdyism'.

---

25 August

SWEET FA

Few of us would be hard pushed to decode the initials in the phrase 'sweet FA'. But there is more to this than you might think. The alternative version, still used by older generations in Britain today, is 'sweet Fanny Adams', and it involves one of the grisliest murder cases of Victorian times.

On this day in 1867, in Alton, Hampshire, a 24-year-old solicitor's clerk named Frederick Baker was arrested for the brutal murder and dismemberment of eight-year-old Fanny Adams. Baker was charged with abducting Fanny on a hot afternoon near her home, killing her, and, in a bizarre and frenzied dissection, cutting her body up into dozens of pieces, some of which were never found. On Christmas Eve the same year, Baker was hanged outside Winchester Gaol before the vengeful eyes of 5,000 spectators.

Such was the impact of this unusually bloody and distressing case that the name of Fanny Adams became lodged in the public imagination for years. With a hefty dose of black humour, sailors in the British Royal Navy hijacked it for the new rations of tinned mutton that were introduced in 1869, likening them to the dead girl's remains.

As for 'sweet FA', the name of the poor victim proved a useful euphemism for the expletive 'Fuck All'. It's an ironic twist that one of the darkest tales of the nineteenth century has provided a dismissive byword for 'nothing at all'.

26 August

TELEGRAPH

On this day in 1858, the first news dispatch was sent by telegraph, and run in the afternoon edition of the *New York Tribune*. The headline promised startling news of 'highly important intelligence of peace with China', referring to the diplomatic conflict between China and a French and British coalition during the Opium Wars. After just a few lines on the topic, the dispatch focused on the new medium by which the news was being transmitted, which was arguably the bigger news. The word 'telegraph' was based on Greek *tēle*, 'from afar', and *graphein*, 'to write'.

The day after the momentous first communication, the *Tribune* mused on the importance of relating current events 'as they happen'. Its editorial commented wryly on the disgust of one 'excitable individual' who, upon seeing the paper's promise 'News by the ocean telegraph, direct from London!', scanned it before throwing it down and declaring: 'Thunder, what cheats! The boys said it was "right from London". It is a day old!' The paper's editor responded, with a hefty dose of sarcasm, 'Can't we have it a little quicker? Half an hour? Can't we have it in half a minute?' A century and a half later, half a minute is pretty much the expectation of the modern reader when it comes to the latest news.

Not everyone celebrated the arrival of telegraph dispatches. An editorial in the *New York Times* described the fear that such communication instilled in many:

> . . . there can be no rational doubt that the telegraph has caused vast injury. Superficial, sudden, unsifted, too fast for the truth, must be all telegraphic intelligence . . . What need is there for the scraps of news in ten minutes? How trivial and paltry is the telegraphic column? It snowed here, it rained there, one man killed, another hanged.

The parallels with critics of social media and fake news are unmissable.

27 August

FREE

On this day in 1963, 200,000 people marched upon Washington, D.C. in an event that became a key point of the civil rights movement; one that is especially remembered for Martin Luther King Jr.'s 'I Have a Dream' speech.

His oration remains one of the most searingly articulate in modern history. It ends with a plea that many still make in the new century:

> When we allow freedom to ring – when we let it ring from every village and every hamlet, from every state and every city, we will be able to speed up that day when all of God's children, black men and white men, Jews

and Gentiles, Protestants and Catholics, will be able to join hands and sing in the words of the old Negro spiritual: 'Free at last, free at last, thank God almighty, we are free at last.'

The word 'free' first appears in the writings of King Alfred. It comes from an ancient root meaning 'to love', from which we also get 'friend'. The word evolved to its modern meaning because the terms 'beloved' and 'friend' were given to the free members of one's clan – as opposed to slaves. In this it shares its history with the Latin *liberi* – a word that, for the Romans, described both those who were free, and one's children. This ancient equation between freedom and love is still unsolved today.

---

28 August

TOSSPOT

In the late summer of 1930, British newspapers found a rare cause for celebration amid the slump of the nation's profound economic depression. Statistics suggested that drunkenness was at its lowest level in two decades, along with arrests of those intoxicated on methylated spirits. Both numbers reflected the impact of a heavily increased excise duty, which was even more punitive amid mass unemployment.

Those who had reluctantly turned their backs on alcohol might have been glad of the term 'hydropot', an eighteenth-century and somewhat friendlier term for a water-drinker. Their livers, if not their souls, would have been grateful for this step away from their previous role as a 'tosspot', a plain descriptor at the time for a hardened drinker's nightly habit of 'tossing' back their pot of beer and promptly reaching for the next one. (Today's use of the word for a contemptible fool is more likely to be a riff on 'tosser', a word with very different, and usually non-alcoholic, origins.) Synonyms of the day were just as colourful: a 'gulchcup' was a greedy drainer of the glass, as was a 'swill-bowl', 'malt-worm', and 'pot-leech'.

By the time of the newspapers' report on the reduction in drinking levels, the temperance movement known as 'tee-totalism', that had begun in Preston, Lancashire, was already a hundred years old. The 'tee' here stood, not for tosspot, but as a re-duplication of the initial 't' in 'total', which added extra emphasis to the pledge of abstinence. It's said that members of some temperance societies would sign a T after their name to reiterate their promise.

The distance between a tosspot and a teetotaller seems vast, but signs suggest the Covid-19 pandemic pushed many along this path, albeit in both directions. For now it seems we measure out our lives not in coffee spoons, but pint glasses. Those statistics a century ago tend to suggest it was ever thus.

---

29 August

COOL

This day in 1920 saw the birth of Charlie Parker, aka Yardbird, one of the most influential soloists and bebop artists of the Jazz Age.

Parker was indisputably 'cool', a word that flourished during the 1930s and 1940s, the heyday of jazz filled with the tunes of such artists as Dizzy Gillespie and Miles Davis. They were the hepcats, first defined in *Cab Calloway's Cat-alogue: A 'Hepster's' Dictionary*: 'A hep cat is a guy who knows what it's all about.'

'Hip' and 'hep' are developments of a nineteenth-century use of both words to mean 'shrewd', which is said to have come in turn from 'Hep!', the exhortation of the ploughman or driver urging his horses to 'Get up!' and get lively. From hepcat came the 'hipster' and, eventually, the 'hippy'.

But 'cool's' story began earlier still: the first record in Jonathon Green's *Green's Dictionary of Slang* is from 1766. The adjective went on to become slang in Eton College, where a 'cool fish' was a cocky, self-possessed pupil. And, while it may have flown below the radar for a century or more, the slang sense of 'cool' has refused to go away. It was definitively propelled into the mainstream when Charlie Parker recorded, in 1947, his composition entitled 'Cool Blues'.

30 August

SARDONIC

In 1708, the capture of Menorca saw a British–Dutch alliance occupy Sardinia and Menorca, wresting them from the hands of Spain on behalf of Charles VI, Holy Roman Emperor and claimant to the Spanish throne.

Whether or not Spain managed a sardonic smile is not recorded. If they had, it would have been entirely fitting, for the word 'sardonic' (as well as the better-known 'sardine') was geographically inspired by the island of Sardinia.

The Greek epic poet Homer used the word *sardanios* for bitter, scornful laughter. Later Greeks and Romans altered this to *sardonios*, 'Sardinian', and pointed to a 'Sardinian plant', *herba Sardonia*, that if ingested was believed to cause extreme facial convulsions resembling hideous laughter, invariably followed by death.

Sardonic laughter is duly characterised by derisive mocking and a lip-curling sneer. In medicine, a *risus sardonicus* is an apparent fixed grin on those afflicted by tetanus.

31 August

ZWODDER

As the end of the summer holidays beckons, the final entry in Joseph Wright's *English Dialect Dictionary* will prolong the sensations of a lazy, daydreamy summer's day. 'Zwodder' is defined there as simply 'a drowsy, stupid state of body and mind'. Its beginnings may lie in a warm, cosy tavern rather than the sunny banks of a river: another dialect word *swadder*, means 'to grow weary with drinking'.

Either way, zwodder and zwoddery carry the perfect sound for such a sleepy, foggy-brained sensation.

SEPTEMBER

FURLOUGH

September takes its name from the Latin *septem*, 'seven'. The Roman year omitted the winter months and originally started in March; January and February were added only later when Julius Caesar introduced the Julian calendar. Charlemagne, Emperor of the West at the start of the ninth century, refused to accept the name of September and insisted instead on 'Harvest-Month'. For the Anglo-Saxons, it was *Gerstmonath*, or Barley Month, a nod to the crop that was harvested in the autumn.

For many of us, the approach of September marks the end of our summer leave. This sense of 'leave' is a sibling of 'furlough', a word that moved from relative obscurity into the mainstream during the pandemic of 2020.

The dictionary defines 'furlough' as a temporary suspension of employment or leave of absence granted to an employee. It is first recorded in the seventeenth century, when it was used of soldiers given permission to be absent from duty for a certain period of time.

The origin of the word is the Dutch *verlof* and the German *Verlaub*, both meaning permission given as a sign of trust and which are related to the Old English *leaf*, 'leave'. Other relatives include 'belief', the trust that we put in another, and also 'love' – when we trust someone with our affection. All of which put 'furlough' in one of the most prized and ancient families English has to offer.

2 September

MUBBLE FUBBLES

Most of us are familiar with the sense of dread and impending doom that besets us at the end of a long summer break, or on a Sunday evening. In the sixteenth century, a mood such as this was known as the 'mubble fubbles', a term whose softness might take the sting out of even the gloomiest of prospects.

No one quite knows how the expression originated, but it may be a riff on a contemporaneous expression, 'mulligrubs', describing a fit of despondency and melancholy.

We can perhaps take heart from the promise made by a character in a Christmas play from 1607, to one who is clearly similarly downcast: 'And when your brayne, feeles any paine, with cares of state & troubles / We'el come in kindnesse, to put your highnesse out of ye mubble fubbles.'

3 September

TRUMPERINESS

James 'Whitey' Bulger, born 3 September 1929, was an Irish-American organised crime leader, who was finally brought to book at the ripe old age of eighty-one, when he was indicted for nineteen murders. Such was his notoriety that his life was brought to the screen in the Oscar-winning film *The Departed*, starring Jack Nicholson, Leonardo DiCaprio, and Matt Damon, and he was later portrayed by Johnny Depp in the 2015 biopic *Black Mass*.

Bulger was also exposed as an undercover FBI informant, in return for which the FBI had allegedly ensured that his criminal enterprise was overlooked. Bulger had thus been a stool pigeon – an expression born in the practice of setting dead or stuffed birds upon a stool as an enticement to other birds, which would then be sitting ducks (to mix a metaphor) for hunters. The 'stool', originally spelled *stale* was also used of a thief's assistant or stooge. Prospero, in Shakespeare's *The Tempest*, uses it in this way: 'The trumpery in my house, go bring it hither, / For stale to catch these thieves', introducing many of us to an even older word for deception and guile: 'trumpery'

Trumpery is defined in the *Oxford English Dictionary* as imposture or trickery, and dates it right back to the 1400s. By Shakespeare's time it had the added meaning of something of less value than it seems – a precursor of 'trumpery finery'. Trumperiness, meanwhile, is a useful and potentially topical noun for something highly flashy and pretentious, but ultimately pretty worthless.

---

4 September

GENERICIDE

Google was founded on 4 September 1998, its name famously deriving from the number googol (1 followed by 100 zeros: *see* 23 May). The world's largest search engine has since dominated the market, to the extent that it might be accused of 'genericide'.

Genericide is a legal term, coined in 1972, for a branded product that has become so ubiquitous it becomes the noun's generic name. Famous examples include 'hoover', 'aspirin', and 'band-aid'. Legally, a trademark can be revoked if a brand is judged to have lost its distinctive identity. In some ways, such companies have been destroyed by their own success. In all but a few dictionaries, although the search engine itself remains capitalised, the verb to 'google' has now lost its capital letter, thereby fulfilling in part the meaning of 'genericide': 'death by becoming generic'.

5 September

YEN

This day in 1839 saw the First Opium War begin in China. It triggered a series of military engagements that pitched Britain against the Qing dynasty over the seizure of opium stocks at Canton. China had stopped the transportation of the drug in an effort to enforce a ban, while the British government insisted that the principles of free trade should be upheld (not least to allow the vast amounts of income that the drug delivered) and the opium merchants granted free travel. The British navy defeated the Chinese, and the trade was allowed to continue, despite the increasing addiction levels to the drug in the country, and its depleting effect on the Chinese economy.

Before it became an essential part of the jazz lexicon in the 1930s, the adjective 'hip' had already been used of opium smokers, lying on the 'hip' as they smoked what was known as 'yen', from the Chinese *yan*, opium. It is the drug addict's craving for it that gave us our modern sense of 'yen', for a desire or longing.

6 September

CHEAP

In September 1916, the first self-service store was born. The Piggly Wiggly supermarket was opened by the US grocer Clarence Saunders, in Memphis, Tennessee. It stocked four times as many items as the traditional counter store, and by

1923 there were 1,200 Piggly Wiggly stores across North America. Surprisingly little has changed since it introduced its aisles, baskets, and checkout tills. Saunders had correctly identified an enormous appetite among Americans for greater choice at cheaper prices.

The word 'cheap' first meant to bargain or barter. Eventually displaced by those two terms from Old French, it went on to deliver the associated message of inexpensiveness: a 'good cheap' was a good buy. The original, Old English sense of the term survives only in place names such as Cheapside, Chipping (Norton, Camden, etc.), and Chepstow – all of which roughly correlate to 'marketplace' – as well as in the word 'chap'. The latter is from 'chapman', an Old English term meaning a merchant or trader and subsequently the customer bargaining with them. 'Chap' finally moved on to become another term for a 'bloke' or man on the street.

---

7 September

HUMICUBATION

On a scorching day in Australia, 1902, the entire nation offered up prayers for rain. An unprecedented period of drought had destroyed livestock and devastated crops. Dame Nellie Melba, the country's operatic soprano and one of the most famous singers of the late Victorian era, spoke with pain of what she had seen as she travelled: 'I have seen with my own eyes the brown, burnt paddocks extending for hundreds of miles, with no vestige of grass left upon them. I have seen starving sheep leaning against the fences, too weak to move . . . It is simply appalling.'

On 8 September, the newspaper *Argus* wrote of the previous day's offerings 'of humiliation and prayer for rain'. The paper reported the words of a Methodist minister from Box Hill, a suburb of Melbourne:

The peril of Australian life and of Australian politics was found in the temptation to regard God as a being that could be safely ignored. And God in terrible drought was writing on the very face of the Continent his warning against that madness. Perhaps Australia had not properly learned its lesson.

Many other observances across the country urged repentance as the requisite of rain. Accordingly, when it did come, it was believed by many to be by the grace of God.

'Humicubation' is a word for lying on the ground, typically as an act of penitence or humiliation, just as might have been observed by the hopefuls of 1902. In far less tragic circumstances, it was used in stereotypical descriptions of a husband arriving home late from work, the worse for wear, and lying prostrate in front of his wife (in which case he might also bring along a gift of appeasement, known in Germany as *Drachenfutter*, 'dragon food').

8 September

MACGUFFIN

This day in 1960 saw the nationwide release of Alfred Hitchcock's *Psycho*, starring Anthony Perkins and Janet Leigh, and based on the 1959 novel of the same name. When Hitchcock was asked why he wanted to make it, he answered simply, 'I think the murder in the bathtub, coming out of the blue, that was about all.' The infamous 45-second shower scene, depicting the most (indirectly) graphic murder that most US cinema-goers had ever seen, required a total number of 78 camera set-ups, and 52 cuts, and took an entire week to film.

While the scene is pivotal to the entire film, there is another element upon which much of the plot hinges, namely the sum of $40,000, stolen by Leigh's character, Marion Crane, and the motivation for her every action. For the viewer, it has far less significance. Hitchcock liked to term such plot-driving elements as 'MacGuffins'. When asked for elucidation, the director himself put it a little more opaquely:

> It might be a Scottish name, taken from a story about two men on the train. One man says, 'Well, what is a MacGuffin?' You say, 'It's an apparatus for trapping lions in the Scottish highlands.' Man says, 'But there are no lions in the Scottish highlands.' Then you say, 'Then that's no MacGuffin.'

Hitchcock's films contain many plot drivers that recede from view, such as the radioactive ore in *Notorious*, and the silent plane engine in *The 39 Steps*. The MacGuffin has been freely interpreted by directors since, including Quentin Tarantino, in whose *Pulp Fiction* characters vie violently for the contents of a glowing metallic suitcase. Even at its conclusion, the case's contents are never revealed.

9 September

SLOGAN

The early days of August in 1859 saw the launch of the world's first advertising slogan. Beecham's Powders promised relief from all 'Bilious and Nervous Disorders', a 'Wonderful Medicine recommended by the Medical Faculty as the Best and Safest Family Medicine, Suitable for Sufferers of All Ages'. They were, the ad stated, 'worth a guinea a box', but while they eventually sold for a fraction of that price, their usefulness was disputed by a few people from the start. In 1912, the British Medical Association tested their ingredients, one of which was found to be powdered soap. They did, however, have some positive effects on the digestive system, and for the average citizen Beecham's were considered to be a magical cure-all and panacea, not unlike Benjamin Brandreth's pills on the other side of the Atlantic, whose maker also harnessed the new technique of mass advertising. Production of Beecham's mighty medicine did not halt until 1998.

The word 'slogan' began in another imagination altogether. It is first recorded in the year of the Battle of Flodden, fought on this day in 1513, when the English army defeated the invading Scots under their monarch King James IV. The term is one with unexpectedly bellicose roots, coming from the Scottish Gaelic *sluagh-ghairm*, from *sluagh*, 'army', and *ghairm*, 'shout'. It was, in other words, a war cry, used by Scottish Highlanders and Borderers in their many battles against the English.

Over time, the 'slogan cry' left its roots and became instead a distinctive note, phrase, or cry – particularly that of a brand vying for attention in the marketplace.

---

10 September

BITCH THE POT

Tea and gossip go together. At least, that's the stereotypical view of a tea gathering: a group of women gathered around the teapot exchanging tittle-tattle. As popularity of the beverage imported from China ('tea' comes from the Mandarin Chinese *cha*) increased, it became particularly associated with women, and above all with their tendency to gossip. Francis Grose's *Classical Dictionary of the Vulgar Tongue* lists various slang terms for tea, including 'prattle-broth', 'cat-lap' ('cat' being a contemporary slang for a gossipy old woman), and 'scandal broth'.

To pour tea, meanwhile, was not just to 'play mother', as

one enduring English expression has it, but also to 'bitch the pot' – to drink tea was to simply 'bitch'. At this time a bitch was a lewd or sensual woman as well as a potentially malicious one, and in another nineteenth-century dictionary the phraseology is even more unguarded, linking tea with loose morals as much as loquaciousness: 'How the blowens [whores] lush the slop. How the wenches drink tea!' The language of tea had become another vehicle for sexism, and a misogynistic world view in which the air women exchanged was as hot as the beverage they sipped. 'Bitch party' and 'tabby party' (again the image of cattiness) were the terms of choice for such gossipy gatherings.

Men, it seems, were made of stronger stuff, and drank it too. Furthermore, any self-respecting man would ensure his wife and daughters stayed away from tea. The pamphleteer and political writer William Cobbett declared in 1822:

> The gossip of the tea-table is no bad preparatory school for the brothel. The girl that has been brought up, merely to boil the tea kettle, and to assist in the gossip inseparable from the practice, is a mere consumer of food, a pest to her employer, and a curse to her husband, if any man be so unfortunate as to affix his affections upon her.

In the twenty-first century, to 'spill the T' has become a firm part of drag culture slang for gossiping. T here may stand for either 'truth' or the drink, but either way 'weak tea' has come to mean a story that doesn't quite hold up – and it's often one told by women.

Perhaps it's time for bitches to make a fresh pot.

11 September

GROUND ZERO

On 6 August 1945, an atomic bomb, nicknamed 'Little Boy' by the US military and capable of producing 2,000 times the blast of the most powerful bomb ever used before, was dropped on the city of Hiroshima. The city was destroyed in a blinding instant, with the estimated death toll reaching 140,000. The surface area closest to the detonation became known as Ground Zero – 'Zero' had been first used as the code name for the site of the so-called Trinity test, involving the very first detonation of a nuclear device.

Ground Zero subsequently came to be used for the points of most severe damage or destruction after other violent events, either natural or man-induced, including earthquakes and epidemics. In 2001, it became firmly tethered to the terror attacks of September 11th upon New York's World Trade Center. The finality of the phrase, and the annihilation it described, seemed fitting. For others, however, it signalled both an end and a beginning; Ground Zero remained the term for the site of the World Trade Center while the gruelling recovery work continued, and restoration began. On the 10th anniversary of the attacks, the then-city mayor Michael Bloomberg urged that the name be finally withdrawn: 'the time has come to call those 16 acres what they are: The World Trade Center and the National September 11th Memorial and Museum'.

Nevertheless, like the shorthand 9/11, it is unlikely that Ground Zero – a tragic epithet since its earliest incarnation – will lose its precise associations for several generations.

12 September

CONKER

September is the month when we gather the seeds of the horse chestnut tree, and marvel at their deep, mahogany lustre. Some replay the game of their childhood by threading them with a piece of string and waging war in a game of conkers.

The word 'conker' probably comes from a dialect word for a snail shell, making it a sibling of 'conch', because these shells were among the earliest objects used to play the game. The word quickly became associated with 'conqueror', which then became another name for the knockout contest. And, as you might expect from such a popular children's game, a whole lexicon of slang terms for sizes, colours, and categories of conker grew up around it. A player would gather their ammunition – including 'obblyonkers' and 'cheggies' – and divide them into such groups as the 'cheeser' (a conker with a flat side to it), or the 'laggie' or 'seasoner' (conkers hardened by age or by the illicit use of nail varnish, industrial resin, etc. – though one old 'foolproof' method of hardening was apparently to pass the conker through a pig). A new conker is a 'none-er' because it hasn't yet conquered any other conkers – the player must say 'addy addy onker' if they want to christen it. As soon as it does break another it becomes a 'one-er', then a 'two-er', and on it goes. And if the strings become entangled, the first player to shout 'Stringsies!' has an extra turn. To seal a victory is to nab a 'kinger'.

All of which might sound quaint and highly jolly. Anyone hearing the thwack of a conker during a serious contest, however, or observing the bruised knuckles of the *conkistadors*, knows differently.

13 September

CALLIPYGIAN

On this date in 1501, Michelangelo began work on his statue of the Goliath-conquering David, which is chiselled from a single piece of marble. Half a millennium later, newspapers were reporting his creation's first bath in 130 years, during which the restorers noticed that David's buttocks were not quite as perfect as one might imagine.

The icon of Renaissance beauty has apparently quite a few purple blemishes on his backside, the result of bacteria produced by damp. The cleaning attempts attracted huge controversy, as restoration often does. But no matter which method is used, it seems unlikely anything will have much impact on the figure's fundament – in other words, he may no longer be described as 'callipygian', a Greek word for 'possessing beautiful or well-shaped buttocks' that was first ascribed to Aphrodite and then to a sculptural representation of Venus.

If David were able to object, he might call those responsible for his upkeep 'prats' – which would be fitting, since 'prat' first designated a single buttock (hence a comedy 'pratfall') before the more figurative 'butt' of everyone else's jokes.

14 September

SPANGLE

In 1814, the American lawyer and amateur poet Francis Scott Key wrote a poem entitled 'Defence of Fort M'Henry'. He penned the verse while witnessing, from a ship in Baltimore Harbor, the British bombardment of Fort McHenry during the War of 1812. The American forces successfully defended their base, and on the morning of 14 September a storm flag was replaced with a large garrison flag. It was this ensign that inspired Key's poem:

Oh say can you see, by the dawn's early light,
What so proudly we hailed at the twilight's last
　gleaming,
Whose broad stripes and bright stars through the
　perilous fight,
O'er the ramparts we watched, were so gallantly
　streaming?
And the rockets' red glare, the bombs bursting in air,
Gave proof through the night that our flag was still
　there.
Oh say does that star-spangled banner yet wave
O'er the land of the free, and the home of the brave?

The poem was published in a newspaper a week later. Key also took it to a music publisher, who duly set the lines to the tune of 'To Anacreon in Heaven'. A century after its publication, 'The Star-Spangled Banner' was formally adopted as the American national anthem, a resolution signed by President Herbert Hoover. Its status is not without controversy – it is increasingly viewed by many as a celebration of the land of the already free, and not of the slaves who were still heavily oppressed at the time Key was writing.

'Spangle' conjures up images of glittering metal or sparkly ornaments (and, for some of us, fruity sweets from the 1980s). In Old English, a *spang* was a buckle or clasp – whose shininess eventually became the prevailing meaning of the word.

15 September

SLEUTH

'Unless you are good at guessing, it's not much use being a detective,' said Hercule Poirot in *The Mysterious Affair at Styles*. 'Use your little grey cells, *mon ami*.' His creator Agatha Christie was born on this day in 1890, one of the most prolific and celebrated crime writers in history, whose characters Miss Marple and Hercule Poirot have become some of the most recognisable fictional detectives of all time. Marple and Poirot are sleuths, a shortening of 'sleuth-hound', once a synonym for a bloodhound that followed the 'sloo' or track of their quarry. That *sloð* was a word inherited centuries earlier from the marauding Vikings, who were equally tenacious in the pursuit of their booty.

Christie's two detectives, had they been born in the United States, would also have been known as 'private dicks', a word that has puzzled many but which might be explained as a shortening of 'detective' or, alternatively, derived from the language of Romani in which *dikh* or *deek* means to 'see' (and which is related to the phrase 'having a dekko').

16 September

LIKE

One of the greatest perceived linguistic offences of the twenty-first century is the use of 'like' in natural conversation. It is seen as a sure sign of English spiralling into chaos before it hits oblivion.

In 2019, the British media had a field day when a contestant on the reality TV show *Love Island* used the filler seventy-six times in under five minutes. This series is seen as a laboratory of language, one in which contestants try out new phrases, or new senses of existing words, as their signature brand. Flipped meanings of 'muggy' (duplicitous) and 'melt' (a bit wet) have flown into mainstream slang as a result of the show, whose lexicon also includes 'prangy' (anxious) and 'pied off' (jilted). It also gave us the 'ick factor', that overwhelming feeling of revulsion you suddenly discover towards your partner-turned-ickee. Such is the programme's influence that several schools decided to ban 'like' from their pupils' conversation: an edict that, like every one that has gone before it, stands a zero chance of success.

'Like' is generally seen as lazy at best and, at worst, as a sign of a highly deficient vocabulary. Both viewpoints can, of course, be justified, but it's worth remembering that we have employed natural pauses, ums and ers, and words such as these since language began. From 'indeed' to 'innit', the fear is always the same. But the evidence suggests it is unjustified. One linguistic experiment played two separate groups an audio recording of the same message. All white noise was stripped out of one, while the other was unedited, and contained all the hesitations and fillers that pepper normal conversation. The result was surprising: the more natural recording was the one that was most readily understood by the participants – our verbal sprinklings apparently allow the listener time to absorb our message, while also adding an authentic rhythm.

The word 'like' began in Old English a millennium before it became the must-have linguistic accessory of the Islanders. It is a shortening of *ylike*, from the Germanic *gelich*, in which *lich* meant a 'body' (usually a dead one, hence a church's 'lych-gate' under which the dead would await the clergyman on the way to the cemetery, or the 'lich' or 'screech' owl, once seen as the foreteller of death). The idea is of one thing having a similar 'body' or form to another. By the fourteenth century, it was being used in such formulations as 'like mad'. And finally it moved to what we think of as its most modern incarnation: the equivalent of 'so to speak' or 'as it were', and a conversational filler or intensifier. As for the *Oxford English Dictionary*'s first record of this kind of usage, the answer may again surprise: it is from 1778, and the novel *Evelina* by Fanny Burney: 'Father grew quite uneasy like, for fear of his Lordship's taking offence.' Those who take offence at the Islanders may be reassured that, as in most things, our current bugbears are anything but new.

17 September

FREELANCER

'Freelance' is one of the best examples there is of a word that wears its heart on its sleeve. Just as secretaries were originally keepers of secrets – 'privy' officers in the literal sense of the word – and just as heathens lived on the heath, away from 'civilised' villages and towns, so the first freelancers were knights who were free to use their lances in the service of people who paid them. Unattached to any lord or manor, they were military adventurers who followed the money. The word was not actually coined in medieval times – instead it was a retrospective term introduced by Walter Scott in his novel *Ivanhoe*. It shifted for a time to mean a political maverick with no fixed affiliation, before returning to the sense of an individual hiring themselves out for work.

Our language is full of words whose origin is written into their name, but which we pass by, often because their sound has changed or their history has long since receded. It's easy to overlook that illustrators add lustre, that to eat breakfast is to break our fast, and that a cupboard was a board or table for cups. All are words you can take at face value – as, in fact, any freelancer who touts their metaphorical lance will agree.

18 September

GOSSAMER

As autumn approaches, we might begin to see the soft, filmy threads of cobwebs spun by small spiders and draped across foliage and grass, or floating on the air.

The whispering consonants of the word 'gossamer' suggest a poetic origin, and Shakespeare took full advantage in such lines as these in *Romeo and Juliet*:

> A lover may bestride the gossamer
> That idles in the wanton summer air,
> And yet not fall; so light is vanity.

The truth is a bit more prosaic: 'gossamer' is probably a simple shortening of 'goose-summer', and a nod to the autumn months when geese were eaten and on whose warm days gossamer is usually seen. Alternatively, perhaps the downy appearance of gossamer spread over a grassy surface called to mind the fluffy feathers of a goose.

19 September

PAMPHLET

In 1796, the US President George Washington delivered a valedictory address to the nation that has come to be regarded as one of the most important speeches, and subsequent documents, in American history. The 'Address of Gen. Washington to the People of America on His Declining the Presidency of the United States' was published some ten weeks before the country's citizens cast their votes for the next incumbent of office, in the *American Daily Advertiser* on 19

September. It had, in fact, been written some four years earlier, when Washington was reluctant to run for a second term, but he had been convinced by others – including Thomas Jefferson – that it was his duty to the nation to maintain a stable government.

The speech was published in newspapers up and down the country. Such was the subsequent demand that it was reprinted in pamphlets and distributed as widely as possible. This may have been the last time the word 'pamphlet' inspired any degree of excitement in anyone.

But not the first, for the origins of 'pamphlet' are unexpectedly fiery. They begin with a Latin comedic play on the subject of love, called *Pamphilus de amore*, or *Pamphilus* for short. Its plot involves the eponymous hero and the object of his deep affections, Galatea. The story recounts her seduction and apparent rape by the youth, who is instructed in a life of violence by the goddess Venus and a female go-between. It is far from the traditional romantic epic with a happy ending.

The name 'Pamphilus' is from the Greek for 'loved by all'. Whatever the morals and integrity of the story, it was clearly loved by many, and the comedy was made into hundreds of small booklets known as 'pamphilets', or 'little Pamphiluses'. It is thanks to these that the often turgid literature that drops through the letter-boxes around election time are known as 'pamphlets', with, regrettably, all trace of passion long forgotten.

---

20 September

INDIAN SUMMER

In 1812, a clergyman from New England wrote poetically about the unexpectedly balmy, hazy days of autumn:

Two or three weeks of fair weather, in which the air is perfectly transparent, and the clouds, which float in a sky

of the purest azure, are adorned with brilliant colours
. . . This charming season is called the Indian Summer,
a name which is derived from the natives, who believe
that it is caused by a wind, which comes immediately
from the court of their great and benevolent God
Cautantowwit, or the south-western God.

The clergyman's sermon seems to give a definitive answer to
the origin of 'Indian summer', an expression reserved for those
days in late autumn when the sun shines as fiercely as it did
in June.

And yet evidence for the etymology is mixed. The *Oxford
English Dictionary* surmises that it may echo a derogatory use
of 'Indian' to suggest something different, substitute, or ersatz:
'Indian bread', for example, was one made from cassava starch
and so not the 'real thing' – just as warmth in autumn does
not mean the return of summer. Alternatively, the expression
may have arisen from the fact that the region in which these
meteorological conditions were originally noticed was still
occupied by the American Indians. Certainly there is much
Native American folklore associated with the unseasonably
warm weather of these months.

In Bulgaria they call such balmy times 'gypsy summer', a
nod perhaps to the original meaning of 'gypsy' – a traveller
thought to come from Egypt – while in Germany it is known
as *Altweibersommer*, 'old women's/hags' summer', who are well
into the autumn of their years. Lastly, Gaelic gives us the lovely
fómhar beag na ngéanna, 'little autumn of the geese' (*see* 18
September).

For English-speakers, we associate an 'Indian summer' with
a warmth as gratifying as it is unexpected, as well as the
glowing autumnal tints of foliage: an extra bonus from nature.

21 September

A FLICK OF HARES

There are few areas of language that get people going quite as much as whether the correct term for a bunch of politicians is a posse or an odium (or worse), while lexicographers have long been looking for their own group name – a sentence (though the judges have already taken that one)? The only boring thing about collective nouns is their name.

The majority of group terms that we know and love today – 'a gaggle of geese', 'an exaltation of larks', 'a murmuration of starlings' – sprang from the medieval imagination. Created by the elite for the elite, they were written down in books of etiquette aimed at instructing the nobility on how not to embarrass themselves while out hunting, hawking, or fishing. For the medieval nobleman, knowing that the correct term for a group of ferrets was a 'busyness', for hares a 'flick', and for hounds a 'mute', was a badge of honour. A handling of these terms would not only avoid humiliation, but would mark the gentry out from the peasants.

Our primary source for such terms is the fifteenth-century *Book of St Albans*, a three-part compendium on aristocratic pursuits. Its authorship is attributed to Dame Juliana Berners, Prioress of the Sopwell nunnery in Hertfordshire. Not only did her work contain over a hundred and sixty group names for beasts of the chase and characters on the medieval stage, but it also boasted the first images to be printed in colour in England. It was an instant hit, reprinted and reissued many times both by William Caxton and the (superbly named) printer and publisher Wynkyn de Worde. Its popularity extended far beyond the nobles for whom it was originally intended.

More than half a millennium on, we still use many of these medieval concoctions, relishing the knowledge that congregated crows form a 'murder', and that foxes come together in a 'skulk'. Others among those fifteenth-century lists prove that collective nouns have invited wordplay from the start. You only have to hear 'an incredulity of cuckolds' or 'a misbelief of painters' (such as portrait artists, who rushed to broaden the shoulders and embellish the eyebrows of their subjects) to eavesdrop on the medieval sense of humour. 'An abomination of monks' made fun of those who took solemn religious vows but who were frequently the lecherous party animals of the Middle Ages.

Some of our enduring favourites have had complex pasts. Before a 'murmuration' settled upon starlings (inspired by the sound of the birds when flocking together), the collective noun was 'mutation', thanks to the belief that the bird shed a leg at the age of ten and then promptly grew a new one. An 'unkindness of ravens' arose from the belief that these huge, dark carrion birds were omens of doom.

Some from the past deserve to be brought back: such as a 'drunkship of cobblers', born in a time when ale was safer to drink than water. And then there are those that are surely due a revival: today's postal workers would enjoy 'a diligence of messengers', while pub landlords and landladies might happily join a 'laughter of hostelers'.

Today, there is no official list of collective nouns, and the search for new ones goes on. Modern choices, submitted whenever the topic trends (and it does, often), include a 'foothurt of Lego', a 'pedant of Oxford commas', a 'blur of opticians', and a 'wunch of bankers'. The search for the name for a group of politicians goes on.

22 September

REMORSE

On this day in 1988, the Canadian government apologised for the internment of Japanese-Canadians during the Second World War. Over 90 per cent of the total Japanese-Canadian population in British Columbia was interned 'for the sake of national security' and in retaliation for the attacks on Pearl Harbor. The majority of those who lost their jobs or were forced to repatriate to Japan were Canadians by birth.

The term 'remorse' has biting regret at its heart. It comes from the Latin *mordere*, to bite, and refers to the gnawing distress arising from a profound sense of guilt.

English is equally grisly when it comes to other emotions, including 'sarcasm'. This is from the Greek *sarkazein*, to 'tear flesh', and refers to the caustic nature of a sarcastic remark, which might metaphorically rip through the skin of its recipient. The word is a sibling of 'sarcophagus', the stone coffins whose name translates as 'flesh-eating', thanks to the properties of the limestone once used, which was designed to rapidly decompose the body lying within it.

23 September

BOYCOTT

On this day in 1880, Captain Charles Cunningham Boycott wrote a letter to *The Times* in order to exemplify what he saw as the disproportionate power of the Irish National Land League, a political organisation of the late-nineteenth century which sought to help poor tenant farmers by abolishing landlordism:

The locks on my gates are smashed, the gates thrown open, the walls thrown down, and the stock driven out on the roads. I can get no workmen to do anything, and my ruin is openly avowed as the object of the Land League unless I throw up everything and leave the country. I say nothing about the danger to my own life, which is apparent to anybody who knows the country.

Boycott was an Englishman working at Lough Mask House, near Ballinrobe in County Mayo, serving as an agent for an absentee English landlord, Lord Erne. During this period, the Land League were campaigning for a major reform of the system of landholdings, and encouraged the tenants of Lord Erne to demand a 25 per cent reduction in their rents. Boycott refused and subsequently became the target of mob rule.

The president of the Land League, Charles Stewart Parnell, announced that one clear way of forcing Boycott's hand was for all those under his rule to refuse to interact with him. As a consequence, his labourers downed tools, and local shop-keepers refused to serve him and his family. When his crops had to be harvested that autumn, he was helped by fifty volunteers from outside the county, who themselves were put under the protection of almost a thousand soldiers. By the end of the 1880s, there were reports of boycotting from all over Ireland.

Such was the passion and fury that the debate provoked, on both sides of the argument, that Boycott's name became an involuntary eponym for collective ostracism. Other languages borrowed it too: the French have *boycotter*, the Dutch *boycotten*, and German *boykottieren*. Nor is its journey in English over: a recent riff includes 'girlcott', an attempt to focus on the rights or actions of women.

24 September

FALL

There are many who mock the Americans' use of 'fall' for autumn, deriding its simplicity and all-too-obvious nod to the falling of leaves from the trees. In fact, the very same term was common in British English right up until the seventeenth century, where 'fall of the leaf' was the successor to the Old English 'harvest', just as spring, for centuries, was known in full as the 'spring of the leaf'. It seems curious to argue with the poetry of either.

In the days of the first settlers in North America, both autumn and fall were used, and it wasn't until the eighteenth century that each nation decided to claim their own. Autumn is from the French *l'automne*, chosen by the British perhaps because, even long after 1066, French continued to be seen as the language of the rulers, and of prestige and beauty.

25 September

BOONDOGGLE

Today in 1066, Harold Godwinson, the last-crowned Anglo-Saxon King of England, won a decisive battle over a Norwegian force led by King Harald Hardrada at the Battle of Stamford Bridge. His triumph was short-lived: three days later, William the Conqueror landed his invading army in Sussex. Harold was forced to turn his troops around and route-march them southwards to intercept the Norman army. He, together with around 4,000 of his men, died in the battle.

Harold's efforts might, in much later parlance, have been dubbed a 'boondoggle'.

In today's political lexicon, a boondoggle is a wasteful and entirely unnecessary project, whose initiators carry on regardless. The term seems to have begun innocently enough in the Boy Scouts Movement, in which a 'boondoggle' was a hand-made leather bracelet or lanyard. Perhaps the activity wasn't a success for all, as the term shifted to embrace other activities whose participants were simply going through the motions. In today's boondoggles, time and cost overruns are a common denominator – there are consequently plenty of candidates.

More happily, the name was also chosen for a craft beer designed, as its makers describe it, 'to savour and satisfy'. Two verbs which certainly didn't apply to Harold Godwinson, whose success did not last long enough for savouring of any description.

---

26 September

ACCOLADE

In 1580, Francis Drake completed his circumnavigation of the world, sailing into Plymouth aboard the *Golden Hind*. Upon his arrival, Queen Elizabeth I made the captain a knight on his own ship.

Whether the monarch gave Drake a hug is not recorded. But it is entirely possible, for the very first meaning of the word 'accolade' was the bestowal of a knighthood by means of a friendly royal embrace – an early and far cuddlier alternative to the touch of a sword upon the shoulder. At its heart is the Latin *ad*, 'to', and *collum*, meaning 'neck' (hence our word 'collar').

The position of 'knight' was once nothing more than that

held by any boy or youth. The Old English *cniht*, a borrowing from the German *Knecht*, 'boy', and pronounced with a hard 'k', eventually moved to mean a servant and, finally, a servant of the realm and a military man of honourable rank. It remains to this day an accolade of the highest order, even if a royal hug is no longer on the table.

27 September

GRICER

Today is a key anniversary in the history of the railways, marking the date in 1825 when George Stephenson's 'Locomotion No. 1' became the first steam locomotive to carry passengers on a public rail line, the Stockton and Darlington Railway. Such was the pace of innovation in the industry that it was to become obsolete within a decade. Such was the pace on the day (15 mph at its highest speed), that at least one passenger was so unnerved he fell off the wagon.

The first known trainspotter was a fourteen-year-old girl named Fanny Johnson, who kept a notebook of the trains that boomed through London's Westbourne Park in the 1860s. The names she recorded in her journal, such as *Firefly, Eclipse,* and *Morning Star*, reveal the extent to which the steam train romanced the teenage imagination.

Today's trainspotters enjoy a large lexicon that marks out the devoted members of their tribe. The enthusiasts fall into several categories, according to their level of passion and expertise. A 'gunzel', once a mark of derision, is a highly enthusiastic railway fan, particularly one who's so intent on taking a good photo that they become rather reckless: the nickname may be rooted in US slang for a gunslinger.

A 'gricer' is an equally fanatical railway enthusiast. The name may be a humorous representation of an upper-class pronun-ciation of 'grouser', because a railway fan 'bags' trains as a grouser bags birds, but some believe it to be a homage to Richard Grice, a trainspotter who became legendary for having travelled the entire rail network.

'Crank' is the name for an old-style rail fan who shoves people out of the way when boarding a train in order to get the best window position, while a 'basher', contrary to expectation, is a collector of train numbers and mileage statistics. When certain milestone numbers are reached, such as 10,000 miles by one engine, the basher will observe certain rituals, usually involving the swearing of oaths.

As for the rest of us, we range from the 'normals', or 'berts' (the non-enthusiasts), to the 'baglets', i.e. female enthusiasts, once looked upon with considerable disdain.

---

28 September

HELLO

On this day in 1968, the Beatles' 'Hey Jude' made number one in the charts, where it was to remain for nine weeks.

'Hey' is still very much part of the hip lexicon today, and its sounds are unmistakably modern. 'Hello', on the other hand, might now seem so old-fashioned that, if asked, we'd probably date it back to Old English. In fact, its first recorded use is less than two hundred years old, which makes 'hey' very much the winner in the age stakes.

English-speakers have been using similar formulations to greet others since Anglo-Saxon times, and most of them began with the letter 'h'. 'Hey' and 'ho' are first recorded in the thirteenth century, while 'hi' is already there in the 1400s, some four hundred years before 'hello' came on the scene.

A familiar greeting used by Anglo-Saxons was *hal*, meaning 'whole', or 'be healthy', the beginnings of both 'hail' and the 'hale' of hale and hearty. *Was hail* was a wish that the recipient 'be in good health': an expression that became the 'wassail' that we remember in 'Here we come a-wassailing'. But it wasn't until the 1800s that 'hello' emerged, with a whole host of spellings.

Hello's day finally came when the telephone was invented. A conversation opener became essential – how else to let the other caller know you were there? The telephone's creator, Alexander Graham Bell, had a preference for 'ahoy', but it was Thomas Edison, who later adapted the telephone by adding a microphone, who shouted 'hello' into the mouthpiece of his device when he discovered a way of recording sound on this day in 1877. Within a decade, the women who were employed as the first telephone operators had adopted the title of 'hello girls'.

It's an odd thought that we might today be shouting 'ahoy!' into our handsets when answering a call. Odder still that we might have adopted an earlier version of ending one: the no-nonsense formulation 'That is all'.

---

29 September

MALL

Samuel Pepys's diary for 2 April 1661 records a venture 'into St James's Park, where I saw the Duke of York playing at Pelemele, the first time that I ever saw the sport'.

This new sport had in fact been around in Europe for some time, and was known by several other names including 'paille maille' and 'pall mall'. It was broadly similar to croquet although requiring more vigour – illustrations suggest the need for a powerful backswing – so much so that it was considered a prime source of exercise for those involved, including royalty. The game saw players using a mallet to drive a boxwood ball through an iron ring suspended at the end of a long alley, itself also called a 'pall-mall'. The name comes, via French, from the Italian *pallamaglio*, literally 'ball mallet'.

Some thirty years before Pepys's first glimpse of the game, a Frenchman named John Bonnealle had laid out a long alley-like playing surface – Britain's first – for playing pall mall on the south side of St James's Square, London, in an area known then as St James's Field. When Bonnealle died, the court was apparently obliterated by a house built by the king's shoemaker. He was later ordered to demolish the house, and a new pall mall alley was laid out. There was a problem, however: the dust from the coaches travelling along the old highway gusted over the wall, leading commentators of the time to grumble that it was 'Very troublsom to the players at Mall'. As a result, in July 1661, posts and rails were set up 'to barre up the old way', and by September a new road on the site of the old pall mall alley had been railed in and opened to public use. This new road took its name from the sport – Pall Mall – and was officially inaugurated in September of the same year. Many other cities still have long straight roads or promenades which evolved from the alleys in which the game was played: Hamburg's Palmaille, Paris's Rue du Mail, the Avenue du Mail in Geneva, and Utrecht's Maliebaan. It is from precincts such as these that we acquired today's shopping 'mall'. All because of a fairly ancient game of croquet.

---

30 September

ON YOUR TOD

James Forman Todhunter Sloan was an American thorough-bred horse jockey who achieved the unthinkable on this day in 1898, riding five consecutive winners at Newmarket. The pioneer of the sitting position known as the 'monkey crouch', still used by jockeys today, Sloan went on to garner huge prestige, riding for a time for the stables of the Prince of Wales.

In his day 'Tod' Sloan, as he was best known, became a major celebrity, thanks as much to his flamboyant lifestyle as his success on the tracks. His spectacular career came to an abrupt end when he was suspected of betting on races in which he himself was riding, leading to an outright ban on competing in both Britain and America. His money gone, Sloan tried his hand at both the restaurant business and motion pictures, but his name had lost its shine, and he died early from cirrhosis of the liver. Although historians have subsequently exonerated him from the betting charges, Sloan ended up isolated and alone, which is how his name became a byword in cockney rhyming slang – 'on one's tod (Sloan) = alone'.

OCTOBER

INWIT

The International Day for Older Persons, which is marked on 1 October, is a cumbersomely named but well-intentioned celebration of the wisdom that comes with age, voted for by the United Nations General Assembly in 1991 and initiated the following year.

Had it existed seven hundred years ago, it might have been known as International Inwit Day, for a person's inner sense of right and wrong, their wisdom, and their conscience, were collectively known as their 'inwit', in which 'wit' is a synonym for the mind as the seat of consciousness and thought. At this time, the 'wit of man' was less a means of making others laugh, and more an expression of human intellect – a sense preserved today in such phrases as 'at one's wit's end', and 'scared out of my wits'. 'Common wit' was common sense, and 'to wit' meant 'to be sure'. By extension, one's intrinsic nature or 'inward' knowledge was thus the inwit, and a 'clean inwit' was a pure heart. One's 'outwit', on the other hand, was an external or physical sense, linked to the faculty of observation and perception. In all of these, 'wit' is an etymological sibling of 'wise'.

As for someone with no wisdom or knowledge at all – they are, of course, a nitwit.

BROADCASTING

This day in 1925 saw John Logie Baird live-transmit a human face onto a greyscale image for the first time in history. It would be the first real incarnation of a working television set, and his demonstration the following year paved the way for a new medium of broadcasting that dramatically and literally changed the way we see the world.

The word 'broadcasting' came to us not through the airwaves, but from early agriculture. The original sense of the word referred to the act of dispersing seeds by hand, literally 'casting broadly' – it is still used in this sense today – but by the late seventeenth century it had already acquired a figurative sense of anything common or widespread.

Agrarian society gave English many other words we now use metaphorically. An 'aftermath' was an 'after-mowing': a second crop or new growth of grass after the first had been harvested. (This sense of 'math' preceded 'mathematics' by over five hundred years.) A 'foreigner', meanwhile, was an outsider in the literal sense – one who inhabited 'uncivilised' spaces. The word comes from the Latin *foranus*, 'outside', which is also at the heart of 'forest'.

---

3 October

ATONE

At midnight on this day in 1990, East and West Germany were finally reunified, less than a year after the destruction of the Berlin Wall. The day is celebrated as *Tag der Deutschen Einheit*, or Unity Day.

The 'oneness' that is inherent in the German word *Einheit* is hidden in another that might also have resonance on this day – 'atone'. Like 'alone', which was originally 'all one' in Old English before it came together and sent 'lone' and 'lonely' on their way, to 'atone' was to be 'at one' – in other words, to desire reconciliation so as to be in complete accord, or oneness, with someone again.

4 October

THRILL

In 1883, the Express d'Orient, which was later renamed the Orient Express, departed on its first official journey. The train arrived at Vienna, its original terminus, on 4 October. (In 1889, the train's eastern terminus was extended to Varna, Bulgaria, and then, later that year, to Constantinople, now Istanbul.) The train became the symbol of luxury and comfort, and even intrigue, at a time when most rail journeys were rough, ready, and occasionally dangerous. On board that day were royalty, nobles, diplomats, business leaders, and other members of the bourgeoisie. Each of them was no doubt thrilled to be a visible part of its sumptuous ostentation.

The word 'thrill' is more suitable to Hercule Poirot's experience with the Orient Express than today's luxury train passengers. It comes from the Old English *thirl*, a hole, and first described the running of a sharp weapon into a human body, with the effect of perforating it. By the fifteenth century, to thrill was to penetrate an enemy line, before encompassing the action of non-material forces and the piercing of the heart with emotion or with sound.

Those 'thirls' pop up elsewhere, such as in the Old English word 'eye-thirl', which was sadly pushed out by a Viking word for lookout 'holes' in a roof or wall – 'vindauga', or 'eye of the wind', which became our 'window'. As for the holes in the human body – our nostrils were originally 'nose-thirls': the holes beneath our nose that enable us to breathe.

5 October

MAUSOLEUM

The body of Vladimir Lenin, founder of Leninist political ideology and of the eventual Soviet Union, and for whom St Petersburg was renamed Leningrad, had its last guard of honour on this day in 1993. Seventy-one years earlier, his corpse had been embalmed and put on display in a mausoleum in Red Square, watched over by a guard of honour known by the people of Moscow as the 'Sentry No. 1'. The post was disbanded after the events of the constitutional crisis, when President Boris Yeltsin was at odds with the Russian Parliament – in 1997, it was reinstated at the Tomb of the Unknown Soldier on another side of the Kremlin. Lenin meanwhile was taken to the graveyard of the Novodevichii Convent in Moscow, the very place that Yeltsin himself would later be buried.

The term 'mausoleum' takes its name from a Persian king, dating as far back as the fourth century BC and an ancient kingdom in Asia Minor named Caria. King Mausolos was not a remarkable leader, but events did not demand that he should be. He was, however, adored by his wife (and sister) Artemisia who, upon his death, was said to be so inconsolable that she added a portion of his ashes to her daily drink. But before her death she had gathered the best sculptors in the land, and had them construct at Halicarnassus a tomb in memory of her husband. The sculptors took their inspiration from the Nereid Monument of Xanthos, which was a city in ancient Lycia, Turkey. The building was up to 40 metres (131 feet) in height and was extravagantly decorated with a large amount of sculptures, carved both in the round and in relief. Such was its beauty that it was long regarded as one of the Seven Wonders of the Ancient World. When ruins of the building were excavated in 1857, it was found to be cased with glorious marble, and to have included a statue of Mausolos himself, housed today in the British Museum. The pyramid roof was crowned by an enormous marble four-horse chariot.

The edifice was still standing at the time of the Crusades, but was mostly destroyed by the knights of St John of Jerusalem, who occupied Halicarnassus in 1402 and who desired the marble and other materials for their own castle. Nevertheless, one legacy survives intact from the great love between Mausolos and Artemisia: the word 'mausoleum', now used for many monumental tombs, including that of Lenin.

6 October

SILVER SCREEN

On 6 October 1927 audiences flocked to view *The Jazz Singer* on the silver screen. Billed as the first feature-length movie to include lip-synchronised speech (and singing), it caused a huge sensation and drew to a close the era of silent movies.

The term 'silver screen' derives directly from the earliest cinema screens, which were coated in silver paint. The added reflectivity enhanced the picture quality of the primitive monochrome projectors, and gradually the term 'silver screen' became a metonym for cinema in general. Today, such metallic screens are making a comeback thanks to their use in projecting 3-D films.

The Jazz Singer could be aptly described as an early 'block-buster'. The use of this term dates back to the 1940s, when it referred to a type of high capacity aerial bomb that was said to contain enough destructive capacity to destroy an entire building or street. The notion of a hugely explosive impact delivered by a film was first used to promote the 1943 movie

Bombardier, described, with as many exclamation marks as the copywriter could muster, as 'The block-buster of all action-thrill-service shows!!!' (*see* 'screamer', 16 January).

---

7 October

HAPLOLOGY

A handsome double-decker steamboat named *Washington* arrived in New Orleans on this day in 1816, after her maiden voyage on the Mississippi.

The name of the great river is one of the biggest challenges of any spelling test. Too many of us have written it as 'Missippi', or with any number of 's's and 'p's shoved in. Linguistics has a term for the accidental omission of a letter or word when it should occur twice in close proximity: 'haplography'. It is a combination of the Greek *haplo*, 'single', and *graphy*, 'writing': you might write 'mispell' for 'misspell', for example, or ask 'Is there anyone I can talk to resolve this issue?' instead of 'Is there anyone I can talk to to resolve this issue?' You might even employ a 'bookeeper' for your accounts.

A close cousin of haplography is 'haplology'. This is what happens when we 'eat' part of a word when saying it: 'secetry', for example, for 'secretary', or 'probly' for 'probably'. We're particularly guilty of this when the full spelling is quite difficult to get out: 'Febry' for 'February' is a classic, or 'libry' for 'library'.

Finally, if you end up putting in *more* letters than you should: that's 'dittography'. As in 'literatature', or 'possessesses'. Or, perhaps fittingly for those on whom all of this grates: 'irritatation'.

8 October

WAG

This day is clearly a good one for comedy. In 1927, the short silent film *The Second Hundred Years* was released, featuring one of the best-loved double acts, Laurel and Hardy. A decade and a half later, on 8 October 1942, the duo Abbott and Costello launched their weekly radio show on Camel Cigarettes, NBC Network. All four stars are acknowledged to be among the best wags in the business.

'Wag' seems a curious epithet for a joker or comedian. In the sixteenth century, the word denoted simply a young lad, particularly one full of mischief. The same idea of a rascal appears in Samuel Johnson's definition of the term in 1755: 'any one ludicrously mischievous; a merry droll'. From here emerged the sense of a habitual joker that we know today. Comedy may be dark, but the etymology of the word is surely even darker: 'wag' is a mocking abbreviation of 'waghalter': one whose behaviour makes them fit for nothing but the gallows, in whose halter they would ultimately swing.

These wags of course have nothing to do with the beloved WAGS of the tabloids, namely the Wives And Girlfriends of football players, even if the comedy headlines might make you think otherwise.

9 October

FRANK

On this day in 768 Charlemagne was crowned King of the Franks, a Germanic tribe that occupied what is now present-day Belgium, France, Luxembourg, the Netherlands, and western Germany. It was Charlemagne's mission to unite all Germanic peoples into one kingdom, and convert his subjects to Christianity, albeit primarily through warfare. On his death in 814, Charlemagne's empire encompassed much of western Europe, hence his reputation today as the father of Europe.

Centuries before Charlemagne rose to power, the Franks had conquered Gaul, and were to give their name to modern France, as well as the country's old currency. The Franks themselves were named after their preferred weapon, the throwing spear, known as a *franca*. After the conquest, full political freedom was granted only to ethnic Franks or to those among the conquered they invited to come under their protection. Consequently, *franc* came to be used as an adjective meaning not only 'free', but also 'superior', thanks to the rank of the victors compared to their slaves. 'Franc' kept this sense when English took it over in the fourteenth century and changed the 'c' to a 'k'.

In both French and English, 'franc/frank' took on extended meanings of liberal values and generosity, and with them the concomitant virtue of honesty: we still speak of talking 'frankly' today. But a trace of sovereignty can still be detected in such words as 'frankincense', from the Old French *franc encens*, 'superior incense'.

---

10 October

TUX

In the latter years of the nineteenth century, the then Prince of Wales, Edward VII, was fitted with a rather special garment. Savile Row tailors Henry Poole & Co. had produced a bespoke ensemble for him that gave a touch of casualness to the traditional tailcoat, and a touch of class to a standard lounge suit. By the early years of the twentieth century, the 'dinner jacket' had become one of the hottest ticket items in tailoring, and was taken to the United States by admirers of the prince who coveted the same look of suave sophistication.

On 10 October 1886, the first such jacket was worn to an autumn ball under the name of 'tuxedo'. The ball was held at Tuxedo Park, New York, a place whose native Algonquian name is thought to mean 'meeting place of the wolves'.

11 October

NAIL ONE'S COLOURS TO THE MAST

One of the most significant actions of the French Revolutionary Wars took place on 11 October 1797. The Battle of Camperdown saw British and Dutch forces at loggerheads, and ended in a decisive victory for the British thanks to their strategic cunning and superior firepower. The defeat was to linger long in the minds of the Dutch for years afterwards. The British had definitely 'nailed their colours to the mast'.

The colours in this idiom, which is thought to have emerged in the direct aftermath of Camperdown, refer to nautical battle colours. If all of a ship's masts were broken as a result of gunnery by the enemy, the captain had little alternative but to surrender. If, however, the captain decided to fight on, this was marked by hoisting his ship's battle colours on the remnants of the ship's rigging.

This was the case on board the *Venerable*, the flagship of the British commander during the historic encounter, Admiral Adam Duncan. At the start of the battle, the *Venerable*'s main mast was struck and its blue standard brought down. Determined that this should not be interpreted as a sign of surrender, one of the ship's sailors, Jack Crawford, shinned up what remained of the perilous mast and nailed the standard back so that the rest of the British fleet could see it and understand the signal to fight on. The brave act was to prove crucial in the battle.

On returning to his native Sunderland, Jack Crawford was hailed a hero, and became the darling of the people, celebrated in engravings and pamphlets across the country and culminating in an accolade from the king. His actions ensured that the British navy had the enduring reputation of being resilient and formidable.

12 October

UNASINOUS

In 1773, America's first 'lunatic asylum', as it was known at the time, opened in Williamsburg, Virginia, reflecting the belief that institutionalisation was the best solution for treating those considered to be 'mad', a word whose ultimate root lies in an ancient word meaning 'changed'. At this time, modern psychiatric treatments were in their infancy, but the setting up of establishments such as the Public Hospital of Williamsburg marked the beginning of a more humane attitude towards mental illness. Previously, those considered insane were frequently destitute and taken in by prisons or workhouses, whose sole remit was to keep their inmates away from society. The recognition that patients could be helped as well as harnessed was a significant step in asylum reform. Nonetheless, the 'madman' remained an ambiguous figure for some time.

Like those described as mad, real-life and theatrical 'fools' stood apart from the Renaissance social order. Royal and aristocratic households often employed fools or 'naturals' for recreation – those considered to have a mental deficiency and inability to comprehend social demands, and who could consequently be freely laughed at. Other fools, such as those populating Shakespeare's plays, were professional entertainers whose madness was a guise for wisdom and an uncensored channel for the unpalatable truth.

Synonyms for a much-weakened sense of 'fool' in the *Oxford English Dictionary* number over a hundred. They include 'saddle-goose' and 'buffard' from the 1400s, 'little Witham' from the 1500s (apparently after a village whose inhabitants were well known for their stupidity), 'niddicock', 'noddypeak', and 'dizzard' from the 1600s, leading up to today's 'nincompoops', 'wallies', and 'plonkers'. In all but a few, the true sense of 'madness' has been lost, replaced by the accusation of stupidity.

If collectively such fools came together and acted in extreme combined idiocy, they could be described as 'unasinous', a word with only a single quotation in the *OED*, from 1656. It means 'united in stupidity', and comes from the Latin *unus*, 'one', and *asinus* 'ass'.

13 October

BLACK MARIA

On 13 October 1832, an American thoroughbred filly named Black Maria won the arduous Union Course race at what is now Woodhaven, New York City, gaining a spectacular pot of money for the Jockey Club. She was to win so many races that her total winnings exceeded $15,000, an extraordinary sum for the times. The name of the beautiful mare, who knocked spots off so many male rivals, became lodged firmly in the public mind.

In the same decade, black police vans used in United States for the transportation of prisoners were dubbed 'Black Marias'. A connection with the beloved racehorse seems likely, but there is another contender to the origin, featuring Maria Lee, an African American proprietress of a sailors' lodging house in Boston, Massachusetts. Lee was said to be so tall and strong that the police frequently asked for her assistance in apprehending and detaining criminals at large. Her own notoriety might well have inspired the affectionate nickname for the police vans among the city's officers, though most etymologists give the plucky filly the edge.

In the First World War, Black Maria lived again, this time as a nickname for a heavy German shell filled with TNT that emitted volumes of dense black smoke upon exploding. Such monikers were not uncommon in the black humour of the trenches, which also christened Silent Susan and Big Bertha – more lethal weapons of war.

14 October

RATIOCINATOR

On this day in 1892, a collection of twelve stories by Arthur Conan Doyle was published, having previously appeared in twelve monthly issues of *The Strand Magazine*. Sherlock Holmes and his amanuensis Dr Watson appear in every one.

Conan Doyle's Holmes is the ultimate logician, a detective whose powers of deductive and inductive reasoning (the one top-down, beginning with an accepted premise; the other extrapolating from what is observed) border on the fantastical, while also foreshadowing future developments in forensic science. He is, in short, the embodiment of 'ratiocination', a rare word derived from Latin that means the capacity to reason with logic and precision.

Few ratiocinators compel as much as Holmes, even now, with the exception perhaps of *Star Trek*'s Mr Spock. As the great man tells his ever-accepting companion: 'I am a brain, Watson. The rest of me is a mere appendix.'

---

15 October

GORMFUL

P. G. Wodehouse was born on this day in 1881, a man who went on to inspire laughter and deep affection for his literary creation of Bertie Wooster. He was also single-handedly responsible for giving the world the possibility of being 'gruntled': 'He spoke with a certain what-is-it in his voice, and I could see that, if not actually disgruntled, he was far from being gruntled' (*The Code of the Woosters*, 1938).

'Gruntled' is just one of many positive states of mind and body that were abandoned long ago. When it comes to many English adjectives, the glass seems to be decidedly half full. The language contains a large number of terms that, at some point in their past, have lost their mojo and now travel on alone. These are the 'unkempts', 'uncouths', 'underwhelmeds', and 'nonplusseds' – terms that linger on the bad, sad, seamy side of life. Those that can never quite be gruntled without being dissed as well.

As it turns out, many of the happier siblings of words like these were once alive and well. 'Kempt' is from the German for 'combed', and is a useful byword for being neat and tidy. To be 'couth', back in the fourth century, was to be affable and agreeable; you can still be 'couthie' in Scotland. (Being couth has always been critical to dating success, apparently – as Chaucer liked to warn: 'uncouth, unkissed'.) Any 'ruly' person, meanwhile, was pretty good at sticking to the rules. And so it goes on: our ancestors had the chance to be 'pecunious' (rich), 'toward' (obliging and hopeful), 'ruth' (full of compassion), and 'wieldy' (handy with a weapon). You may also be 'mayed' (possessing power), 'ept', 'flappable', 'peccable', 'bridled', and 'descript'. (But *never* 'promptu', 'petuous', 'shevelled', 'chalant', or a 'nomer'.) The category is so full that today's survivors have been given their own linguistic moniker: 'orphaned negatives'.

And so to 'gorm', which today only ever appears with 'less' in its wake. To *gaum*, for the Vikings, was to take heed; to be 'gaum-like' was to have an intelligent look about you. Gaum became gorm, and all positivity slipped away.

16 October

FAN-BLOODY-TASTIC

The play *Pygmalion* premiered on 16 October 1913, at the Hofburg Theatre in Vienna, having been translated into German by Shaw's literary agent, Siegfried Trebitsch. Shaw's chosen actress for the British production, Mrs Patrick Campbell, had suffered a mild nervous breakdown, thereby delaying London performances for several months.

The play's infamous line 'Walk? Not bloody likely!' – a perceived profanity that was to provoke both horror and adoration in its British audiences – was translated into German as the far-milder '*Dreck! Bish!*' When Mrs Patrick Campbell dared to say the English line on stage, according to a review in the *Daily Telegraph*, she 'brought the house down'. Today, it seems almost quaint: in the *Harry Potter* stories, 'bloody hell' is used with regularity among the children of Hogwarts. In Australia, 'bloody' is used as such a regular filler in conversation that its past is surely long forgotten.

That past is murky, but not with the smear of a taboo. Numerous theories have been put forward to account for its transfer from a simple descriptive adjective (as in Byron's 'But here, where Murder breathed her bloody steam'), to an expletive causing uproar. Some point to oaths referring to the blood of Christ, the drinking habits of priests, the Catholic doctrine of transubstantiation, a mangling of the phrase 'By our lady', and the pursuit of heretics by a Bishop of London called 'Bloody Bonner' (drunk, the story goes, only on the smell of fresh blood).

The reality may lie elsewhere, with the aristocratic rowdies or 'bloods' of the late seventeenth and early eighteenth centuries, whose behaviour was so objectionable and arrogant that the public were all too aware of them. To be 'bloody drunk' was to be as drunk as a blood – in other words 'very drunk indeed'.

Perhaps bloody's favourite modern outings are as an infix, whereby it is sandwiched between parts of another word. 'Fan-bloody-tastic', for example, is a popular companion to 'abso-fucking-lutely', both the result of a linguistic process that is also known as 'tmesis', from the Greek meaning to 'cut'.

---

17 October

CUDDLEMEBUFF

A beer flood for most of us sounds anything but tragic. But for eight people living in a London slum known as the St Giles Rookery on this day in 1814 it was to prove devastating. At Meux & Co.'s Horse Shoe Brewery, a 6.7-metre wooden vat housing fermenting porter burst dramatically, releasing up to a million litres of alcohol and destroying both the building itself and many of the dwellings at the Rookery. The brewery, which was to continue making beer until the 1960s, moved away, and its premises were eventually taken over by the Dominion Theatre.

Before London built proper sanitation, beer and ale were considered far safer to drink than water. Even children would drink watered-down alcohol, known as 'small beer'.

Hardly surprising then that the dictionary has hundreds of slang terms for the drink. One of the best has to be 'cuddlemebuff', a general term for 'intoxicating liquor' of any description, but one that conjures up cosy images of a pint of the best, supped by the hearth or at the local kiddly-wink (aka an alehouse, in nineteenth-century parlance).

---

18 October

RIVAL

'Call me Ishmael' is one of the most famous opening lines from literature in the modern age. It comes from *Moby-Dick*, published as *The Whale* on this day in 1851.

The name of Melville's creation was apparently suggested by an article published in the New York *Knickerbocker Magazine* a decade earlier. Entitled *Mocha Dick: or The White Whale of the Pacific*, it recounted the capture of a giant white sperm whale that had been terrorising whalers and their ships. The whale had been frequently sighted in the vicinity of the island of Mocha, hence its name, while 'Dick' was simply a generic name similar to others mentioned by Melville, such as Jack and Tom. Melville's choice of 'Moby' was clearly not dissimilar to the name of the actual albino whale that loomed large in the minds of the fearful sailors.

Moby was, of course, the great rival of the captain, Ahab, on board the whaling ship *Pequod* (whose crew includes the chief mate Starbuck, a name that would become a leviathan in its own right). The word 'rival' has equally watery beginnings. It is a sibling of 'river', and once denoted someone who competed for water from the same source as another, and hence was in pursuit of the same thing. It is part of a family to which 'derive' also belongs – originally a verb meaning to conduct water from a reservoir or stream into another place.

19 October

ABUSES AND ABSURDITIES

Jonathan Swift died on this day in 1745. The author of
Gulliver's Travels brought several words into the lexicon,
including 'Brobdingnagian', a byword for 'enormous', thanks to
his fictional land Brobdingnag, which was occupied by giants.
The *Oxford English Dictionary* credits Swift with over a hundred
more neologisms, including 'bantering', 'big-endian' (and 'little-
endian'), 'dupe', 'screamer', and of course 'Liliputian'.

Swift wasn't just concerned with words, though. He was
writing at a time when many fellow educators were lamenting
a decline in good grammar. His *Proposal for the English Tongue*
turned up the volume of that criticism considerably. The
'proposal' in question, submitted to the leader of the government of Robert Harley, was for the establishment of an academy
with the power to 'fix language forever'.

Swift complained to Harley that 'our Language is extremely
imperfect; that its daily improvements are by no means in
proportion to its daily Corruptions'. Among his damning
observations of the 'Abuses and Absurdities' of English is that
'Most of the Books we see now a-days, are full of those
Manglings and Abbreviations'. Loanwords were also roundly
condemned. As far as Swift was concerned, 'Proper Words in
proper Places, makes the true Definition of a Style'. Ironically,
given his dread of foreign imports, the large amount of capitalisation he used was probably brought over by printers from
the continent, who would be familiar with the capitalisation
of nouns in German.

No such academy was ever created, and English remains a
democracy in which the only perceived arbiters are dictionaries. But the desire for linguistic government has never gone
away, and the transformations in communication we have
witnessed this century have created a parallel fear that English

is descending into a chaotic cesspit, intensifying the need for black and white rules.

In many cases, those rules to which we aspire are the very same as those clamoured for by Swift. Who knows what the writer would have thought about the harnessing of 'little-endian' and 'big-endian' – and indeed 'endianness' – by modern technology, in which they refer to the sequences of bytes stored in a computer's memory.

20 October

DOUBLET

Elvis Presley's *Jailhouse Rock* opened on this day in Memphis, Tennessee, in 1957. The movie involves a young man sentenced to prison for manslaughter, who is then mentored by his cellmate to develop his musical talents.

English has two spellings of 'jail', both of which come from French. *Gaol* was a borrowing from Northern or Norman French, while *jail* is from Central or Parisian French. This type of double borrowing is not uncommon – 'warranty' and 'guarantee' both come from French, but entered English via different routes and at different times, as did 'guardian' and 'warden', 'pâté' and 'paste', 'fete and 'feast', and 'chattel' and 'cattle' (cattle were once so central to livelihoods that they became a token of all property, hence 'goods and chattels'). In linguistics, such linked groups are known as 'doublets', even though more than two borrowings are often involved, such as 'clock', 'cloak', and 'cloche', all of which are linked to bells or are bell-shaped.

Other languages also get involved: 'Slav' and 'slave' are from the same root, reflecting the historical subordination of many Slavic nations, while the odd line-up of 'charity', 'cherish', 'cheer', and 'whore' are all ultimately from an ancient Proto-Indo-European language meaning 'dear' or 'loved'.

21 October

SHOTCLOG

At some point in our lives, most of us will have endured the pub bore – he or she who tells the same stories, at length, to the same crowd they regaled the week before. The pub is unique in British culture in that it is almost beyond linguistic law – it offers a kind of conversational lockdown in which complete strangers can strike up an extended conversation. It is also home to a number of characters who are replicated in drinking establishments up and down the land.

Chief among these is the 'shotclog', Elizabethan slang for the companion in the tavern who is only tolerated because they are buying the next round. They go well alongside the 'snecklifter', the money-pincher who quietly lifts the 'sneck', or latch, of the pub door to see if they know anyone who might stand them a drink. And, if they are lucky, they might just chance upon the local tosspot (*see* 28 August).

22 October

CORONACOASTER

Like other major events of the past, Covid-19 has spawned a lexicon all of its own. Much of it was trailed by previous events – self-isolation has been promoted for a century or more in the face of such dangers as the flu and leprosy. Our modern sense of quarantine began in the fourteenth century, when sea trade between Europe – in particular Italy – and countries of the Far East was increasing. In 1348, at the peak of the Black Death, the authorities of the port of Venice imposed a period of isolation upon the crews of arriving ships, establishing a station on an island in the lagoon.

The minimum number of days required was forty, and the period was known in Venetian dialect as *quarantena*, from *quaranta*, 'forty'.

But there have been many new additions to the dictionary that have been fuelled by the pandemic. WFH (working from home) is now in Oxford Dictionaries, as is 'hot zone', 'flatten the curve', 'PPE', and 'contact tracing'.

Other neologisms relating to the virus and its consequences are lighter-hearted, a counterpoint to our sombre mood. One of the first to emerge was 'covidiot' – someone who wilfully flouts the rules of social distancing. A 'quarantini', meanwhile, is an experimental cocktail made from ingredients found at the back of the cupboard, and 'Covid 15' is the fifteen pounds gained from nervously eating our way through the fridge. 'Doughverkill' is the new way of describing the surfeit of pictures posted on social media of home-baked sourdough, while 'dinfluencer' is someone who similarly photographs every supper created from the remnants of their lockdown larder.

The writer Michael Hogan has noted some new ones on the list. 'Bored-eaux' is the wine drunk when there's nothing better to do, while a 'claphazard' is someone so caught up in the enthusiastic and deserved applause for our key workers that they ignore every distancing guideline (thus giving an entirely new meaning to 'space invader'). Finally, a 'co-runner virus' is the spread of the infection by heavily panting runners who leave hundreds of droplets in their wake.

It's hard to say whether any will last the course, but as we ride the coronacoaster, the certainty is that there will be more to come.

23 October

MOLE

International Mole Day, celebrated annually on 23 October, has nothing at all to do with the furry subterranean creatures that take their name from a Germanic word meaning 'lizard'. This mole refers instead to one of the seven SI (*Système international*) base units, the others being seconds, metres, kilograms, amperes, kelvins, and lastly candelas for luminosity. 'Mole' is the base unit for substance. Sometimes referred to as the Avogadro number, it is defined as precisely 6.02×10^{23} and allows us to calculate the number of elementary particles (usually atoms, ions, or molecules) in a certain mass of a given sample.

At 06:02 a.m. on 23 October, the time and date could (in America at least) be written as 6:02 10/23, bringing a very specific and specialised joy to physicists around the world.

24 October

NORMAL

The definition of 'normal' was severely challenged in 2020. In the autumn of 1929, things were anything but normal, as panic gripped the Wall Street stock market on a day that would be known thereafter as 'Black Thursday'. Ironically, the number of times the market has been thrown into turmoil since that bleak day have almost made the dramatic slumps the new normal, with at least twelve crashes, including that of 2020 in the face of the Covid-19 pandemic. On Black Thursday, those walking in confusion around the streets of New York's financial district witnessed such strange scenes as a luxury motor car bearing a placard '$100 WILL BUY THIS CAR MUST HAVE CASH LOST ALL ON THE STOCK MARKET'.

The word 'normal' has, fittingly, meant many things over the years. It came to English in the seventeenth century from the Latin word *normalis*, meaning 'at a right angle'; it is based on the Romans' use of *norma* for a carpenter's square, which consists of two straight arms at right angles. In a 1658 dictionary called *The New World of English Words*, 'normal' is defined as 'done exactly, according to the rule, or square'. It is from here that we get the idea of a 'norm' or standard set of affairs, as well as the modern sense of 'normal' to mean conforming to a regular pattern.

From this same trail came 'enormous', from *e*, 'out of', and *norma*, 'standard', used originally for something undesirably unusual before settling on size, as 'abnormal' took on its negative side.

As for 'normal' itself, the word has continued to change and grow, matching the fluidity of our situations. As we have been learning throughout history, the question 'What is normal?' is never as simple as it sounds.

25 October

BALACLAVA

On this day in 1854, at the height of the Crimean War, the Battle of Balaclava took place, named after a small fishing village close to a British supply base. The event was memorialised in verse soon after by Tennyson in 'The Charge of the Light Brigade'.

During the conflict, knitted caps covering the head and neck, with holes for the eyes, nose and mouth, were sent to British soldiers to protect them against the bitter cold. They were given the name 'balaclava' thanks to the village near the camp where they were first worn.

Clothing for cold weather has a varied lexicon with origins right across the globe. The parka was originally a long hooded jacket made of skins and worn by the people of the Arctic. It is one of very few words to have passed into English from Nenets, a language of the Arctic peoples from the Ural mountain range in Russia.

'Anorak' is a Greenland Inuit word, and in its early days, in the 1930s, was a colourful, beaded item worn by Greenland brides. By the 1950s it had become such a hot fashion item that it was featured in the pages of *Vogue* magazine. The transfer of the word to the people who wore it seems to have begun in 1984, when the *Observer* newspaper used it as a metonym for Dutch pirate radio fans.

Closer to home, when Britons were encouraged by the then PM David Cameron to 'hug a hoodie', he probably wasn't thinking of the hooded crow, which is the first hoodie recorded, in the late 1700s. Like anorak, the term has come to describe the people inside the clothing rather than the clothes themselves, this time disaffected youths whose hooded sweatshirts saw them controversially banned from many public places.

---

26 October

HENGE

In 1918, Cecil Chubb donated what was to be one of Britain's most treasured, and mysterious, monuments to the nation. He had bought it three years earlier for £6,600 – as a present to his wife, some say, while others believe he wanted to ensure it stayed in British hands. Chubb was made a baronet by a grateful government, an event which the barrister marked by having a coat of arms designed bearing the legend '*Saxis Condita*': 'Founded upon the Stones'.

Stonehenge exerts a powerful force in the imagination to this day, not least because its origins and purpose remain elusive. Lord Byron's poem *Don Juan* presents the same head scratching: 'The Druid's groves are gone – so much the better: / Stonehenge is not – but what the devil is it?'

Even the name of the monument is the subject of debate. It is first recorded in a glossary from the tenth century, in which 'henge-cliff' is given the meaning 'summit', and 'henge' is related to 'hang'. Consequently 'Stanheng', as it was known at the time, might be translated as the stones 'hanging in the air'. Half a millennium later, William Stukeley, who pioneered the early investigation of Stonehenge and nearby Avebury, concurred: 'Pendulous rocks are now called henges in Yorkshire . . . I doubt not, Stonehenge in Saxon signifies the hanging stones.'

Another theory extends the sense of 'hanging' to infer the shape of a gallows, based on Stonehenge's two uprights with a lintel stretched across them – a far darker interpretation of the Druids' use of the mystifying formation.

27 October

TICKER TAPE

The Statue of Liberty was dedicated by President Grover Cleveland to the American public this week in 1886; an event that was followed by the first recorded ticker-tape parade, celebrated by thousands who gathered in New York City.

The term 'ticker tape' first referred to the paper output from telegraphic messages recorded in a tape-machine, and to devices used in the financial sector to relay stock-market quotes. The machines would produce a *tick-tick-tick* sound as they worked. The traditional parade route for events such as those in 1886 ran through lower Broadway and on through the Financial District, and was dubbed the 'Canyon of Heroes'.

Ultimately the tape was replaced by confetti, Italian for 'something prepared' – originally sweets (the word is a sibling of both 'comfit' and 'confectionery'). It was customary during Italian carnivals to throw little sweets at those being fêted, before the sugary treats were replaced with tiny plaster balls, which would explode in a cloud of white dust as they landed. By the end of the nineteenth century, today's tradition of small paper petals was fully established.

28 October

JERUSALEM ARTICHOKE

'Tis the season for artichokes, and if you have ever wondered what the exotic vegetable has to do with the Holy City of Jerusalem, you are not alone. The answer is absolutely nothing – the term is a classic example of what is known as an 'eggcorn', with a bit of folk etymology mixed in.

An eggcorn is a slip of the ear that somehow makes perfect sense, and which may become so widespread that it replaces the standard term. The name for the phenomenon was the creation of the US linguist Geoffrey Pullum in response to an article by his colleague Mark Liberman, who had recounted the case of a woman who grew up thinking 'acorns' were 'eggcorns' – an understandable substitution given the closeness of sounds in US English, and the fact that acorns do resemble tiny eggs in eggcups.

In the past decade or more, Oxford's vast dictionary data-bases have picked up examples of 'lack toast intolerance', of chickens coming home to 'roast', of a child being a 'pre-Madonna', the act of nipping something 'in the butt', and of people following a new fad 'like lemmings to the slaughter'.

The Jerusalem artichoke is much older, and belongs in the category of stories that we spin in order to avoid a hellish foreign pronunciation. The word began with the Italian *girasola* and French *girasole*, both of which mean 'turn towards the sun' and describe the artichoke plant's heliotropic properties. The impossibility of this on the English-speaking tongue made us turn to the only thing '*girasole*' sounded remotely akin to – and Jerusalem suddenly became not just its name, but also its fictional origin.

---

29 October

SMELLFEAST

René Goscinny's cartoon *Astérix* was first published in the magazine *Pilote* on this day in 1959, with now iconic illustrations by Albert Uderzo. Asterix is the indomitable hero of a village of Gauls who comically but powerfully resist Roman occupation. Goscinny, a Jew, is thought to have modelled much of this theme on the German occupation of France, which had seen many members of his family slaughtered.

Asterix's sidekick is the barrel-stomached Obelix. Like 'Wimpy' in *Popeye*, his appetite is infinite. He is what those in the sixteenth century would have termed a 'smellfeast', defined in the *Oxford English Dictionary* as 'one who scents out where feasting is to be had'. It is a useful term for any friend who magically appears whenever good smells emanate from the kitchen.

The equivalent, from the same century, for those friends who turn up whenever they smell a fine wine or pint of beer is a 'lickspigot'. Clearly some human characteristics never change.

---

30 October

UGSOME

The language that eventually became English arrived in the fifth century on board the ships of Germanic warrior tribes. The Anglo-Saxon historian Bede later documented the 'groans of the Britons' who suffered at the hands of these barbarians.

But the image of an invading fury is one more usually associated with invaders from other shores some two centuries later, whose very name meant 'pirate' or 'freebooter'. With the arrival of the Vikings (ultimately from *wic*, 'camp'), England and its language were once more under siege. The defining characteristic of the words we inherited from the plunderers–cum–settlers is their directness: you can almost smell their history. From 'ransack' and 'slaughter' to 'freckle' and 'egg', 'blunder' and 'heathen' to 'happy' and 'Yule', the words inherited from Old Norse are as pithy as they have proved enduring.

Among the word-hoard brought over by the Norsemen was 'ugsome': a lesser-known but equally useful expression that, curiously, failed the test of time. For them, 'ug' represented everything repulsive to the eye and the senses. To 'ug' was to be filled with an unparalleled sense of fear and dread. Something ugsome, it followed, was, as the *Oxford English Dictionary* defines it, 'horrible, horrid, loathsome' – what the less punchy classical scribes translated as *abhominabilis*. It survives, of course, in our word 'ugly' – once an adjective with a sting not unlike the one delivered by the Vikings themselves.

31 October

FASCINATE

All Hallows' Eve, the Eve of All Saints, is thought to be the Christianised successor of a festival that marked the last night of the year in the old Celtic calendar. Celebrants of Samhain believed that this was the time when the barriers between the physical and spiritual world broke down. Today's Halloween is little different: it's a time when folklore and superstition come together to provide both menace and thrills, as well as painted cheeks puffed with chocolate.

Belief in devilry and the supernatural once inspired all kinds of spells and incantations designed to counter the threat of evil. Many were contained in the 'grimoire', a magician's book of sorcery and magic used for calling up spirits (*see* 'grammar', 13 January). Its spells might seek to protect against the evil eye of those who, with just a look, were thought to possess the power to bring misfortune, illness, or death.

For the superstitious Romans, a practitioner of such magic was known as a 'fascinator', one capable of causing, according to later historians, 'impairment of function, especially the sexual function . . . headache, hiccoughs, and yawnings'. As fascinators weren't obvious to the eye, the custom arose of wearing an amulet or *fascinum* to ward off evil – even cattle bore similar talismans around their necks. Such amulets were usually phallus-shaped, because the virility implied by an erect penis was believed to divert the gaze of the eye. When 'fascinate' first arrived in English in the early 1600s, it meant to cast the evil eye upon someone – to bewitch them so entirely that they fell completely under an evil spell. Not every use was malevolent, however: as late as the 1600s, a Medical Dispensatory spoke of the promise to 'fascinate and cure stinking breaths'.

As for the incantations used to mitigate any wrongdoings

from ghosts and goblins on this of all nights, they were once known as 'nightspells' – special words to protect you at night. The idea of 'telling' such magic gave us the non-spooky but potentially equally scary 'spellings' tested in schools today.

NOVEMBER

HEART

This month takes its name from the Latin *novem*, ninth, on account of its original place in the ancient Roman calendar. For the Anglo-Saxons, it was called *Blotmonað*, Blood Month, as this was the month where surplus livestock would be slaughtered in preparation for the winter season, or sacrificed and consecrated to the gods.

In Shakespeare's time, the first day of November was known as 'Hallowmas', the feast of All Saints, a Christian festival during which saints both known and unknown are celebrated. For the Bard himself, Hallowmas 1604 saw an early performance at court of his tragedy, *Othello*.

Othello is an individual posthumously described as 'great of heart'. Iago, in the same play, says he will not 'wear my heart upon my sleeve'. By this time, the heart-shaped symbol of love had already been established; four centuries later, it has become the second most used emoji in electronic communications (just pipped to first place by the 'crying with laughter' face; *see* 21 July).

The modern symbol is quite a pictorial departure from the complex fist-shaped organ we rely on to pump blood around the body. Its origins are slippery, but one theory links it with a now-extinct plant called *silphium*, said to have aphrodisiacal powers. Around the fifth century BC, the heart symbol was used to depict silphium seeds – archaeologists have for example uncovered coins with the heart-shaped seeds embossed upon them. Similarly, the heart shape was used in heraldry to denote the leaves of the water lily.

Years later the Middle Ages would tie the heart symbol to its modern interpretation, although it was to undergo a couple of slight transformations along the way. A fresco by Giotto in Padua's Scrovegni Chapel depicts the personification of Charity holding up a pear-shaped heart to Jesus Christ – this slightly more anatomically correct 'pine cone' shape was almost always depicted upside down. At the beginning of the fifteenth century we begin to see not only its inversion, but also the addition of the cleft, or dent, at the top, as seen in European playing cards of the day.

The use of the symbol as a substitute for the word 'love' was popularised in the late 1970s with the ubiquitous pop-culture T-shirts proudly stating 'I ♥ New York'. The symbol has become so intrinsically linked with love that the verb 'hearting' is now recognised as a modern synonym for loving. Though not for the first time – in *Othello*, once again, Shakespeare went before, as he so often did. Iago speaks about his cause being 'hearted': fixed in his heart, seen as the seat of intelligence as much as emotion (*see* 20 November).

---

2 November

ON A WING AND A PRAYER

This day saw the first and only flight of Howard Hughes's enormous Spruce Goose (aka the Hughes H-4 Hercules), a wooden seaplane that would hold the world record for the largest wingspan of any aircraft for the next seventy years. The plane, which despite its name was constructed almost entirely of birch, was intended to be used during the Second World War for the transportation of troops and equipment across the Atlantic, where Allied shipping was taking a battering from German submarines. In the event, it wasn't completed in time, and was flown only once.

The phrase 'on a wing and a prayer', used of any risky course of action that has but a slim chance of success, had taxied into the wartime zeitgeist around four years earlier in a popular wartime song 'Comin' in on a Wing and a Prayer', where a fighter plane, badly damaged by enemy fire, is coming in to land with only one engine. (You might think 'winging it' evolved from similar aviation challenges. In fact, it refers to an unprepared actor furiously trying to learn their lines in the wings before going on stage.)

Aviation has contributed other, less obvious, idioms to the language. We owe 'pushing the envelope', for example, to aeronautics, where it refers to the flyable portion of the atmosphere enveloping the earth – its boundaries would be pushed when pilots tested the speed of a new aircraft. Today, the expression is used metaphorically for anything that goes beyond commonly accepted boundaries. In which case some might be 'flying by the seat of their pants', a phrase that harks back to the early days of aviation when navigation aids were few and pilots were reliant upon little but their instinct.

3 November

HOMME DE BIGOTE

This week also marks the beginning of Movember, when men the world over try to grow 'lip foliage', 'double hamsters', 'nose bugs', 'old bullet proofs', 'face lace', and 'fanny dusters' in order to raise awareness of men's health issues, such as prostate and testicular cancer.

The first recorded instance of the word 'moustache' in English is from 1585, and comes from a travel journal by Nicolas de Nicolay, who notes during his *Navigations, Peregrinations and Voyages Made into Turkie* that the native people 'suffered no haire to grow, but only the moustaches betwixt the nose and mouth'. Since then, numerous synonyms have emerged for the fashion, including 'umbrage' (1600s), 'mousetail' (1800s), and the more familiar 'tash', 'taz', and 'mo'. On the same list, however, is something a little more strange: 'bigote'.

In eighteenth-century France, an *homme de bigote* was a

334

moustachioed, spirited man, full of verve and bravado. The connection between this and our modern sense of 'bigot' is a mystery – perhaps some religious fanatics were also partial to facial hair. But there is a parallel in English: 'bizarre' may be an adaptation of the Basque word *bizarra*, a beard – for those unused to the sight of a bearded man, such an individual may have seemed both eccentric and strange. Some 'pogono-phobes' (beard-fearers) might well feel the same.

4 November

EXSIBILATE

This was the day in 1963 when John Lennon spoke to the audience at a Royal Variety Performance in London, and delivered lines that are remembered to this day: 'Will the people in the cheaper seats clap your hands? And the rest of you, if you'll just rattle your jewellery.' The applause was loud from all parts of the theatre.

The word 'applause' comes directly from the Latin *plaudere*, to clap. It has an unlikely sibling that lies far beyond the confines of the stage. In the Roman theatre, inferior performers would be jeered off to the sound of slow and insistent hand-clapping. The noise made by the disgruntled audience must have been loud indeed: because *explaudere* (to 'clap away') eventually shifted into English as 'explode', with the meaning of violently ejecting someone and, eventually, ejecting gunpowder from a gun.

Within the curious applause lexicon is another Latin word, 'exsibilate', which loped menacingly into English to mean, specifically, to hiss a poor performer off the stage.

5 November

GUY

Sparks are guaranteed to fly on Bonfire Night – the annual commemoration of a conspiracy against James I that placed thirty-six barrels of gunpowder in a cellar beneath the House of Lords. The plotters were hunted down, and the survivors tortured and executed, among them Guy Fawkes. The fifth of November was duly designated by Parliament a day of national thanksgiving, along with the obligation that any citizen must take an oath of allegiance to the king over the pope. To this day, the Houses of Parliament are still searched by the Yeomen of the Guard, brandishing lanterns, before the state opening.

The events of that day reverberate through more than ceremony and celebration, Catherine wheels and sky-lit chrys-anthemums: there are ripples in language, too. Fairly near the top of any modern list of bugbears is the use of 'you guys' as a sweeping catch-all for any gender. The blame is usually laid at the feet of North America, and yet it is British English that provided the inspiration for 'guy', and its notorious namesake is Guy Fawkes himself.

While it's true that American English was the direct source of expressions such as 'fall guy', 'wise guy' and 'you guys', the conduit was Fawkes. Before it came to be applied to people, 'guy' was used, as it still is today, to describe an effigy of the explosive expert, traditionally burned on a bonfire on 5 November, or carried and 'guyed' around the streets in the hope of securing a few coins.

It seems a curious leap from a grotesquely grinning effigy to a generic name for a man (and, eventually, a woman), but the gradual shift is there to see in such books as *Tom Brown at Oxford* – 'He was such an old guy in his dress' – and, by 1893, in *The Swell's Night Guide*: 'I can't tonight, for I am going to be seduced by a rich old Guy'. By the end of the nineteenth century, 'guys' had become entrenched as a form of address to a group of people, irrespective of gender, and with all painted notoriety forgotten.

---

6 November

AI

Artificial intelligence (AI) gained a hero on this day in 1990, when the inventor Ray Kurzweil published his *The Age of Intelligent Machines.* The award-winning book predicted both the internet and the deeper philosophical questions AI will pose for all of us, when we encounter machines that are potentially more intelligent than we are.

One 'intelligent' aid we are already familiar with is the spellchecker, designed to eliminate typos and, some would say, the need to ever learn spelling properly at all. Most, but not all, are grateful. Typos can be costly. One allegedly committed by NASA in 1962 led to the crash of a probe that was to deliver invaluable data on Venus. A single missing hyphen in NASA's coding is said to have caused the craft to malfunction within minutes of its launch. It was, the sci-fi writer Arthur C. Clarke mooted, 'the most expensive hyphen in history'.

Typos, of course, are usually slips of the finger rather than blips of the brain – no one would assume that one London cafe actually meant to offer a daily 'vaggie special', but polls consistently maintain that 40 per cent of us rely on spell-checkers for accuracy.

English spelling is one of the gnarliest there is. Its quirks and eccentricities make a mastery of its spelling and grammar one of the trickiest educational journeys any of us will ever have to make. Our language is awash, for example, with silent letters, many of which were inserted by a single anonymous hand at some point in its history. We must thank Renaissance scribes for the 'b' in doubt – eager to show off their classical education and to bolster language's Latin inheritance, these scholars discarded the straightforward 'dowt' and looked to bring the word closer to the Romans' *dubitum*. Spelling moved on, but our sounds refused to budge.

All of this history means that we can be utterly forgiven for misspelling such words as 'archaeology' and 'phlegm'. The eccentricity of our language makes us all fallible, with no need for the spin doctors of spelling. According to his aide, Tony Blair was being flamboyantly 'playful' when he produced 'toomorrow' three times in a single document. Trump apparently knew exactly what 'covfefe' meant; it was the rest of us who didn't.

Spellcheckers are our frenemies. On the one hand, complacency creeps in the moment we see a wavy line, lulling us into the sense that our back-up bot will haul us out of the gutter. But then even the most scrupulous of spellers can dig a hole and fall in it. Artificial intelligence has distinct disadvantages – no amount of automated intervention would, for example, pick up the difference between a 'revue' and 'review', nor would it bat an eyelid over a comment below an article on Madonna's latest album, encouraging the public to give 'Madonna and her elk' the recognition they deserve.

Research suggests you have to be pretty good at spelling and grammar if a spellchecker is going to be effective. 'I don't worry about artificial intelligence,' wrote the former CIA spy Robert David Steele, 'I worry about artificial stupidity.'

7 November

COVER-SLUT

Jean-Paul Sartre's controversial play *La Putain Respectueuse* premiered in Paris on this day in 1946. It was later translated into English under the title *The Respectful Prostitute*. Sartre is said to have taken his inspiration from the Scottsboro case in America in 1931 when two white prostitutes accused nine black teenagers of rape on a train travelling through Alabama.

The French term *putain* is an extension of the word *pute*, meaning 'dirty woman'. Terms for sex workers in the English language are just as revealing, not least of a long-standing male bias that has shaped our vocabulary for centuries. Some of the terms we today associate exclusively with women started off as labels for men – the first harlots, 800 years ago, were 'vagabonds, rascals, low fellows'. The word flipped gender in the fifteenth century to describe any similarly 'low' woman of unchaste morals and character – in other words, a 'strumpet'. The latter is a term with elusive origins, although Francis Grose's *Classical Dictionary of the Vulgar Tongue* of 1755 includes the apparently related verb 'to strum', with a curiously double-sided definition: 'TO STRUM: to have carnal knowledge of a woman; also to play badly on the harpsichord'.

Then there is the Old English *huse-wif*, a female who managed her household skilfully and economically. When, as it usually does, promiscuity crept in, 'huse-wif' became 'housewife' and its sluttish alter-ego became the alternative, shortened version of the word, 'hussy'.

'Slut' is a word that has almost been reclaimed as an affectionate term among women towards women. This too seems to have begun as a term for a 'careless man' before it arrived at a 'dirty, slovenly, or untidy woman; a foul slattern' (thus a man writing in 1402). The word didn't settle upon sexual connotations until later, in the sixteenth century. Originally, it was all about imperfection or untidiness: 'slut's pennies' were hard pieces in a loaf of bread from inadequate kneading; a 'slut's corner' was one left uncleaned, and a 'slut-hole' a place or receptacle for rubbish. A 'cover-slut', meanwhile, was something most of us have resorted to at some point. It is defined in the dictionary as a seventeenth-century term for 'something worn to cover sluttishness; an outer garment put on over untidy attire' – in other words, something that hides a stain, hole or other unsightliness in a piece of clothing underneath.

The figurative 'stain' on a slut's reputation went on to become something quite different.

---

8 November

X FACTOR

This was the day in 1895 when a professor of physics at Germany's Würzburg University discovered electromagnetic waves. Working in his laboratory with a cathode-ray tube, Wilhelm Röntgen noticed a fluorescent glow of crystals on a table nearby. The ray, he realised, was being emitted from the tube, with the capability of passing through heavy paper and most other substances. During his investigations of the ability of various materials to stop the rays, Röntgen introduced a small piece of lead while a discharge was occurring. So it was that he witnessed the first radiographic image, a flickering, ghostly picture of his skeleton on the barium platinocyanide screen.

The 8th of November was a Friday, and Röntgen repeated his experiments and wrote them up over the weekend. He gave his discovery the temporary name *X-Strahlen*, 'X-rays', using the standard mathematical designation of X for something unknown that had already been established by René Descartes during the Scientific Revolution of the seventeenth century. For many years, however, the official name bore a tribute to Röntgen's disovery: *Röntgenstrahlen*.

It seems an odd trajectory to go from an X-ray to the X Factor, but the quantity of an unknown remains the same. The earliest use of the X Factor is from 1930, when it first refers to the unidentified cause of disease or psychopathology. Today, it is generally perceived as something that sets a person apart – something indefinable, if not indescribable (a word whose euphemistic potential is occasionally useful to followers of reality TV).

9 November

SEGREGATION

Today is a key date in the sempiternal fight against segregation. At a plenary meeting of the UN General Assembly, gathered on this day in New York in 1982, the President of the African National Congress, Oliver Tambo, delivered a powerful address. The politician and revolutionary spoke of the 'worldwide revulsion and condemnation' provoked by apartheid, and of the need for a united international effort to free political prisoners such as Nelson Mandela and countless others, some of whom awaited execution. He listed many of the injustices of his country's regime:'. . . we have even reached the extraordinary situation where the police have the power to prohibit public funerals, alternatively to tell the bereaved what hymns to sing at the graveside, what sermons to read, what to include and what to exclude in a funeral oration.'

Tambo made clear that those fighting against apartheid, a word that in Afrikaans means 'apart-hood', sought to liberate not just themselves, but all those around the world who suffered – and continue to suffer – similar segregation.

The word 'segregation' is made up of the Latin *segregare*, to separate from the flock, in which *se* means 'apart from' (there in 'separate', and in 'secret'). The second element is based on the Latin *grex*, a flock or herd, which also gave rise to such words as 'gregarious', someone who enjoys the company of the flock, 'aggregate', to gather as one, and 'egregious': originally one whose qualities distinguished them from the crowd. In segregation, separation from the 'main' flock implies exile from a group that is considered both primary and dominant.

Today is also the anniversary of the dismantling of the Berlin Wall – a construction that for many black Americans and Europeans became a metaphor for the segregation and division in their own lives. US cities had their own boundaries: 'color lines' that hindered mobility for black citizens, a model that was replicated across the world. When the Attorney General Robert Kennedy visited the divided city of Berlin a year before his brother's momentous '*Ich bin ein Berliner*' speech, he commented: 'For a hundred years, despite our protestations of equality, we had, as you know, a wall of our own – a wall of segregation erected against Negroes. That wall is coming down.'

As events continue to prove, that wall remains still very much in evidence, but the impetus for its erosion is strong.

10 November

JINX

In 1956, the infamous Hope diamond was donated to the Smithsonian Institution by diamond merchant Harry Winston. It has a well-documented and bloody history, leading many people to believe it is cursed. Among other things, it is said to have been responsible for the beheadings of Louis XVI and Marie Antoinette, from whom *le roi bleu*, the diamond from which the Hope was eventually cut, was stolen. The Sun King, it was said, had been jinxed by the most breathtaking jewel in history.

The word 'jinx' came into modern use in America in the early part of the twentieth century, but its links with the occult go back much further. The ancient Greek word *iunx* was the name given to a type of woodpecker, known as a 'wryneck', a bird closely associated with magic, and incorporated in soothsaying rituals and spell-casting. In mythology Iynx, the nymph-daughter of Pan and Echo, is best known for casting a spell on Zeus. The god is made to fall in love with the mortal Io, which leads his enraged sister-wife Hera to transform the nymph into a wryneck as punishment.

By the seventeenth century, the word 'jynx' was still being used to refer to a spell; the modern sense of the word wasn't popularised until the late nineteenth century with the comedic stock character Jinks Hoodoo, who appeared in an 1887 play *Little Puck*. The cast list in the *New York Daily Tribune* described the character as 'a curse to everybody', and his name has been synonymous with bad luck ever since.

11 November

CHAPEL

Today is St Martin's Day, which commemorates the funeral of St Martin of Tours, a fourth-century Roman soldier to whom is attached one of the most enduring stories of charity and benevolence. It is the story that also gave us the word 'chapel'.

As a soldier in Gaul, Martin is said to have encountered a shivering beggar during a perishingly cold snowstorm. Many stories relate how Martin insisted upon cutting his military cloak in half in order to warm the man. That night, he dreamed of Christ wearing the half-cloak he had given away, and saying to the angels: 'Here is Martin, the Roman soldier who is now baptised; he has clothed me.'

Upon Martin's death, the halved garment was kept as a holy relic in a sanctuary that became known as the *cappella*, from the Latin for 'little cape'. It was protected and presided over by the *cappellani*, whose name would eventually enter English as 'chaplains'. *Cappella* meanwhile became 'chapel', and was used to mean any private sanctuary or holy place.

The musical term *a cappella* is an added layer of the linguistic story. Its literal meaning is 'in the manner of the chapel', referring, in the 1800s, to church music written for unaccompanied voices in religious services. By the twentieth century it referred to unaccompanied vocal music more generally.

12 November

POWWOW

When the earlier settlers arrived on American shores, they were inventors by necessity. Names were needed for the flora and fauna they encountered for the first time, and for their interactions with it. They had, of course, brought a native language with them, with all its complexity, including all the varieties of local dialects, a heady spelling system that was far from standardised, and place names that might give them a jot of familiarity in the new land. But improvisation was essential. When, for example, they settled on a tract of land whose shape resembled the neck of an animal, they created the descriptor 'neck of the woods', still in use today. These were the original trailblazers – a word born in the necessity of 'blazing' or marking a trail by tearing off pieces of bark from trees, enabling others to follow their path.

Their home-grown English was never going to be enough for this new world; they needed to borrow from indigenous peoples a vocabulary that had existed long before they came ashore (*see* 14 May for more examples). Figurative expressions also emerged from those early encounters, including 'burying the hatchet', which arose from a native American custom of burying weapons as tokens of peace. In Captain John Smith's accounts of his voyages to the Jamestown colony in Virginia, we hear of a 'cawcawwasssough', which he defines as 'priests and their assistants among the Chickahominy Indians', and which may have given American English the word 'caucus'.

'Powwow' is another example of a native language borrowing, from the Algonquian spoken by one of the most widespread indigenous peoples of North America. Meaning 'he who dreams', it was first applied to a priest, shaman, or healer. Edward Winslow, an American Pilgrim leader on the

344

Mayflower and one of the first to arrive, described the role of the powwow (or powah) after first encountering one: 'The office and dutie of the Powah is to be exercised principally in calling upon the Devill; and curing diseases of the sicke or wounded.' From that point on, the *Oxford English Dictionary* offers plenty of examples of the attempt by Christian missionaries to convert the *powwows*, not least because their magic was associated with the worship of the Devil ('Their Pow-wows betaking themselves to their exorcismes and necromanticke charmes', as one witness would have it), or with the cunning pretence of conversing with spirits. Two hundred years on, the first mention of a 'powwow' as a meeting of powerful people emerged, a development of the idea of a religious or magical ceremony held by early Native Americans.

---

13 November

HYPNOSIS

In Greek mythology, Hypnos was the god of sleep, and the son of Nyx, or 'night'. Hypnos lived in a cavern of perpetual darkness and mist, through which flowed the waters of Lethe, the river of forgetfulness. Surrounding Hypnos, as he reclined on a couch, were numerous sons, collectively called the Dreams. Most notable among them was Morpheus, who together with Hypnos was sometimes called upon to intervene in human affairs. While Hypnos induced a state of sleep, Morpheus would make human forms appear to dreamers.

Such gifts of the gods were to reappear in eighteenth-century complementary medicine, when sleep and dreams began to be seen as able to foster healing and recovery. This was when Franz Anton Mesmer began to set out his belief in the existence of a mysterious fluid that permeates all matter, which he called animal magnetism. Denounced as a practitioner of magic in his native city of Vienna, Mesmer made a name for himself in Paris, attracting the attention and support of the aristocracy and even the monarchy, including Marie Antoinette. Contemporary accounts described patients sitting in circles, hands held, around a large tub of sulphuric acid from which several iron bars protruded. These had previously been touched by Mesmer, and were consequently believed to be imbued with animal magnetism. The result, according to these witnesses, were 'crises' of the body that preceded a total cure.

Not everyone suspended their disbelief. In 1784, King Louis XVI appointed a joint committee to investigate Mesmer and his claims. It concluded that the 'cures' were the result of psychosomatic relief, and nothing more.

Years later, as Mesmer fled Paris in the wake of the French Revolution, it was recognised that what he promoted, by then known as 'Mesmerism', was a trance-like, 'mesmerising' state that induced the mind to effect recovery. In 1843, Scottish surgeon James Braid turned to the name of the Greek god of sleep to create the alternative term 'hypnotism', the science of artificially inducing a sleep-like trance as a way to recovery.

As for the god of dreams, he too inspired an eponym of sorts. Thanks to its own deep-sleep-inducing properties, in addition to its relief of pain, Morpheus became the basis for the name of the drug morphine.

14 November

POPPY

This is a time of remembrance, when Armistice Day has passed and Remembrance Sunday falls, and when millions of poppies recall the lives of all those in the armed forces who have died in the line of duty. In English folklore, the poppy, long valued for its narcotic and medicinal properties, symbolised sleep, particularly the sleep of death. The explicit associations of the poppy with the battlefield were established during the Napoleonic Wars. Records of the time noted that, in the aftermath of battle, poppies became abundant on fields where soldiers had fallen. It was these that first drew the comparison between the vivid colour of the poppies and the blood spilled during conflict.

The flower's use as a symbol of respect, reverence, and remembrance began after the First World War. In one of the most famous war poems of a generation, 'In Flanders Fields', John McCrae presents the soft lament of the dead:

> Take up our quarrel with the foe:
> To you from failing hands we throw
> The torch, be yours to hold it high.
> If ye break faith with us who die
> We shall not sleep, though poppies grow
> In Flanders fields.

The ultimate origins of the word 'poppy' are unknown. Its recorded history began with the Romans' name for the flower *papaver*, which may in turn contain an ancient word meaning 'to swell'. Its relationships are often surprising: the Greek *mekonion*, 'poppy juice', inspired the English 'meconium', the dark faecal matter discharged by a newborn infant, thanks to the similarity in colour. Perhaps there is something to be valued in the flower's association with birth as well as death. For now, in these dark months of November, it is the poppies of remembrance that occupy our buttonholes and our minds.

15 November

PEA

On this day in 1969, the first colour TV advertisement aired in the UK, interrupting an episode of *Thunderbirds* to promote Birds Eye frozen peas.

The name of the humble pea is a good example of how speakers mistakenly create words by working back from a false assumption. You could not in fact eat a 'pea' until the mid-seventeenth century. The word originated in the Greek *pison*, which came into English as 'pease' – a word that just about survives in pease pudding and pease pottage – and which people understandably interpreted as a plural. The logic was that if you had a handful of pease, you must be able to have one pea.

The same process was at work with the 'cherry'. This we took from the Old French *cherise* (now *cerise* in modern French), and which we once again worked backwards to a single 'cherry'.

16 November

JACK THE LAD

Who were Billy-no-Mates, Clever Dick, and the plucky Jack-of-all-trades? English is littered with phrases that use a person's name as shorthand for a particular type of person or character attribute. Most of them never (as far as we know) sprang from a particular individual.

There are, thankfully, exceptions – ones that make up for all the anonymous personalities that pepper our idioms. Jack the Lad is one of these. His namesake is a thief, gaol-breaker, and one of the most celebrated folk heroes of his day.

Jack Sheppard was born in Spitalfields in early 1702. His father died early, and he was sent by his mother to a workhouse near St Helen's Bishopsgate at the age of six. In 1717, he became the apprentice to a carpenter in Covent Garden, where he is said to have worked diligently at his trade. Diligently, that is, until he discovered the Black Lion Tavern off Drury Lane, where he fell under the spell of gangsters such as Joseph 'Blueskin' Blake, who was to become his partner-in-crime.

Sheppard became a competent pickpocket and burglar, but it is for his improbable and apparently impossible escapes from justice that he is best remembered. On the first occasion, Sheppard fled from a temporary prison by breaking through a wooden ceiling and lowering himself to the ground with a rope made from bedclothes. Still wearing irons, he is said to have distracted the gathering crowd's attention by exclaiming that the felon was on the roof, and then hotfooting it away.

Amazingly, three more escapes followed, despite the desperate measures of the authorities (involving leg irons that were stapled to the floor). Sheppard became a working-class hero, idolised by the poor and eulogised in ballads of the day. Such was his fame that his gaolers are said to have charged high society visitors four shillings to see him. He was even painted by the king's portrait artist.

When Sheppard's luck finally ran out, he refused to inform on his associates, and was duly sentenced to death. On 16 November 1724, he was taken to the gallows at Tyburn and hanged. His execution is said to have been attended by 200,000 people, most of whom adored him – and who knew him simply as Jack the Lad.

17 November

THWANKIN

Thomas Hood was not a fan of November. The nineteenth-century writer of puns and comic verse took to paper to express his loathing of the month's shivery cheerlessness.

No sun – no moon!
No morn – no noon –
No dawn – no dusk – no proper time of day. . . .
No warmth, no cheerfulness, no healthful ease,
No comfortable feel in any member –
No shade, no shine, no butterflies, no bees,
No fruits, no flowers, no leaves, no birds! –
November!

English has hundreds of words for various states of cold – for when it really is emphatically cold, so cold that you might freeze ('freezing') or even die ('perishing'), and for when it's cold, but not *that* cold, when it's just 'chilly'. 'Baltic' and 'bitter' are now UK-wide, while 'nithered' is a favourite in northern England and Scotland, and 'shrammed' survives in the south and south-west; there is also the evocative 'hunchy' in Cambridgeshire. These words are often derived from dialect verbs meaning 'to shrivel' or 'to make numb'.

Hood might also have been a fan of some now long-lost English dialect words that describe November's comfortless elements. They include the word 'gwenders', defined in the *English Dialect Dictionary* as 'a disagreeable tingling sensation in the extremities during cold weather'. 'Devil's smiles', in Yorkshire, are gleams of sunshine among the darkest clouds, while 'thwankin', from Scots, is a thudding term applied to clouds that gather together in thick and gloomy succession.

18 November

BASILISK

On this day in 1626, the new St Peter's Basilica was consecrated in the Vatican. The largest church in the world, it is one of only four major basilicas in the Catholic Church.

The word 'basilica' comes to us via the ancient Greek word *basileus*, meaning 'king'. The *stoa basilike* was the name given to the royal portal or portico of the official who dispensed justice in Athens. The Romans adopted the word 'basilica' for the new churches springing up during the reign of Constantine.

Beyond the grandeur of architecture, the basilica has some unexpected relatives. The South American lizard, the 'basilisk', shares its regal etymological root; this 'little king' has a crest on its head said to resemble a crown, much like its fearsome mythological namesake who was said to be capable of killing with a mere glance. And the herb 'basil' is another member of the family, although scholars have debated the reason why. Some argue that it was believed to be an antidote to the basilisk's venom. The *Oxford English Dictionary*, however, suggests its use in 'some royal unguent, bath, or medicine'.

19 November

PERISSOLOGY

Long-windedness is never a virtue, and is generally viewed by any verbose speaker's audience as evidence of a 'bloviator' (someone who loves the sound of their own voice, and a blower of hot air), or of a 'circumbendibus' – words or actions that go round and round without ever getting to the point. But there is 'waffle', and there is 'perissology', a crime defined in the dictionary as simply 'the use of far more words than necessary'. The term is rooted in a word from ancient Greece, where it was used for anything super-fluous or redundant.

On this day in 1863, in the course of the Civil War, President Abraham Lincoln delivered an address on the battlefield near Gettysburg, Pennsylvania, that would show any perissologist how things should be done. In fact, some newspapers would comment on the speech's 'inappropriate' brevity the following day. For most, however, this was a speech destined, as one listener put it, 'to live down the ages'. He spoke of the need to remember the fallen, 'that we here highly resolve that these dead shall not have died in vain – that this nation, under God, shall have a new birth of freedom, and that government of the people, by the people, for the people, shall not perish from the earth'.

John Hay, a close friend of the president, recorded the reception to the speech: 'He did not read, but spoke every word in a clear, ringing, resonant, vibrating voice. His speech occupied only a few minutes in delivery. It was listened to with breathless attention and when it came to an end there was at first no cheering, but an audible indrawing of deep breath as from an audience that had been profoundly moved.'

Lincoln's speech consisted of just 271 words.

20 November

ACCORD

In 2014, President Barack Obama announced a new policy on immigration, laying down in law the path to citizenship for millions who lived undocumented and illegally, many of them for decades. They were, Obama insisted, quoting his predecessor George W. Bush, 'part of American life'.

At just over fifteen minutes, the president's speech was short and direct but, characteristically, not without poetry: 'Scripture tells us that we shall not oppress a stranger, for we know the heart of a stranger – we were strangers once, too. My fellow Americans, we are and always will be a nation of immigrants. We were strangers once, too.'

Obama used the word 'heart' to evoke honesty, integrity and love – the traditional associations of this organ that since ancient times has been regarded as the seat of life. But this wasn't always the way the heart was understood. For the Anglo-Saxons, the heart was not just the house of the soul, but of understanding and thought too. The idea that it was the repository of intellect as well as emotion explains such phrases as 'to learn by heart', and such words as 'record', which hides the Latin *cor*, 'heart', because to record something is to register it in one's memory.

In the following centuries, it was the emotional governance of the heart that began to take hold. That same Latin *cor* gave us the words 'courage' (strength of heart), 'accord' and 'concord' (hearts brought together), 'discord' (hearts torn apart), and 'cordial' (as an adjective, hearty and warm; as a noun, a tonic designed to invigorate the heart). And this is where it has stayed: the heart, as a word and as a symbol (*see* 1 November) embraces love, while the brain has become the seat of the intellect.

21 November

BALLOON

In 1783, the first free hot air balloon flight carrying human passengers was made by two men, Jean-François Pilâtre de Rozier and François Laurent d'Arlandes. The word 'balloon' has, fittingly, enjoyed quite a journey, from an early form of rugby to a ball full of fireworks.

In the sixteenth century, a popular ball game involved players kicking a large and heavy ball of strong leather, or striking it with their arms or hands that were protected by a wooden brace. The ball they played with was known by the French name of *ballon*. By the eighteenth century, the word had become anglicised to 'balloon', and the sport had become known as the 'balloon game'.

A century later, as pyrotechnics gained favour as a source of entertainment, a favourite firework was a cardboard ball propelled from a mortar and designed to fly into the sky, where it would explode with a shower of bright sparks. This, riffing on the popular ball game, was also called a balloon.

Back to 1783, and the hot air balloon, originally designed by the Montgolfier brothers, was a far larger ball, consisting of a bag filled with hot air. They had borrowed for their invention a name that already defined an inflated round object, creating not just a unique flying machine but also, unwittingly, the forerunner of party balloons everywhere.

22 November

WALRUS

On this day in 1967, the BBC banned all playing of the song 'I Am the Walrus' by the Beatles, thanks to its explicit use of the word 'knickers'. It went on to become one of the most notorious B-sides in the music business. Today, it is regarded by many as seriously silly or glorious nonsense, fittingly perhaps, given it contains brief hints of Lewis Carroll and Edward Lear.

The word 'walrus' has an altogether different, and more straightforward, significance for lexicographers, although it involves another writer of fantastical tales. J. R. R. Tolkien, author of the truly classic *The Lord of the Rings* and *The Hobbit*, and *The Silmarillion*, worked at the very start of his career on the staff of the *Oxford English Dictionary*. He was to say later that he 'learned more in those two years than in any other equal period of my life'. Tolkien was steeped in the history and culture of Anglo-Saxon England, which was to thrum beneath the surface of the fictional lexicons he went on to create.

Tolkien's distinctive handwriting can still be found in the *Dictionary*'s archives, on slips of paper for entries from *waggle* to *warlock*. He seems to have been particularly good at words with elusive or complex etymologies – one of which was 'walrus'. The Anglo-Saxons, like the Vikings, seem to have perceived a resemblance between the curious-looking mammal and a horse, for they called it a 'horse-whale'. This eventually became reversed to 'whale-horse', and then shortened to 'walrus'.

That was not the end of Tolkien's association with Oxford. In 1989, the editor of the *Supplement* to the *OED*, Robert Burchfield, who had studied under Tolkien at Oxford, wrote an appreciation of 'the puckish fisherman who drew me into his glittering philological net'. And he had asked, of course, for his mentor's help in compiling the entry for 'hobbit'. Tolkien's touch can still be felt within the pages of the *Dictionary* he had loved.

---

23 November

WELL DONE, *CUTTY SARK*

On this day in 1869, the clipper *Cutty Sark* was launched in the Scottish town of Dumbarton. Built for the China tea trade, it carried a vast array of cargoes during its career. It is one of the last surviving tea clippers of its kind.

The ship took its name from a poem by Robert Burns, 'Tam o' Shanter', in which 'cutty sark' means simply a 'short undergarment'. It is also the nickname of the poem's young, attractive witch, who wears a short nightie that fitted her as a child but which is clearly too short for her now:

Her cutty sark, o' Paisley harn,
That while a lassie she had worn,
In longitude tho' sorely scanty,
It was her best, and she was vauntie.

So taken is Tam by the sight that he exclaims 'Weel done, Cutty-sark!' His tragic end is a warning to men of the dangers of falling for skimpy underwear. Such was the popularity of the poem that, for a while at least, 'Well done, Cutty Sark!' entered Scots and English as a form of enthusiastic 'Bravo'.

24 November

EVOLUTION

Charles Darwin, whose *On the Origin of Species* was published on this day in 1859, rarely used the word 'evolution', preferring instead the term 'descent with modification'. Perhaps this was because 'evolving' implied some preordained design. The first edition of his book includes no mention of the word at all, and in subsequent editions he introduced it just once, through the use of 'evolved' in its final sentence:

There is grandeur in this view of life, with its several powers, having been originally breathed by the Creator into a few forms or into one; and that, whilst this planet has gone cycling on according to the fixed law of gravity, from so simple a beginning endless forms most beautiful and most wonderful have been, and are being, evolved.

Almost in spite of his efforts, 'evolution' soon became attached to what was to become the dominant unifying concept of modern biology.

'Evolve' itself, from the Latin *evolvere*, is a metaphor from the once physical act of unrolling a book or parchment (to 'involve' was to wrap it back up again). History unfolds just as, for the Romans, a piece of parchment or papyrus was unrolled to reveal its script.

25 November

SPHALLOLALIA

This is the feast day of Saint Catherine, commemorating the martyrdom of Catherine of Alexandria, one of the Fourteen Holy Helpers – a group of Catholic saints who, together, are thought to have miraculous powers.

On this day, tradition in France holds that all unmarried women may pray for a future husband. Conversely, it also honours women who have reached twenty-five years of age without marriage, who are known as 'Catherinettes'. Friends of the single women make hats for them – usually ridiculous ones – whereupon the duly behatted kneel at the feet of the statue of St Catherine and beseech help in finding a partner, lest they remain spinsters and be consigned to wearing St Catherine's bonnet for ever.

Catherinettes might be all too familiar with the romantic disappointment of 'sphallolalia'. This recent concoction, which is Greek for 'stumble-talk', is a pithy if unpronounceable term for 'flirtatious talk that goes absolutely nowhere'. It is perhaps the likely outcome of any romantic situation that is 'imparlibidinous': in other words, one characterised by an unequal state of desire between two people.

---

26 November

MERRYTHOUGHT

This happy day is fast approaching – the turkeys are gobbling and growing fat, the chickens are crowing and getting plump, and the oxen are eating corn and pumpkins, that the pilgrims of Massachusetts may have a feast, and their sons and daughters may have a frolic with wishbones and mince pies! There is no day like it among the nations of the earth.

Thus an article in the *Baltimore Sun* from November 1842, lauding the approach of Thanksgiving in the old Bay state. To this day, the pulling of the wishbone remains a custom on both sides of the Atlantic during feasts of great significance.

The custom of pulling apart the wishbone dates back to at least Roman times. It may have evolved from the Etruscan practice of 'alectryomancy', which involves divination of the future by means of rooster clavicles. According to Roman legend, the Etruscans selected the wishbone because its V shape resembled a human groin, the repository of life. Thus, the wishbone was seen as an appropriate way to unravel life's mysteries.

One writer from the seventeenth century puts it rather more bluntly: ''Tis called the merrythought, because when the fowle is opened, dissected, or carv'd, it resembles the pudenda of a woman.' Another account from the same period adds a wistful note: 'The Original of that Name was doubtless from the Pleasant Fancies, that commonly arise upon the Breaking of that Bone.' Men in love were even said to grow pale and lose their appetite upon the plucking of a 'merrythought'. The tradition soon arose that whoever ended up with the longer piece of the merrythought would marry first, and see their greatest wish fulfilled.

Unrelated to this meaning of the word (perhaps) was a secondary, now obsolete, use of the term for a construction of wire designed to increase the size of a woman's bust.

27 November

DYNAMITE

In 1850, following in the footsteps of his inventor father, Alfred Nobel learned of the work of Ascanio Sobrero, the chemist who invented nitroglycerine. More powerful than gunpowder, this highly explosive and unpredictable liquid captivated him. His experiments began, and he proceeded to look for a practical application. After several explosions, including one that killed Alfred's brother, authorities banned nitroglycerine tests within Stockholm's city limits.

Undeterred, Nobel moved his lab and began experimenting with additives, including one that transformed nitroglycerine into a malleable paste that rendered it more manageable. This he named dynamite, from the Greek *dynamos*, meaning power.

Nobel seems to have taken the view that scholarly discovery is a neutral endeavour, which can be used for both good and bad. He believed, at least initially, that the use of his invention in weaponry was likely to have a strong deterrent effect. But in 1888, another of his brothers, Ludvig, died while visiting Cannes, and in a case of mistaken identity a French newspaper published Alfred's obituary, condemning him for his invention of military explosives and entitling the piece *Le marchand de la mort est mort* ('The merchant of death is dead'). Nobel was said to have been appalled by this interpretation of his work.

Nobel signed his last will and testament on this day in 1895, giving the lion's share of his fortune to a series of prizes in Physics, Chemistry, Physiology or Medicine, Literature, and Peace – the Nobel Prizes. The complexity of a scientist's responsibility was voiced by Albert Einstein half a century later, when physicists saw the atom bomb dropped over Japan: 'Alfred Nobel invented an explosive more powerful than any then known – an exceedingly effective means of destruction. To atone for this "accomplishment" and to relieve his conscience, he instituted his award for the promotion of peace.'

28 November

CHARING CROSS

If there is one place in London that is seen as the centre of the capital, it is Charing Cross. Since the late 1800s, it has been the point from which distances from London are calculated.

In Old English, a *cierring* was a turning. The hamlet of Charing, as it was once known, is skirted by a bend in the River Thames. The 'Cross' element, however, takes us to a different period in history, and refers to one of twelve 'Eleanor Crosses' erected by a disconsolate Edward I when his wife Queen Eleanor of Castile died, on this day in 1290.

Grief-stricken, Edward ordered that Eleanor be embalmed, and her entrails buried at Lincoln Cathedral; her body was then carried to Westminster Abbey in London. At each place where the procession stopped for the night, Edward had a memorial cross built in her honour. The cross in the hamlet of Charing eventually gave its name to the whole district. The playwright George Peele, who chronicled the career of Edward, put it so:

> Erect a rich and stately carved cross,
> Whereon her statue shall with glory shine;
> And henceforth see you call it Charing Cross.

Now only the crosses at Waltham Cross in Hertfordshire, and Geddington and Hardingstone in Northamptonshire remain.

Nevertheless, Eleanor has a permanent memorial in the name of the junction in London where six roads meet.

Today, folk etymology will tell you that 'Charing' is a corruption of *chère reine*, 'dear Queen'. It may be wrong, but the sentiment behind it, given the true story, seems entirely fitting.

29 November

ANTIC

A memorial service for arguably the most famous clown of the twentieth century took place on this day in 1974, in London's St Paul's Cathedral. Nikolai Poliakoff, aka Coco the Clown, is said to have run away to the circus at the age of eight – travelling 300 miles by train to Belorussia (our modern Belarus) where he persuaded the proprietor of a circus to take him on. He was later put under the tutelage of experienced clowns, acrobats, and stars of the Soviet stage.

Technically, Coco was an *Auguste*, a performer who is traditionally the stooge of another clown and who follows a chiefly slapstick routine. Coco would wow audiences with the distinctive make-up that was to become the stock-in-trade of clowns everywhere; he also had giant boots, said to be a size 58, and trick hair, which he could comically raise as an expression of surprise.

The word 'clown' has an elusive past, one that leads us to several European words for a 'clod, clot, or lump', perhaps with the extended idea of a boorish lout. Such an epithet might please those suffering from 'coulrophobia', a distinct fear of clowns and their antics, and a word apparently invented in the 1990s: in the absence of an ancient Greek word for 'clown', it seems neologisers settled for the nearest equivalent: a walker on stilts.

The antics of circus comedians have an authentically ancient origin – 'antic' comes from the Italian *antico*, which in turn gave us our English 'antique'. The term was originally applied to fantastic, 'grotesque' representations of human, animal, and floral forms that were found by archaeologists while exhuming ancient remains in the grottoes of such Roman buildings as the Baths of Titus. 'Antic' was later extended to anything similarly incongruous or bizarre, including the stage shenanigans of Coco the Clown.

30 November

ILL-WILLY

The Scots language has a knack of filling gaps in English that you either never quite knew existed, or which would otherwise take an entire sentence to describe. Where would we be without 'kerfuffle', 'dreich', and 'braw'? Bibulous people might be fond of the word 'bonailie' meaning a 'grace cup', or drink taken just before parting from friends. A 'curglaff' is the shock of cold water when you plunge into it or step trepidatiously into the shower, while 'gnashgab' is not just any old gossip, but the particularly malicious kind. A 'bumfle' is an unsightly bulge in your clothing.

And then there are 'well-willy' and 'ill-willy' – meaning, respectively, full of good will and benevolence, and cherishing meanness, thereby neatly characterising what kind of day we intend to have. In the sixteenth century there were in fact two further siblings in the willy family – 'evil-willy', an epithet for someone with extremely malevolent desires, and the cheery 'good-willy', meaning 'generous' and ever-ready to help.

DECEMBER

A SURFEIT OF LAMPREYS

In the autumn of 2018, an unusual set of keratin 'teeth' were identified in London's archaeological record for the first time. They belonged to the gruesome lamprey fish – a primitive lineage of eel-like fish that pre-dates the existence of dinosaurs. The discovery was made by Alan Pipe from Museum of London Archaeology, in the course of examining environmental samples from excavations near Mansion House Underground Station in the heart of the City. It was an important find: the most memorable physical trait of the fish is its disc-shaped, suction-cup mouth, ringed with sharp, horny, tooth-like structures used for latching on to any fish it identified as prey.

Lampreys were a popular delicacy among the nobility in medieval Britain. It is famously said that Henry I, who died on this day, had such a hankering for them that his doctor deemed the cause of his untimely death 'a surfeit of lampreys', thereby enshrining an unlikely collective noun in the dictionary (*see* 'a flick of hares', 21 September). Some historians believe this to be a flight of fancy on the part of the king's chronicler, Henry of Huntingdon, but their enjoyment among the monarchy is undisputed. King John is said to have fined the City of Gloucester the equivalent of £250,000 in today's money for failing to deliver his Christmas lamprey pie, and a special lamprey pie was made for the coronation of Queen Elizabeth II in 1953.

For the rest of us, the origin of the fish's name appears to be equally unappetising: it descends from the Latin *lambere*, 'to lick', and *petra*, 'stone', because the lamprey has a habit of attaching itself to stones with its rasping mouth.

2 December

STORY

If there was ever a time to dive into the imaginary stories of films and books, Christmas is surely it. Whether it's the traditional story of the nativity or the tear-jerking narratives of movies like *It's a Wonderful Life*, it's time to bring on a bit of magic. The word 'story' has a suitably long and involving history, which takes in the Romans, Normans, and today's social media, where we can share stories in very different ways.

In fact, the words 'story' and 'history' were once fairly inseparable in meaning. The original 'stories' were oral or written narratives of past events, accepted as true by virtue of great age or a long tradition. The word comes from the Latin *historia*, but was 'reborrowed' into English after 1066 from the French word *estoire*. By the 1500s, 'story' described dramatic representations of real events, which could contain either fiction or fact. We retain this ambiguity today, when we can read the story of a book, or a story in a newspaper (some would say the two aren't always too far apart).

'Storey' with the added 'e', meaning the floor of a building, is essentially the same word. It originally referred to tiers of painted windows or sculptures used to decorate the facades of buildings, each depicting a historical subject – so each storey told a different story.

3 December

TEXT

The test engineer Neil Papworth sent the first text message to a mobile phone on 3 December 1992, when he wrote 'Merry Christmas' on his personal computer and sent it to the phone of the Vodafone director Richard Jarvis (whose device weighed in at over 6 kg). Jarvis had no technological means of returning the message, and the communication ended there. Today, texting has a grammar and vocabulary all to itself – it is a language whose conventions make it one of the greatest tribal languages in existence today.

The roots of that simple word 'text' are ancient, and like so many other words in English, their basis is the metaphor of clothing. Text's story began, not unexpectedly, with 'textile': cloth that is 'woven' and that comes from a form of the Latin *texere*, to 'weave' or 'plait'. The written texts that we write and send today each have a 'context', with which they are 'woven together'.

This new written-spoken language demands that we are, above all, succinct, a word that also began with a garment – this time a Roman toga tied with a girdle or belt and which was consequently *succinctus* (*sub*, meaning 'under', and *cinctus*, 'girdled'). Our messages today, limited by speed demands and character constraints, are 'tucked in' just like an expanse of billowing cloth.

---

4 December

FRENCH FRIES

The fast-food chain Burger King opened its first restaurant in December 1954, further entrenching the inseparable partnership of 'burger and fries' in the Western culinary lexicon. In those days, the must-have accessory to the 'broiled beef burgers' would have been known more fully as 'French fries' – a distinction still used today if chunky chips are also on the menu.

Our love of fried potatoes apart, the trajectory of the adjective 'French' has not been a positive one. In the fifteenth century, 'French fare' denoted extremely polite behaviour, a connotation that was to become obsolete as political conflict got in the way. By the 1700s, the French had become firmly tethered to the idea of explicitness, particularly when it came to sexual adventure. The writer of one lampoon from 1682 describes how the young wife of a much older man 'swears and fucks and all the while's *so* French!' Henry Fielding whisperingly spoke of 'certain *French* novels', and 'French' was for centuries the only description needed for fellatio: a work from 1890 entitled simply *Stag Party* lists the offerings: 'Common, old fashioned f—k $1.00 . . . Tasting (French) $2.50. French fashion with use of patent balls $3.50.' All of this, one would hope, with a 'French letter', recorded at around the same time.

It's perhaps not surprising that sexually transmitted diseases were also invited into the French lexicon. Syphilis was variously dubbed French pox, French compliment, French disease, French evil, French goods, French marbles, and French measles – though to be fair, every nation decided to blame the disease on each other (*see* 26 April).

Such implications of explicit behaviour, and language, are still there in 'French' kisses and 'pardon my French', while a certain Gallic laziness is imputed in 'to take French leave' (to which the French promptly retaliated with *filer à l'anglaise*, to leave the 'English way').

French fries have, it seems, little to do with this curious history. The idea appears to have been American from the start – Thomas Jefferson had 'potatoes served in the French manner' at a White House dinner in 1802, and 'French fried potatoes' are later recorded in a cookery manual for maids. When the United States and France were at cross-purposes over the invasion of Iraq, French fries had a brief outing as 'freedom fries', before the term was quietly thrown in the bin.

5 December

MINUTE

As advent calendar doors are eagerly opened each morning, most children will be counting down the minutes until the big day. For adults, this tends to be a time of 'betwitterment' – anticipation and excitement mixed with fear.

The counting of hours and minutes has its origins in traditions dating back thousands of years. Today, the most widely used numeric system is decimal (base 10), a system that probably originated because it enabled humans to count with their fingers (the word 'digit' is from the Latin *digitus*, 'finger'). The civilisations that first divided the day into smaller parts, however, used different numeral systems: the Egyptians, for example, used the duodecimal system (base 12), perhaps because it reflected the number of lunar cycles in a year or, as some believe, because it enabled counting by the number of finger joints on each hand (three in each of the four fingers, excluding the thumb).

The Egyptians eventually developed advanced sundials they knew as shadow clocks: a T-shaped bar in the ground, calibrated to divide the interval between sunrise and sunset into 12 parts. The astronomers of the time also first observed a set of stars known as 'decans', whose appearance marked the passage of night. The period of total darkness was marked by the sight of 12 decans in the skies, resulting in 12 divisions of night.

Once both the light and dark hours were divided into 12 parts, the concept of a 24-hour day was in place. Hours, though, were of different lengths: daytime hours were typically longer than night-time ones, and varied with the seasons. These only became fixed after mechanical clocks arrived in Europe at the end of the fourteenth century.

The historical picture is more complex still, as the subdivision of the day into hours, minutes, and seconds is a nod to the ancient Babylonians, who preferred 60 as the basis for counting. An hour was divided into 60 parts once – creating *prima pars minuta*, the first diminished part, or 'prime minute' – and then divided again, for the *secunda pars minuta*, or 'second minute'. Their names were eventually shortened to 'minute' and 'second'.

Whether a sundial or hourglass, quartz watch or atomic clock – or advent calendar – the counting of time never seems quite so important, or stressful, as in the run-up to Christmas.

6 December

CHESTNUT

Steaming braziers of glossy brown chestnuts are the sweet-smelling advents of Christmas across the globe. The word 'chestnut' is a translation of the botanical Latin *castanea*, making it a sibling of 'castanets', so-named on account of their shape. The sweet chestnut is unrelated to the unpalatable fruits inside the thorny husks of the horse chestnut tree, once considered to be a remedy for chest diseases in horses and which belong to a different genus, the *Aesculus*.

In extended use, a 'chestnut' – especially an old one – has become a metaphor for a story that has been told many times before. The origins of this sense have long proved elusive – is it a reference to a horse, nut, tree, or to something else entirely?

According to the *Oxford English Dictionary*, the usage may have been inspired by an early nineteenth-century melodrama, *The Broken Sword* by William Dimond, first performed in London in 1816 to rave reviews and which became a must-see of its time. The relevant scene involves Captain Zavior, a character who monotonously retells his old exploits in the presence of his much-pained and long-suffering servant Pablo, who clearly knows them by heart:

Zavior: Let me see – aye! it is exactly six years since,
   that peace being restored to Spain . . . I mounted a
   mule at Barcelona, and trotted away for my native
   mountains. At the dawn of the fourth day's journey,
   I entered the wood of Collares, when suddenly
   from the thick boughs of a cork tree—
Pablo (*Jumping up*): A chesnut [*sic*], Captain, a *chesnut*.
Zavior: Bah! you booby, I say, a cork.
Pablo: And I swear, a chesnut – Captain! this is the
   twenty-seventh time I have heard you relate this
   story, and you invariably said, a chesnut, till now.

The use of a chestnut as a jokey byword for anything worn
out and hackneyed might well have travelled from this hugely
popular play into theatrical slang and on to the mainstream.
At least the real thing, popping on an open fire or the fiery
cylinders of a street-vendor, is anything but old and tiresome.

---

7 December

GREMLIN

The US comedy horror film *Gremlins* was released in
Britain on this day in 1984. The film, which was a
commercial success, was criticised by some for its unsuitability
for a younger audience, who might be seduced by the cuddly
gremlins before witnessing their evil menace unleashed on
the screen.

But then gremlins have never been friendly. The notion of
mischievous monsters causing havoc is ancient, but they were
given the name of 'gremlin' by RAF fighter pilots during the
Second World War when any unexplained mechanical fault
was blamed on malevolent sprites. The concept was greatly
popularised by Roald Dahl, an erstwhile RAF pilot whose
book *The Gremlins*, published in 1943, features little creatures

prone to causing havoc in planes until they are tamed by the story's pilot protagonist Gus.

Dahl did not coin the word 'gremlin', however. Its origin is, suitably perhaps, vexing. Some suggest it is an alteration of the Irish *gruaimín*, 'gloomy little person', or of the Dutch *gremmelen*, meaning 'to stain or spoil', but supporting evidence for both is lacking. The most plausible theory is that it is a portmanteau of 'goblin' and a brand of Kentish beer called Fremlin's, as a joking suggestion that these were the type of spirits you saw when you'd had one too many. If that's the case, then this makes 'gremlins' a pair with another expression that began in the skies – 'gone for a Burton', apparently coined by pilots during the same war when the planes of colleagues were shot down. 'Burton' had become a general term for beer, a nod to Britain's Burton-on-Trent which was a centre of beer production for over a century. To have 'gone for a Burton', said to have been a slogan for the beer at the time, became a dark euphemism for going missing or dying in the sea, otherwise known as 'the drink'.

---

8 December

TOAST

As the office Christmas party beckons, speeches may be written and rewritten, and toasts to management duly prepared. Not everyone will be cheered by the prospect, nor its inevitable aftermath. There seems to be no single English word to describe the particular crapulence that follows that final glass of warm wine at 1 a.m. *Piblokto* might in this instance be useful: a highly specific term for the condition affecting Inuit peoples in winter, and characterised by episodes of wild excitement and irrational behaviour followed by a period of stupor.

The idea of 'toasting' someone seems a curious cause for celebration. But the tradition of raising a glass to someone's health and happiness had very literal beginnings. It is said to date as far back as the reign of Charles II, when it referred to a woman present at a gathering and whose beauty or success the others wished to acknowledge. During this period, small pieces of spiced, toasted bread were regularly added to wine to add spice and flavour, or to disguise its poor quality. The woman being 'toasted' was regarded as adding zing to the company in the same way as the toast added piquancy to the drink. One eighteenth-century writer noted an account in *Tatler* magazine involving an (unnamed) beauty of the day, who was taking the cold waters at Bath. 'A gentleman dipped his cup in the water and drank it to her health; another in his company wittily (or drunkenly) replied that, while he did not care for the drink, he would gladly enjoy the *toast*.'

9 December

RESPAIR

Few entries in the dictionary seem so entirely necessary to modern times, even while they have fallen completely out of use. 'Respair' is one of those. The word is a clear variation of 'despair', in which *spair* is a descendant, via French, of the Latin *sperare*, to hope. 'Respair' has just a single record in the *Oxford English Dictionary*, from 1525. We can only interpret what the author meant by 'Respaire hade in gude hope agane', but the *Dictionary*'s definition is beautiful in its simplicity: 'fresh hope, or a recovery from despair'.

10 December

WELKIN

Before the sky there was the welkin. A sibling of the German *Wolke*, a cloud, this was a standard term in Old English for the space above our heads and, by extension, heaven. It was eventually nudged out by 'sky' in the thirteenth century.

Welkin became restricted to literary use as well as some regional dialects, such as that of Yorkshire. In her novel *Shirley*, Charlotte Brontë gives Robert Moore the beautiful line, 'I see a fine, perfect rainbow, bright with promise, gloriously spanning the beclouded welkin of life.'

Today, we might remember the word only in the expression of a very loud sound: *make the welkin ring*. What rings is the vault of heaven, the firmament. For the ancients, this was believed to be one of several crystal spheres encircling the earth and carrying the planets and stars, capable of resounding like a bell if you made enough noise.

In 1739, a collection of *Hymns and Sacred Poems* introduced a piece for Christmas by Charles Wesley. It began, 'Hark! how all the welkin rings, / Glory to the King of kings.' Fifteen years later, it reappeared as 'Hark! the herald-angels sing / Glory to the new-born king'.

11 December

SWANK

Swank is a dialect word defined in Nathan Bailey's *Universal Etymological Dictionary* of 1721 as 'the remainder of liquor at the bottom of a tankard, pot, or cup, which is just sufficient for one draught; which it is not accounted good manners to divide with the left hand man, and according to the quantity is called either a large or little swank'. The word was particularly popular, according to Bailey, in Bocking in Essex, though we have no accounts as to why. A century later, 'swank' appeared again, in a *Dictionary of Archaic and Provincial Words*, this time alongside two companions: 'The three draughts into which a jug of beer is divided are called *neckum, sinkum*, and *swank* or *swankum*'. Perplexingly, it would take more than one of each to unravel their etymology: the *Oxford English Dictionary* simply offers a question mark.

If you prefer to sound a little more elegant, you might want to drink less of the swank, and more of the 'supernaculum', Latin for 'on the nail' and a translation of the German *auf den Nagel trinken*, to 'drink to the very last drop'. 'Drinking supernaculum' was an old English custom of emptying a glass of excellent wine or ale before turning it on its head so that the last drop or two might wet the drinker's fingernail.

Suitably, in Francis Grose's collection of eighteenth-century slang, 'supernaculum' appears just above the entry for the mocking title 'Surveyor of the Highways', defined as 'one reeling drunk' – as opposed to 'Surveyor of the Pavement' – although one of course could surely lead to the other.

12 December

THROTTLEBOTTOM

This was the day, in 2019, when Boris Johnson won a landslide victory in the British general election. His self-styled bumbling, mop-headed approach to politics invited various epithets from across the political spectrum, suitable perhaps for one who himself threw at his opposition such insults as 'mutton-headed mugwump', or 'a void within a vacuum surrounded by a vast inanition'.

A riffle through the virtual pages of the *Oxford English*

Dictionary delivers a feast when it comes to political person-alities. 'Quockerwodger' is one, originally the name given to a nineteenth-century toy puppet, whose wooden limbs could be made to jerk and flail about by the person holding the strings. The lip-bending term entered the political lexicon to mean a puppet leader whose strings are pulled by another.

Sycophants are often in servitude to shrewd and unprinc-ipled leadership, otherwise known as 'scallywaggery', a term that has embodied political opportunism for over two hundred years. It could also be a useful collective noun, perhaps for a group of 'snollygosters', a word for a scheming, unprincipled politician that has an elusive past: but that may be an extreme riff on 'snallygaster', a terrifying mythical creature from the folklore of Maryland, said to prey upon chickens and children.

Most suitable of all, perhaps, for this day in history, might be the epithet 'throttlebottom', a shambling, rather incompe-tent person in public office. Its inspiration was Alexander Throttlebottom, a meek and ineffectual vice-president in a musical comedy and political satire from the 1930s, written by Ira and George Gershwin. It has the ring of a word that the PM would surely relish himself.

---

13 December

POP GOES THE WEASEL

In the middle of the nineteenth century, a new dance was added to the Christmas party list. One of the earliest outings of 'Pop Goes the Weasel' was at a ball held in Ipswich on 13 December 1853, where it was played as the grand finale and was described by one of the guests as 'one of the most mirth inspiring dances which can well be imagined'. An advertise-ment from the same period offered dance lessons for this new and 'highly fashionable Dance, recently introduced at her Majesty's and the Nobility's private soirees'.

Quite what the dance entailed is unclear, but it seems the words of the rhyme came a fair bit later, and in multiple versions. One American incarnation features a monkey chasing a weasel all around a cobbler's bench, as well as a Jimmy who has the whooping cough and a Timmy who has the measles. For the British, however, it will always be:

> Half a pound of tuppenny rice
> Half a pound of treacle
> That's the way the money goes
> Pop goes the weasel.

The final recurring line of the rhyme is common to all versions of it and is also the one that attracts most curiosity. Is this really a reference to the strange explosion of a furry mammal?

The most likely explanation takes us to a very different and, on the face of it, equally unlikely source: the pawnbroker's trade. 'Weasel' here is probably operating as rhyming slang, in which a 'weasel and stoat' was a coat. To 'pop' something, meanwhile, was to 'pawn it', and the rhyme proceeds to list all those items that can be bought with the cash exchanged for the coat, including trips up and down London's City Road, and 'in and out the *Eagle*', an eighteenth-century tavern that stands to this day.

If this is indeed the origin, it puts 'Pop Goes the Weasel' in the same stable as the English phrase 'up the spout'. This too originated in the pawnbroker's trade – or more specifically in the pawn-shop lift, known colloquially as the 'spout'. Articles brought in to be pawned were hauled up via the lift to the rooms above, where they would be stored. Belongings that had gone 'up the spout' were entirely out of service to the owner until they were redeemed.

---

14 December

DOOM

Commissioned by William the Conqueror this month in 1085, and completed after his death in 1087, the *Domesday Book* recorded exactly who had held land immediately prior to the Norman Conquest, in the time of Edward the Confessor, and who held it afterwards. It was born out of William's need for an overview of how much he could claim in taxes in order to fund his sizeable army. By the time it was completed, the *Book*, written in Latin in two tomes, contained records for some 13,500 settlements south of the Scottish border. It listed extensively not only the names of landholders, their tenants, and the size of their land, but also such details as animals, fish, and farming utensils owned, and any disputes over such possessions.

The earliest uses of 'doom', an Old English word of Germanic origin that was mostly written as 'dome', were as a neutral term for a 'statute' or 'law'. As Anglo-Saxon society developed, a second sense of the word emerged, meaning a judicial decision that was formally announced, particularly a sentence of punishment. From the early thirteenth century, the word came to be used specifically for the (final) Judgement, which in Christian belief will come at the end of the world. This is the sense of the word for Shakespeare when Macbeth, seeing the phantasms of a line of kings descended from the murdered Banquo, cries out: 'What, will the line stretch out to the crack of doom?'

The name of the *Domesday Book* combined both senses of the word. It reflected the fact that the book was regarded as a final authority and arbiter of the law, but also invited religious associations. The antiquary William Lambarde (1536–1601), in his *Perambulation of Kent*, gives a picture of how the name was understood: 'The booke of the generall survey of the

Realme, which William the Conquerour caused to bee made
. . . and to be called Domesday, bicause it spared no man, but
iudged all men indifferently, as the Lord in that great day will
do.'

---

15 December

GROTESQUE

Nero, traditionally viewed as one of Rome's most infamous
emperors and history's greatest criminals, was born on
this day in 37 AD. New studies of ancient texts suggest he
may not have been the psychopath we have long judged him
to be; there is no evidence, for example, that he caused the
Great Fire of Rome, or that he fiddled his way through it:
these may have been rumours promulgated to discredit him.

Whatever the extent of his criminality, few would argue
that, centuries after his death, it was Nero who created the
birthplace of 'grotesque'. In the ruins of his city's conflagration,
he ordered the construction of a sumptuous villa occupying
300 acres, one that would become known as the *Domus Aurea*,
the Golden House, thanks to the lavish amount of gold used
in its decoration.

The villa housed elaborate frescoes and marble sculptures
(including a bronze likeness of Nero himself), as well as an
enormous pool on which the Colosseum now stands. Slaves
were used to crank a luxuriously embellished rotating ceiling,
symbolising the heavens. It was the pleasure palace of the city.

By the time Nero was declared a public enemy of Rome,
leading to his suicide, the villa had stood for only forty years.
It fell into disrepair, and was plundered for its jewels and gold.
During the reign of Titus, its rooms were filled with earth,
and buried alongside the reputation of its creator.

The Golden House remained silently underground until
the Renaissance, when archaeologists and artists descended

to marvel at the buried palace's fantastical frescoes. Raphael and Michelangelo were among the visitors, as was, later, the Marquis de Sade. The art they witnessed there became known as *grottesca*, from the Italian *grotte*, a grotto or cave. When the word 'grotesque' first appeared in English in the sixteenth century it described the style of decoration found in ruins such as these, including their decorative wall paintings depicting interweaving human and animal forms with flowers and foliage (*see* 29 November).

16 December

ZHUZH

The time is coming when party outfits are dusted off and require a bit of zhuzh – that indefinable '*je ne sais quoi*' that takes something ordinary and kicks it up a notch. The word is as unspellable as a zhuzh is indefinable, and its beginnings are also just a touch elusive.

The story of 'zhuzh' (or 'zhush', 'zhoosh', 'tzush', 'tzuj' . . .) begins in the theatre, whose argot can be unexpected, sumptuous, and as gnarly as a Shakespearean plot. English has borrowed an immense number of terms from the stage, from 'stealing the limelight' to 'waiting in the wings', while others, such as 'corpsing', are still caught within the showbiz spotlight. Steeped in over two millennia of history, it's unsurprising that the theatre has generated not just one, but several tribal lexicons of its own.

Among the most memorable of these is one with few surviving footprints. Its original name, 'Parlyaree', was an anglicisation of the Italian *parlare* meaning 'to talk'. It began as a jargon brought back by sailors who had picked up a working pidgin on their trading trips abroad. Back on land, many turned to the circus or theatre for employment: their fearless ability to climb and build kept them in high demand behind the scenes. And their lingua franca became melded with that of the entertainers they worked with. To this day both professions refer to 'rigging', 'flying', 'working a show', and 'striking' a set.

A little later, the ever-evolving banter found a new home in the gay community, one so marginalised that a new tribal language felt not only fitting but essential. Here it gained a new title, Polari, and was made famous by the ostentatiously camp crosstalk of Julian and Sandy (Hugh Paddick and Kenneth Williams), the unashamedly queeny duo who became staples of the 1960s airwaves as part of BBC Radio's *Round the Horne*. This was Parlyaree with rhyming slang, back slang, and several other elements of wordplay thrown in.

Its vocabulary, from shaving the lallies (legs) to fluttering your ogleriahs (eyelashes) or powdering your eeks (faces), found a natural home in the glitz and chatter of showbusiness. It has largely fallen out of use, but continues to be studied as a lexicon of both joy and isolation. One of its most famous legacies is 'zhuzh'. Onomatopoeic in origin – imitating such sounds as fingers ruffling velvet – it stepped beyond Polari to fill a clear linguistic gap. If only we could decide how to spell it.

---

17 December

MISTLETOE

Puckering up beneath a sprig of mistletoe is a tradition that can strike fear and hope in equal measure. Both emotions do justice to the plant's mythology, which combines high romance with an unexpectedly dark history.

Historically, mistletoe represents love, fertility, and vitality. The ancient Greeks are said to have used mistletoe as a pain-reliever for menstrual cramps, while the Roman naturalist Pliny the Elder noted it could be used as a balm against epilepsy and as an antidote to some poisons. Our modern tradition, however, probably originated with the Druids, who revered it for its ability to blossom even in winter, and applied such generative powers to human fertility.

But while this explains the association between mistletoe and love, its power for malevolence appears in Norse mythology, where it can be a medium for wickedness as well as regeneration. In one story, when the death of the god Odin's son Baldur is foretold, his mother Frigg, goddess of love, secures a promise from all the animals and plants of the natural world that they will not harm her son. But Frigg overlooks one thing: the unassuming mistletoe. The malicious god Loki deceives Baldur's blind brother, and has him make an arrow of mistletoe to slay the otherwise-invincible hero. The violence is tempered in an alternative version that is closer to our modern tradition. Here, Baldur is revived, and his mother's joy is such that her thankful tears turn into mistletoe berries – henceforth it became a symbol of love under which people may pass and kiss.

Such rich tales would suggest an equally layered etymology. Yet in Old English, 'mistel' referred to birdlime, a sticky substance prepared from the plant's berries that is spread upon twigs as a means of trapping wild birds. That 'mistel' is related to the German *Mist*, 'excrement', and probably reflects the fact that mistletoe can be spread by bird faeces. Which means that, pulled apart, 'mistletoe' translates as 'dung on a twig'. It would be hard to imagine a less romantic origin for a plant that has sealed relationships (and lips, depending on the desirability of the kisser) for centuries.

18 December

BRUME

'You can't get too much winter in the winter', wrote Robert Frost, recognising the delights of a season that can be met with a mental as well as physical shiver. Glühwein at the Christmas market, steaming bowls of hearty soup, long duvet days, and a dose of Danish *hygge* (*see* 1 July) all enhance the cosiness and conviviality that can only come from hunkering down in winter-tide. Snerdling (snuggling) with a dictionary is of course an additional pleasure.

First, the weather, full of silent 'froriness' (frosts) and 'clink-abells' (icicles). You may wish to 'crump' across the 'niveous' landscape – a verb that perfectly conveys the sound of walking on compacted snow – or escape the intensity of a 'heller': a bitterly cold winter's day named after the dwelling of the dead.

A heller might well bring its 'brume': a winter mist. The perfect word for the low-lying vapour that shrouds the land on a frosty morning, its roots lie in the Romans' word *brumalis* – 'belonging to the winter'. One of the best chroniclers of the landscape, Robert Macfarlane, also reminds us of the 'myst-hakel' from Middle English, literally a 'mist-cape' – a fog or mist that mantles and cloaks the earth.

Even the beautiful kingfisher plays its part. Its German name is *Eisvogel*, 'ice-bird', while in Russian, as Зимородок, it is 'winter-born'. Both names relish the kingfisher's appearance in new areas when their usual fishing sources freeze over.

---

19 December

HUMBUG

More than a century and a half after its publication in 1843, the reading of *A Christmas Carol* (or the watching with a cast of Muppets) has become a near-sacred ritual for many in the run-up to Christmas. Now the best-remembered of all stories by Charles Dickens, it was an instant hit, with 6,000 copies sold within the first few days. No more than two months after its appearance, eight or more stage shows of *A Christmas Carol* were already in production. Today, 19 December, was a triumphant day for author and publisher, although the cost of production for the lavish book, which included four woodcuts and four colour plates, ultimately meant little financial gain for either.

The story nudged several words onto the English stage – first and foremost the epithet 'Scrooge', even now a synonym for a miserly killjoy. It also ensured the survival of 'humbug', a word already in existence but which today rarely comes without a 'Bah' and a silent nod to Dickens's curmudgeon (*see* 17 May). It is also a word with a frustratingly elusive etymology.

In 1750, the *Student or, the Oxford and Cambridge Monthly Miscellany*, noted this about a new linguistic fad:

> There is a word very much in vogue with the people of taste and fashion, which, though it has not even the *penumbra* of a meaning, yet makes up the sum total of the wit, sense, and judgement of the aforesaid people of taste and fashion . . . I will venture to affirm that this Humbug is neither an English word, nor a derivative from any other language. It is indeed a black-guard sound, made use of by most people of distinction! It is a fine, make-weight in conversation, and some great men deceive themselves so egregiously as to think they mean something by it.

Origins for this 'black-guard sound' are a mystery. One theory suggests it is a mangling of 'Hamburg', referring to counterfeit coins emanating from the German city. More elaborate still, others point to *húm*, a Norse word for 'dusk', and 'bogey', an apparition. The most literal suggestion is that of a humming bug, something small, inconsequential, and irritating.

The longevity of a word can usually be assessed by the number of riffs it produces. In the case of 'humbug', the *Oxford English Dictionary* records the word being used as a verb from the very start, while 'humbuggable', 'humbuggability', and 'humbuggery' have also joined the list. Scrooge, of course, is the ultimate 'humbugger': a word that will see regular outings during this season, when anyone harbouring ill-willy (*see* 30 November) is usually exposed.

20 December

QUAFFTIDE

Gin o'clock, sun over the yardarm . . . Most of us plump for whatever prompt we need to reach for a drink at the end of the day. And in that drink we hope to find a 'nepenthe': the drug in Homer's *Odyssey* that banished all worries from the mind and, by extension, any modern potion that sends us to a happier place. 'Nepenthe' takes its name from the Greek for 'not grief'.

In the 1500s, the single-word announcement that it was time for a restorative drink was 'quafftide', in which 'quaff' nicely imitates the sound of a long, deep draught. Defined in the *Oxford English Dictionary* as simply 'the season for drinking', it unmistakably belongs to Christmas.

21 December

CRUCIVERBALIST

Cruciverbalists (a fittingly complicated term for crossword puzzlers) everywhere should doff their hats to one man today, who on 21 December 1913 decided to fill some space in his newspaper, the *NY World*, with what he dubbed a 'Word-Cross'. While prototypes of such puzzles existed in ancient Rome, Arthur Wynne is generally acknowledged to be the inventor of the modern crossword.

Wynne's puzzle was diamond-shaped; today's black and white grid was to take several decades to evolve. His clues ranged from the ridiculously easy: 'the plural of is' (3), to the puckish 'A fist' (4)* and the downright fiendish 'The fibre of the gomuti palm' (3).**

In 1924, the newly formed Simon & Schuster published a book of similar puzzles. The company's bosses were said to be unsure of its reception, and so omitted the publisher's name from the cover. As it turned out, their fears were unfounded: the book soon sold out, and reprints were hurriedly organised.

Since then, quick, cryptic, and super-cryptic crosswords have become big business, a daily and often ingenious mental challenge for the cruciverbalists in pursuit.

* NEIF.
**The answer, apparently, is DOH.

22 December

SCURRYFUNGE

Few words can be more useful at Christmas-time than this one, borrowed from US dialect where it means to hastily and frenziedly tidy a house just before guests arrive.

It manages to capture in a single term the mad throwing of things into cupboards and under furniture in an attempt to achieve some semblance of order before your family or friends descend. If such efforts come to nought, requiring a tumble of apologies the moment your guests walk through the door, a 'xenium' might prove useful: a present given to a house-guest as a softener.

23 December

BELLY-CHEER

'Abligurition' is the word you need for any excessive spending on food and drink, or, as Nathan Bailey put it in his *Dictionary* of 1724, 'a prodigal spending in Belly-Cheer'.

The lexicon of Christmas fare is as international in origin as it is old. The wherewithal to go carousing is there in most shopping trolleys filled with alcohol of every flavour and description. The more traditional among us will be 'wassailing', from a Viking toast 'be fortunate', to which the standard reply was 'drink-hail', 'drink to good health'.

Tipples (from the Norwegian *tipla*, 'to drip slowly') may include brandy – from the Dutch *brandewijn*, 'burnt wine', champagne (*see* 4 August), and a few crates of beer. The ancestor of the latter is a Latin term used in monasteries: *bibere*, 'to drink', which also gave us 'bib', 'beverage', and, appropri-ately, 'bibulous': 'excessively fond of drinking'.

On to the food, and the prince of the Christmas plate among carnivores is the chipolata: a word believed to derive from the Italian *cipollata*, 'made with onions', referring to a sausage-and-onion stew. Sausages also sizzle behind the original meaning of 'pudding': a savoury dish made from stuffed animal intestines. Their link with our flaming Christmas version is the idea of putting a filling into a casing and cooking it. However glorious it may taste, 'pudding', thanks to its Latin root *botellus*, 'sausage or small intestine', shares its story with 'botulism'.

On a more fragrant note, you might opt for the cascade of meringue and fruit that is pavlova instead of pudding. Anna Pavlova was a Russian ballerina who became world famous for her solo dance *The Dying Swan*. Her tour of Australia and New Zealand inspired chefs to commemorate her in a dessert. The first recorded pavlova was composed of coloured layers of jelly made in a mould that resembled a ballerina's tutu.

However much we 'abligurate' this month, we may never reach the heights, or excesses, of the Roman celebrations of Saturnalia in December, the predecessor of Christmas. The poet Lucian of Samosata describes them thus: 'the serious is barred: no business allowed. Drinking and being drunk, noise and games of dice, appointing of kings and feasting of slaves, singing naked, clapping – such are the functions over which I preside.'

24 December

OVER THE TOP

Christmas in the trenches of the First World War was a season of mixed emotions, a time when the bleakness of weather and conflict were temporarily allayed by gifts from the soldiers' families and from charities. In October 1914 Eleonora French, wife of the army's commander-in-chief, asked the women of Britain to knit 250,000 mufflers to keep the soldiers warm, and Princess Mary tins, filled with chocolate and tobacco, together with a royal Christmas message, were delivered to over 350,000 as a token of thanks and a boost to morale.

For those manning the trenches, rations were still rations, even when topped up by gifts from home. Army biscuit and bully beef were the usual meal on Christmas Day, as they were on almost every other. Bully beef was tinned corned beef (in reality a variety of meats): its name reflecting the picture of a bull on the cans of the popular 'Hereford' brand.

On 24 December 1915, one private wrote of a service and communion in a tent: 'very strange singing *Peace on Earth* and off to kill all we can early next morning . . . We have a cessation midday for Christmas dinner, bully and biscuits.' That year saw no repeat of one of the most famous wartime acts of humanity: the Christmas truce of 1914, during which unofficial ceasefires took place along many parts of the front, with some German and British soldiers even going 'over the top' into no-man's-land to exchange food, cigarettes, and play games of football.

When the conflict resumed, so did the standard meaning of 'over the top': the act of soldiers climbing over the parapet of the trench and entering the battle. Within twenty years, thanks to the unthinkable number of casualties of that war, it became a figurative expression for behaviour that goes too far, beyond the acceptable limits of reason.

┌─────────────────┐
│ **25 December** │
└─────────────────┘

CONFELICITY

Crackers, mistletoe, carols, pudding, joblijocks (a morning disturbance, in this case usually an excited child jumping up and down on the bed at 3 a.m.): everyone has a word that defines their Christmas Day. There is one, however, that is far too seldom used: a rare gem that has had such few outings it rarely appears in print, including dictionaries.

Confelicity is the pleasure you take from the happiness of others. It derives from the Latin *con*, 'with', and *felix*, 'happy', via the French *félicité*.

Today, before the crapulence sets in (the feeling of 'sickness or indisposition resulting from excess in drinking or eating'), may there be confelicity aplenty.

---

26 December

WONDERCLOUT

The *Oxford English Dictionary* defines Boxing Day thus: 'The first week-day after Christmas-day, observed as a holiday on which post-men, errand-boys, and servants of various kinds expect to receive a Christmas-box.' The earliest mention found in print is from 1833, four years before Charles Dickens referred to the joy it brought to many employees in his *Pickwick Papers*: 'No man ever talked in poetry 'cept a beadle on Boxin' Day.'

Other gifts are distributed on this day: alms boxes, for example, placed in churches during the Advent season for the collection of donations. Clergy members traditionally distribute the contents of the boxes to the poor on 26 December, which is also the feast of St Stephen, the first Christian martyr commemorated for his acts of charity.

For the luckier ones, Boxing Day sees merriment continue and even the last Yule-hole (*see* 27 December) stretched to its limits. Plus the chance to inspect more closely the various presents received – perhaps lovingly trying them on, hunting for the correct batteries, or painstakingly reading through nonsensical instructions.

Among them will usually be one or two 'toe-covers', a

word from the 1940s for 'an inexpensive and useless present'. Presumably, a warmer for the toes was considered the ultimate of these, though in the earliest record a 'crocheted napkin ring' is given as the prime example. In among such utterly dispensable presents are the 'wonderclouts'. These belong in a different category, reserved for showy items that look highly promising but actually turn out to be worthless, and which people were clearly receiving in the sixteenth century, when the word was coined. Wonderclouts are perhaps the ultimate examples of the state otherwise known as 'trumperiness' – a surprisingly useful term for something of far less value than it seems (*see* 3 September).

---

27 December

YULE-HOLE

The old English term for December, the tenth month in the ancient Roman calendar (from *decem*, ten) was *Ærra Geola*, 'before Yule'.

Yule comes from an Old Norse word *jól*; it was used of a pagan festival that took place at the winter solstice, and which lasted for twelve days. Germanic and Scandinavian pagans celebrated the festival in late December or early January; when they began to adopt Christianity they simply changed the nature of the festival, and *jól* became Christmas. The merry word 'jolly' may come ultimately from the same Old Norse beginnings.

The entry for 'Yule' in the *Scottish National Dictionary* is long and suitably twinkly. Its list of words in combination is particularly fruitful: there is the 'Yule-blinker', the Pole Star; a 'Yule-fee', Christmas money given to a public official such as a 'town-drummer or minstrel'; and the 'Yule-brose', the seasonal version of a kind of oat porridge onto which was poured the juices from boiled meat. The tradition was to put a ring in the communal bowl of Yule-brose; the person in whose spoon it popped up was predicted to be the first to wed.

The list goes on. All children would want to avoid the 'Yule-skrep', a smack on the bottom at Christmas time. A 'Yule-shard' is 'an opprobrious term for someone who leaves work unfinished before Christmas or the New Year', but which has the curious double meaning of 'someone who has no new piece of apparel to celebrate the season'.

Perhaps the most useful phrase of all, however, is the 'Yule-hole', for which most of us will surely be reaching at some point this season. The term is amply defined in the *Oxford English Dictionary* as 'the hole in the waist-belt to which the buckle is adjusted, to allow for repletion after the feasting at Christmas'.

---

28 December

MERRYNEUM

English lacks a word for the blurring of time during the Christmas holidays, when the usual boundaries of our day recede and we lose all touch with our calendar, remaining blissfully unaware of the date, the day of the week, and the time of day when a drink becomes acceptable.

Equally elusive is an adequate term for the period of limbo between Christmas and New Year. In Germany, it is *zwischen den Jahren*, 'between the years'. For others, it is known as Twixtmas, Taintmas, Witching Week, or Chrimbo Limbo. The cleverest, perhaps, is Merryneum, because this time straddles Christmas and New Year just as the perineum connects the anus and the genitals. Some might also find a connection in the perineum's ability to stretch during childbirth, just as this twilight period may seem – for some, at least – to go on and on, with no apparent end in sight.

29 December

APANTHROPY

'Tis the time for board games with relatives you barely know, and for heated arguments with those you do (too well).

Whatever the subject of the argument – be it the purple Quality Street, the capital of Iowa, the state of your marriage, or whether *zax* is *really* allowed on the Scrabble board – you may need to muster a 'recumbentibus': a knockout blow from which there is no recovery. In the US slang of the 1830s and 1840s, another word for such a winning point in an argument was the 'sockdolager'. This is the decisive finisher which leaves your opponent with nowhere to go but the phrontistery (*see* 18 June), where they must contemplate their defeat.

When a sockdolager just isn't enough, it might be wise to withdraw altogether. 'Apanthropy' is a rare word from the nineteenth century for a state of mind characterised by both a love of solitude and a dislike of other people. It is made up of the Greek *apo*, 'away from', and *anthrōpos*, 'man', and seems perfectly tailored to the time when a surfeit of human company pushes you to the point of latibulation – another pithy word, this time from Latin, for the act of hiding oneself in a corner.

30 December

DOMINO

On this day in 1809, a law was passed in Boston, United States, banning the use of masks at balls and social gatherings. Despite its reputation for puritanical laws (the city also outlawed Christmas for over two decades in the nineteenth century), Boston was not alone – other US cities, and many in Britain too, decided that such disguise encouraged immoral behaviour and illicit acts that could not be tolerated in polite society. Masks, at the heart of the word 'masquerade', were judged the easy tools of the promiscuous and pleasure-seeking.

The letters of Lady Mary Wortley Montagu, an eighteenth-century English writer who challenged contemporary attitudes towards women, recounted the pursuits of some young and wild aristocrats: 'They call themselves Schemers, and meet regularly 3 times a week to consult on Galant Schemes for the advancement of that branch of Happyness which the vulgar call "Whoring".' Such 'happyness', Montagu continued, provided 'the best contriv'd Entertainment in the World, and the only remedy against spleen and vapours occasion'd by the Formality of the Day'.

The Schemers followed strict house rules, including total discretion. Each member, Lady Montagu's *Letters* relate, 'must arrive at the hour of 6 mask'd in a Domine', and swear an oath that they would never, under any circumstances, reveal the identity of the women they encountered. The *domine* in question was a loose cloak with a mask that covered the top of the face. Its name was derived from the Latin *dominus*, 'lord' or 'master', and referred originally to a hood or habit for the head attached to the cape of a priest or canon.

When the *domine*, or 'domino', entered the world of the masquerade, high fashion soon added its own requirements: another prolific letter writer, Fanny Burney, wrote admiringly of a 'Miss Strange' who had 'a white satin domino trimmed with blue'. The domino effect, back at those eighteenth-century secret balls, must have been a powerful one.

Dominoes became particularly popular as carnival costumes, when it was de rigueur to wear a black-hooded robe with a white mask. Today's dominoes are far more likely to be played at Christmas than worn on the back of any schemer: it is thought that the colours of these carnival masks inspired the English name of a board game of spotted tiles.

31 December

KALOPSIA

Logophiles love nothing more than the challenge of creating a new word. Best of all is the chance to base their offering upon Latin or Greek, in the belief perhaps that the voices of the ancients will give immediate credence to the new concoction. 'Kalopsia' is one such word. Seldom found in any dictionary, it nonetheless fills a gap on such occasions as New Year's Eve, when intoxication makes the world look a little better than it did before.

Little mind that the etymology of 'intoxication' itself hides a warning – for the ancient Greeks, a *toxon pharmakon* was the 'arrow poison' in which their weapons were dipped (we preserve *toxon*, 'arrow', in the technical term for archery, 'toxophily'). Intoxication was quite literally the injection of poison.

For tonight, however, all such stories are lost, and what remains are the beer-goggles. 'Kalopsia', a term with a touch more mystique, describes the same effect. Put simply, it is the state in which everything, and everyone, looks beautiful.

ACKNOWLEDGEMENTS

Writing this section is surely the most difficult of all. For a start there's the fear that you've missed out someone important through some catastrophic brain blip. Even more than that, it would be hard even for the most consummate of writers to convey just how much of a difference the contributions the individuals below have made. But here goes and, if I have indeed omitted someone who really deserves to be on the list, I promise copious amounts of shotclogs and a year's worth of humicubation.

Once again, my biggest thanks go to Rosemary Scoular, my agent, and Georgina Laycock, my editor, whose bottomless optimism and sunny disposition never fail to spur me on. Their enthusiasm was the only desirable infection in this darkest of years.

Jonathan Yardley was my most excellent researcher – the book's exploration of mythology in particular owes much to his enthusiasm and knowledge.

Kate Craigie calmly and efficiently wrapped a breakneck production schedule around lockdown requirements – it's thanks to her, to Caroline Westmore, to Charlotte Davey, to Diana Talyanina in production, and to Palimpsest typesetters and Clays printers that this book has seen the light of day.

Thanks are due to Martin Bryant, my copy-editor, and Nick de Somogyi, my proof-reader – their clarity and insight were extremely welcome when the text began to swim before my eyes. And thanks also to Alice Herbert, my brilliant publicist, and Emma Petfield in marketing.

My Twitter followers never fail to surprise and cheer me with their appreciation of what I do. Many of them will, I hope, help me spread the word(s) and revive those that are in danger of slipping away.

My family as ever put up with my witterings over how I would ever get the writing finished, and how it would be received if I did: thank you for your patience and for the biscuits.

Gratitude to the friends, especially Charlotte Scott, Giles Paley-Phillips, Susie Hilton, Gyles Brandreth, Greg Jenner, Gethin Jones, Linda Papadopolous, Simon Brew, and Jo Brand, whose whispers of encouragement (and, when needed, mighty shoves) made all the difference when the world was starting to change.

And thank you for picking up this book and, I hope, embarking on its year of words. It's said that Victor Hugo once sent a telegram to his publisher enquiring about the success of his book, that simply read "?". The book was doing well, and Hugo received the reply '!'. Whether or not I ever receive a '!', I really hope you enjoy *Word Perfect*.

INDEX